WHAT MORE IS THERE TO SAY BUT AMEN

WHAT MORE IS THERE TO SAY BUT AMEN

The Autobiography
of Dr. Oswald C. J. Hoffmann
as told to Ronald J. Schlegel

USED   Nov 09

Town + Country Center, Santana, CA

SAINT LOUIS

Scripture quotations are the author's own translation unless otherwise noted.

Scripture quotations marked KJV are from the King James or Authorized Version of the Bible.

Scripture quotations marked NKJV are from New King James edition, copyright © 1979, 1980, 1982. Used by permission.

Scripture quotations marked NIV taken from the HOLY BIBLE, NEW INTERNATIONAL VERSION®. NIV®. Copyright © 1973, 1978, 1984 by International Bible Society. Used by permission of Zondervan Publishing House. All rights reserved.

Copyright © 1996 Concordia Publishing House
3558 S. Jefferson Avenue, St. Louis, MO 63118-3968
Manufactured in the United States of America

Library of Congress Cataloging-in-Publication Data

Hoffmann, Oswald C. J.
    What more is there to say but Amen : the autobiography of Dr. Oswald C. F. Hoffmann as told to Ronald J. Schlegel / Oswald C. J. Hoffmann
        p.   cm.
    Includes bibliographical references.
    ISBN 0-570-04876-1
    1. Hoffmann, Oswald C. J. 2. Lutherans—United States—Biography. 3. Lutheran Church—Clergy—Biography. 5. Lutheran hour (Radio program) I. Schlegel, Ronald J., 1933-   . II. Title.
BX8080.H545A3 1996
284.1'092—dc20
[B]   96-13788

1   2   3   4   5   6   7   8   9   10   05   04   03   02   01   00   99   98   97   96

To Marcia,
with love

᪣ Art student in Minneapolis and promising
dress designer who married a struggling
preacher

᪣ Mother of four strapping children, and their
educator in the perennial absence of the
same struggling preacher

᪣ Anonymous contributor to one good cause
after another

᪣ Discerner of the spirits with a clear eye
focused upon the Gospel

᪣ Bearer of the burning torch of Christ the
Savior to anyone who has ever met her

᪣

CONTENTS

A Word
from Billy Graham

F EW PREACHERS IN OUR GENERATION HAVE SPOKEN AS ELOQUENTLY and as forcefully for Christ as my friend Oswald Hoffmann. His ministry through radio and in person has touched the lives of thousands, but perhaps equally important has been the example of his life and dedication to countless young pastors and preachers. It has been a special privilege for us to welcome him as a regular speaker at our Schools of Evangelism, where his wise counsel and deep commitment to the Gospel have encouraged and inspired thousands. I have no doubt this story of his life will bless and inspire many as it points them to Christ, whom Oswald Hoffmann has sought to serve throughout his life.

COMMENTS
BY PAUL L. MAIER

I T IS HARD TO IMAGINE ANYONE LIVING A MORE INTERESTING LIFE THAN
Oswald C. J. Hoffmann. Most will assume that this is the life
story of Walter A. Maier's great successor as voice of "The
Lutheran Hour," but they are only partially right, since Dr. Hoffmann was so much more than a Sunday radio institution. He was a
classical and linguistics scholar, professor, choir director, athletic
coach, pastor, public relations director, theological observer, Bible
translator, motion-picture consultant, television and video personality, and member of numerous boards, quite apart from his
more familiar roles as speaker over the radio, on camera, and on
many platforms across the world. His extremely versatile careers
with all their intriguing facets impacted millions across the globe.

Surprises abound in these pages, which unveil episodes and
portraits far beyond the man and the microphone. Readers will
learn how Synod's long-running television show "This Is the Life"
was born in his office, how Dr. Hoffmann nearly had to fire Martin
Luther (that is, the actor who played the lead in the film *Martin
Luther*), and how he—a Lutheran—improved the language in one
of the Roman Catholic documents issued by the Second Vatican
Council.

The backgrounds in these pages are hardly limited to a broadcasting studio. The voice penetrated the globe, but so did the

11

man, as one chapter may have Ossie and his beloved Marcia having a palace chat with Haile Selassie, Emperor of Ethiopia, or with the King of Tonga in the South Pacific. Another will find him preaching to our troops in Alaska or flying in a helicopter over Vietnam.

Dr. Hoffmann's discussions with Presidents Eisenhower, Kennedy, Johnson, and Nixon, as well as his conversations with kings, generals, admirals, and other famous personalities here and abroad should never be written off as "name-dropping." These occasions are not only of maximum interest to the reader, but opportunities in which he was able to make a significant witness for the Christian faith. Not a line in this book is born of pride or self-praise on the one hand, or false humility on the other. Jesus Christ, not Oswald C. J. Hoffmann, is actually the central figure in these pages.

His friends have urged not only that this book be written, but that it be written by Dr. Hoffmann himself—an autobiography— since no one else could have pieced together so many different personalities, memories, and scenes as the man who actually lived them. But it was left to his gifted associate Ronald Schlegel to "worm the stories out of him," and this he has done with distinction, leaving his touch in these pages so transparent that the material speaks directly for itself, as it should. A well-rounded life story is the result, with chapters on work followed by those on play, with reverses acknowledged as well as successes enjoyed.

We all have our Ossie Hoffmann stories, and some of the best were told by the man himself. He always had—and has—a blazing sense of humor that is only augmented when his own laughter takes on a "second wind" and a merely funny joke becomes hilarious. He is a raconteur *extraordinaire.*

I first met Ossie Hoffmann as a dinner guest at our home on the Concordia Seminary campus in the '30s. I looked with a child's admiration at the most brilliant student in my father's Hebrew classes, for which WAM (as the students called him) made him class marker and assistant—a perhaps dubious honor, since no pay was attached to that post in those post-Depression days!

The first time I heard Oswald Hoffmann speak was in 1950, when he gave an address at Harvard University on "Church Union," which was off the cuff but very memorable. He also must have been pleased with it, because he later asked if I could send him an outline of what he had said "as best you can remember." I had not been taking notes, but said I'd try. He was astounded at what I submitted, claiming it was virtually a manuscript of his address *if* he had had a manuscript. Midst his accolades, however, I had to remind him that it was the *speaker,* after all, who had made the profound impression, and that my powers of recall were quite obtuse in the case of many another speaker!

It was not the last time that I received a touch of the Hoffmann generosity. In May 1963, when my book *A Man Spoke, a World Listened* was first published, I was liturgist for a Lutheran Hour rally in Grand Rapids and wondered to myself if Dr. Hoffmann might be gracious enough to give it a passing reference somewhere in his sermon. Passing reference? He *began* his address with the words, "An important new book has just been published."

A great-hearted man, Oswald Hoffmann has never begrudged the responses of thousands of people who have told or written him about how much my father's ministry on "The Lutheran Hour" meant to them. He cheerfully agreed with them! A lesser man, afflicted with the "hard-act-to-follow" syndrome, might have tried to bury this memory in jealous anxiety over comparisons. Not Ossie Hoffmann. Instead, he has continued the Maier ministry in dramatic fashion, and in a manner that would greatly have gladdened the heart of Walter A. Maier, as it has delighted all members of the Maier family.

His appreciation of his predecessor was movingly expressed in the remarkable memorial address he delivered in Manhattan on the Sunday following his professor's death in 1950. An excerpt will also illustrate the classic cadences in the Hoffmann prose:

> It is safe to say that no man in the first half of this century— anywhere in the world—so touched the hearts of the suffering masses in this country and abroad as Walter Maier did. ... In the cultivated accents of Harvard, he spoke of Christ to the common man. Whatever he touched leaped into life. His breath was on the neck of the entire church, urging it forward in its mission for Christ.

The voices of WAM and Ossie may have been different, but their theologies were identical. So were their accents: WAM did all he could to put the Germanic Lutheran Church—Missouri Synod "on the American map" and diminish its insularity and the legalism of some of its leaders. O.C.J.H. continued this effort both as his church's director of public relations and as Lutheran Hour speaker, forging important links with the secular media, mainstream Christianity, and Evangelicalism. His close personal friendship with Billy Graham, with whom he has shared many a platform, is a case in point.

Our paths have crossed many times across the years, at Lutheran Hour rallies, synodical functions, and while filming scenes for *Yeshua.* In recent years, when Dr. Hoffmann was considering retirement, I always urged him to cancel the very thought of it. With many others, I could not conceive of "The Lutheran Hour" without him. Then I recalled that this was the near-universal impression after my father died in 1950, and yet "The Lutheran Hour" not only survived but prospered, thanks to God's blessing and the efforts of the man mirrored in these pages. How glorious that Oswald C. J. Hoffmann picked up the torch and carried it one-third of a century farther with such extraordinary success! Amen indeed!

PREFACE
BY OSWALD C. J. HOFFMANN

EAR READERS: The publication of these memoirs, collected
after being recollected, is due to the noble pressure
mainly of three people. They are Gaylene LaBore, my secretary since before the flood; Ron Schlegel, a member of our staff
at Lutheran Hour Ministries; and Mervin Marquardt, of the editorial staff at Concordia Publishing House.

Ron Schlegel collected material "with prodigious assiduity" (as
William Makepeace Thackeray used to say). His preface explains
how he did his work of collecting material and dividing it into
chapters. The editing and reediting of manuscripts came to a conclusion mainly as the work of Mervin Marquardt, whose contribution is beyond comprehension and also beyond competition.

Lastly, but not leastly, the magnificent and constant revision
of both material and text is due mostly to Gaylene, whose personal interest in the final product was matched only by her ability to perform X rays on the mind of the subject. Anyone who has
enjoyed the command of an extremely competent executive assistant will appreciate what all of this means. She is the one who constantly arranges for me to be out of town when anything important needs to be done. What is more, she is often ably assisted
and abetted by her husband, Dr. Richard LaBore, a scholar in
church history and also for the time being mayor of Crestwood,
one of our prospering suburban commercial communities.

As anyone can plainly see, this is an autobiography for which others need to be blamed, including the authorities at Concordia Publishing House, who faithfully promoted this project in spite of all their decades of experience in book publishing and other endeavors.

Let all enjoy themselves while looking for things to criticize, an old and well-founded habit among Lutherans, not to speak about other Christians!

PREFACE
BY RONALD J. SCHLEGEL

F ROM DECEMBER OF 1993 THROUGH FEBRUARY OF 1995, IT HAS BEEN my great privilege to work with Dr. Oswald Hoffmann on his autobiography. I have had the opportunity to sit with him over 40 hours as he reminisced about his life, shared interesting anecdotes, laughed in his uproarious manner, and above all proclaimed the Gospel. That Gospel proclamation has found its way into this book in many instances. It has also strengthened me personally, for which I am deeply grateful.

I also had the privilege of talking with Dr. Hoffmann's family, friends, and associates all over the United States. That, too, was a moving experience. I was impressed once again by how many lives Dr. Hoffmann has touched with the Gospel of salvation by God's grace through faith in Jesus Christ.

Among those who contributed to this memoir were the International Lutheran Laymen's League, Concordia Publishing House, and Aid Association for Lutherans, who provided funding for the project. We owe a great debt of gratitude to Gerald Perschbacher of the International LLL staff, who has so well organized the archives at the LLL headquarters and made them accessible, and to Dave Kuenzel, the LLL staff photographer, who helped with the selection of photographs. Thanks are due Rev. Roy Ledbetter at Concordia Historical Institute, who was a great help in finding needed dates and names. Rev. Fred and Edith Pankow's book on the history of the LLL, *Seventy-Five Years of Blessing—and the Best Is Yet to Come,* was a valuable resource. We owe a huge debt of gratitude to Dr. Hoffmann's executive assistant, Gaylene LaBore, for assisting with materials from his files and for scheduling times to meet with Dr. Hoffmann in the midst of his nonstop itineraries.

We also owe a great debt to those interviewed. That includes all members of the Hoffmann family: Dr. Hoffmann's wife, Marcia; sons Peter, Paul, and John; and daughter, Kate. Others interviewed were Rev. Ardon Albrecht, Mr. Dave Anderson, Mr. Earl Birkicht, Dr. William Buege, Dr. David Burke, Dr. John Drager, Rev. William Dingler, Mrs. Corinne Duever, Dr. Herman Gockel, Mrs. Susan Hasting, Mr. Elmer Kraemer, Rev. Herbert Kern, Dr. Elmer Knoernschild, Mrs. Gaylene LaBore, Mr. Robert E. A. Lee, Mr. John Meredythe Lucas, Dr. Billy Melvin, Rev. John Meyer, Rev. Louis Meyer, Mr. Jim Miller, Mrs. Ewald (Jean) Mueller, Mrs. Lori Parker, Dr. James Reinhard, Mrs. Edith Simcoe, Mr. Mel Stueve, Rev. Norman Temme, Mr. Tommy Thompson, Gen. John Vessey, Dr. Oswald Waech, and Rev. Mel Witt. Thanks to every one of you for your invaluable assistance.

To you, the reader: I hope you will experience as much joy in reading the book as I have had in helping to shape it. I know I learned new things about Dr. Hoffmann, and I assume you will too. More important, though, may you see beyond him to see again the one whom Dr. Oswald Hoffmann fully and unswervingly proclaimed: our Lord and Savior, Jesus Christ.

To Him be the glory, both now and forever.

CHRONOLOGY

Dec. 6, 1913	Born, Snyder, Nebraska
Dec. 25, 1913	Baptized, St. Peter Lutheran Church, Snyder, Nebraska
1919	Entered St. Peter elementary school at second grade
1921	Family moved to Springfield, Illinois (Concordia Seminary)
1925	Family moved to Chicago, Illinois (St. Luke Lutheran Church)
1926	Graduated from St. Luke Lutheran Elementary School
	Entered Luther Institute, Chicago, Illinois
1928	Transferred to Concordia [Junior] College, Milwaukee, Wisconsin
1930	Family moved to St. Paul, Minnesota
	Transferred to Concordia [Junior] College, St. Paul, Minnesota
1932	Graduated from Concordia College, St. Paul, Minnesota
	Entered Concordia Seminary, St. Louis, Missouri
1934–35	Attended University of Minnesota; took Master of Arts degree
1935–36	Attended Concordia Seminary, St. Louis, Missouri; took Bachelor of Divinity degree
1936–40	Instructor and dean of men, Bethany College, Mankato, Minnesota
1939	Ordained and installed as pastor of English Lutheran Church, Cottonwood, Minnesota

1940-41	Instructor in linguistics and classical languages, University of Minnesota
June 23, 1940	Married Marcia nee Linnell, Redeemer Lutheran Church, St. Paul, Minnesota
1941-48	Professor of Greek and Latin, Concordia Collegiate Institute, Bronxville, New York
June 5, 1942	Son Peter Carl born
June 20, 1945	Son Paul George born
1948-63	Director of the Department of Public Relations of The Lutheran Church—Missouri Synod, New York City, New York
	Assistant to the pastor, St. Matthew Lutheran Church, New York City, New York
May 11, 1950	Son John Linnell born
Sept. 5, 1955	Daughter Katharine Ann born
1955-88	Lutheran Hour speaker
1963	Moved to St. Louis, MO
1988-	Honorary Lutheran Hour speaker

Honorary Degrees and Awards

1952	Doctor of Divinity, Concordia Seminary, St. Louis, Missouri
1952	Doctor of Laws, Valparaiso University, Valparaiso, Indiana
1971	The Saint Martin of Tours Medal, the Armed Forces Commission of The Lutheran Church—Missouri Synod
1973	Clergyman of the Year, Religious Heritage of America
1975	Membership in the "Order of Aaron and Hur," an organization of the Army chaplaincy
1980	The Secretary of Defense Award for Outstanding Service (to military personnel), the United States Department of Defense

20

The Gutenberg Award from the Chicago Bible Society

1982   Doctor of Humane Letters, The Philippine Christian University, Manila, Republic of the Philippines

The Gold Angel Award, "International Media Clergyman of the Year," Religion in Media

1984   The Colonel Koch-Luther (Distinguished Service) Medal, Concordia Historical Institute

1987   The American Bible Society Award

1988   Honorary President of the United Bible Societies

Honorary Lutheran Hour speaker

1989   Named Life Member of the Religious Public Relations Council

The William Ward Ayer Distinguished Service Award, National Religious Broadcasters

1990   The Aeterna Moliri Award, Concordia College, St. Paul, Minnesota

1992   The Gold Medal Award, Religious Heritage of America

1993   The Wittenberg Award, Luther Institute, Washington, D.C.

Books Published

1959   *Life Crucified.* Grand Rapids: William B. Eerdmanns Publishing Company.

1969   *God Is No Island.* St. Louis: Concordia Publishing House.

1970   *Hurry Home Where You Belong.* St. Louis: Concordia Publishing House.

1973   *God's Joyful People—One in the Spirit.* St. Louis: Concordia Publishing House.

1982   *The Lord's Prayer.* San Francisco: Harper & Row.

1985   *There Is Hope.* St. Louis: Concordia Publishing House.

1

CALLED BY
"THE LUTHERAN HOUR"

IT WAS EARLY 1955. TELEVISION WAS STILL IN ITS INFANCY, BUT MANY were predicting the eventual death of radio, now that this new medium had appeared. The headquarters of the Lutheran Laymen's League (the LLL) in St. Louis had the same concern, but the leaders faced a more immediate predicament. Their radio program, "The Lutheran Hour," was in debt for the first time in 20 years.

In January 1950, "The Lutheran Hour" was enjoying immense popularity. Its speaker, Rev. Dr. Walter A. Maier, had taken it to world significance. But his 1949 Christmas Day message was his last. He died January 11, 1950.

Over the next five years, "The Lutheran Hour" struggled with continuity. Rev. Lawrence Acker served as interim speaker for the 1950–51 season, until the 1951 LLL convention. Then Dr. Armin Oldsen was selected to be Lutheran Hour speaker. (Coincidentally, I was the person who installed Dr. Oldsen as the speaker. Pastor Acker was scheduled to do so, but that Sunday at the convention he had a heart attack. As the representative of the Synod at that convention, I was accorded the honor.) However, before he could really build an audience, Dr. Oldsen resigned in 1953 because of health problems. In addition, some people felt that the "music and message" format of "The Lutheran Hour" was not dramatic enough to compete with TV.

Perhaps 1955 should be the year for change, decided the staff and board of the LLL. So they hired Rev. Elmer Knoernschild to write and produce a dramatic program. He had been in charge of religious programming at St. Louis radio station KFUO, a Lutheran station on the seminary grounds, so the choice was an excellent fit. The first of those programs was already complete when the Synod's president, Rev. Dr. John Behnken, and his right hand, Synod Planning Counselor Dr. Lorrie Meyer, counseled otherwise. They urged that the "Hour" should continue to present the best in Lutheran preaching. Paul Friedrich, the executive director of the LLL, acceded. The idea of changing "The Lutheran Hour" was scrapped, and the search for a permanent speaker on the program resumed.

In a few months, in the spring of 1955, a letter appeared on my desk asking me to become the permanent speaker. Its arrival surprised me. I had no idea "The Lutheran Hour" was looking for a speaker—even though I was the public relations director of the denomination at the time and was supposed to know everything that was going on. It was not until some 15 years later that I found out what had happened.

As I understand it, members of the LLL board of directors, LLL executive director Paul Friedrich, and LLL pastoral advisor Lawrence Acker (who had survived his heart attack) sat around a table suggesting names for a permanent Lutheran Hour speaker. After a fruitless while, Friedrich said, "I'm surprised that one name has not been mentioned: Oswald Hoffmann." I am told that at the mention of my name, Acker jumped up from his chair and said, "Of course! He's a natural!" And as a result of all this, I was elected to be permanent Lutheran Hour speaker.

That was responsible for the letter that appeared on my desk on a spring day in 1955. They felt that my election was God's will, so they sent me a divine call—which of course, I accepted. That was the beginning of my 33½ years as Lutheran Hour speaker.

Some people would be pleased that they had "arranged" such a job offer for themselves, but I have never in my life sought a position in the church. I firmly believe that the office should seek the man, not the man the office. You do what God has called you to do, and you do it in the best way you know how. When God wants to use you to do something different, He will let you know. The most important thing you can do is to be God's man wherever you are and in whatever He has called you.

I believe that, by God's grace, I was able to do that as speaker for "The Lutheran Hour" and president of the United Bible Societies—and to do it around the world. Not only was I privileged to preach God's Word over radio waves to the world, I've been there. I have spoken in every province of Canada, including, in 1979 alone, every maritime province. I've been to Mexico, Guatemala, the Dominican Republic, and the Caribbean; to the British Isles, Norway, Sweden, Belgium, France, Germany, Switzerland, Greece, and Russia; to Africa, Ethiopia, Israel, and India; to South Korea, Japan, China, Hong Kong, Taiwan, Okinawa, Thailand, and Vietnam; to the Philippines, Australia, New Zealand, New Guinea, Tonga, and Samoa. And I've preached the Word in every one of the 50 states.

I believe that God in His grace had been preparing me from childhood on for these marvelous opportunities.

2

FOUNDATIONS

I N 1988, I HAD THE OPPORTUNITY TO TAKE MY SECOND SON, PAUL, back to visit the little town where I was born and lived the first seven years of my life: Snyder, Nebraska. (It's on Highway 91, just west of Scribner, in Dodge County, about 70 miles northwest of Omaha.) Although son Paul was already 43 years old and a pastor in California at the time, I wanted him to see the place with me. I had been there just a month or so earlier to preach for the church's 100th anniversary, but I felt the need to visit again. It is important that we have a sense of where we have come from, for that's a part of who we are. Maybe I needed to remind myself again who I truly am behind the well-known voice and face: a small-town preacher's kid—and thankful for it. Actually, my father went on to teach in one of our denomination's seminaries, but the early years of everyone's life seem to have the greatest impact.

My childhood decision to become a pastor was not made in a vacuum. My father, Rev. Carl J. Hoffmann, was a pastor—in fact, the first resident pastor at St. Peter Lutheran Church in Snyder. He originally had studied at Concordia Teachers College in Addison, Illinois, fully intending to become a teacher. However, during a year of student teaching in his home congregation, St. John Lutheran Church, Quincy, Illinois, he changed his mind. He found the study of Greek (under Pastor William Schaller) so interesting that he decided to become a pastor instead. After preparatory courses at Concordia College, Milwaukee, he was graduated from Concordia Seminary in St. Louis, Missouri. My father was the first pastor on that side of the family; his father was a carpenter in Quincy.

My mother's side had two pastors: her grandfather and one of her brothers. Her grandfather Jakob Seidel was among the Bavarians sent to this country by Wilhelm Loehe, who founded the Lutheran colony in Frankenmuth, Michigan, and Concordia Seminary in Fort Wayne, Indiana. (The school later moved to Springfield, Illinois, and is now back in Fort Wayne.) Jakob was graduated as the one and only member of the first class in the then-new Fort Wayne seminary. His first position was as assistant pastor at St. John Lutheran Church, Maryville, Ohio, which was one of the 12 charter congregations of the Evangelical Lutheran Synod of Missouri, Ohio, and Other States (now named The Lutheran Church—Missouri Synod). Jakob's third pastorate was St. John Lutheran Church in Quincy, Illinois. There his son Julius set down roots as an expert leather worker and raised his family. In addition to my mother, the Seidel children included Louis (who became a pastor), Al (who became a doctor), Selma (who married a minister), and Julius (who became a dentist and served as a corporal in both World War I and II).

In due time Carl, the son of the carpenter, met Bertha, the daughter of the leather expert. Carl's first call out of the seminary was to Snyder, Nebraska, and the following year, in June 1912, he and Bertha were married. They moved into the brand new parsonage in Snyder, built according to plans drawn up by Carl's carpenter father.

As I said, my decision to become a minister was not unusual, given that my father, an uncle, and a grandfather were clergy. My younger brother, Kenneth, made the same decision. Personally, though, I cannot remember a time when I did not want to become a pastor. That is all I ever prepared myself for. Anything else that would happen would be a surprise from God.

My father—and my mother too, I believe—certainly influenced us, but they never tried to persuade my brother and me to become pastors. Later, when my father was a professor at Springfield seminary (formerly in Fort Wayne), he said to me, "I've seen too many men become pastors because somebody else wanted them to be one." Since he did not want that to happen to us, he never tried to persuade us to follow in his steps. That way, he said, we could make up our own minds about what we wanted to do.

I was born on St. Nicholas Day, December 6, 1913, the eldest child of Rev. Carl J. Hoffmann and his wife, Bertha nee Seidel. The day was a Saturday—a fact I learned during the church's 100th anniversary. One of the ladies told me, "I remember the day you were born. We lived on a farm about five miles outside of town. It was Saturday morning, and my father had gone to town to go to the bank. When he came home, he said to me, 'The pastor has a son.' "

I was baptized on Christmas Day, 1913, with my two grandfathers as sponsors (although my father's father was represented by a proxy). They named me Oswald Carl Julius—Carl after my grandfather on my father's side, and Julius after my mother's father. (Julius, incidentally, is a biblical name. He was the Roman captain in charge of the prisoners when Paul was taken to Rome. The fact that he is mentioned by name probably indicates that he became a Christian.)

My parents had two more sons: Carl, born in 1915; and Kenneth (the one who also became a pastor), born in 1916. Carl, however, died of a stomach obstruction when he was only about two weeks old. His funeral was on Palm Sunday. That was to have been Confirmation Sunday, but the rite was postponed. The four boys who were to be confirmed donated their lapel flowers as flowers for the funeral. This was quite a donation in those days, since there was no florist in Snyder, and the flowers had to be brought in by train from Omaha. The same boys served as pallbearers. My mother used to say that Carl in his coffin looked like a little doll.

PERSONAL MEMORIES FROM SNYDER, NEBRASKA

I am not sure why my first memories from Snyder have remained with me. For example, when I was about three years old, some workmen were installing our first indoor plumbing and had dug a big hole in our yard. I was playing with my wagon. Somehow I backed up and fell in—one of the first big surprises of my life!

I also recall that our first transportation was by a buggy drawn by our broken-down racehorse, King. In 1918, the congregation purchased a Chevrolet touring car. It was a good car, except that the rear axle always broke down and had to be repaired. When that happened, Harvey Seebeck, the local automobile dealer and member of our church, would let us use one of his cars—a Willys-Overland or something like that. We thought that was pretty special. The best part of having a car was that we got to visit neighboring pastor families: the Nordens, the Ercks, the Pflugs, the Oelschlaegers, the Scheips, and many others.

And I remember being impressed at Christmastime. The church would have a large tree with lots of lighted candles—and an elder standing by with a wet mop to extinguish any embers that might fall on the floor and endanger not only the tree but the whole church!

Other memories are more significant. I know I was impressed by my father's ministering with God's care during the great flu epidemic of 1917–19. If you want to see the terrible toll that epidemic took, all you have to do is visit the cemeteries in Nebraska and look at the number of tombstones from those years, especially those of very young children. Other people remember the graves; I remember the tolling of the church bells, one ring for every year of the person's life. The sound was particularly harsh when they tolled for the second person in a family within the same week.

In spite of the risk to his health, my father ministered to all those in his congregation who got sick. And toward the end of the epidemic he did catch the flu. My mother fixed him a bed downstairs in the dining room. The day when he stood up with his feet on the floor was a day of real celebration at our house! I can remember it to this day.

The second significant thing I remember from those early years was the emphasis on reading and education. Not that we were pushed into it; rather, our parents obviously saw it as important to their lives. Therefore, so did we children. As a pastor, my father had to read and study a lot. My mother too was very intelligent. Before my parents were married, she had taught at Gem City Business College in Quincy, one of the first business schools in the country to teach Gregg shorthand. At 5'2", she was the dominant person in our household. It was she who taught me to read both English and German before I went to school. I had begged her to do it, because I wanted to be able to sing the hymns in church (and we still had both German and English services).

I started school at St. Peter Lutheran School, across the yard from our home, when I was five years old. We did not have many books, so teacher Walter Reese taught us mostly by writing on the blackboard. I remember him writing the word *rat* on the blackboard and telling us to notice the tail at the end of the word: the *t*. That was not the way my mother had taught me to read! She used the phonics system.

Anyway, when Mr. Reese realized that I already had learned to read quite well, he told my parents that I should start in the second grade. At first my parents did not think that was such a good idea, but he finally persuaded them that would be best for me. As a result, I started the second grade at age five. All through school I was the youngest one in my class, but I was a fairly tall boy, and age never really bothered me very much.

Mr. Reese is one of those who had great influence on me. He played a great part in helping prepare me to proclaim the Gospel for all these years. I always like to tell teachers, who sometimes think they are really not accomplishing very much, that they may never know on this earth how many lives they may have influenced along the way.

The third significant thing I remember from Snyder was the emphasis on music. Every child wants to learn to read, but I think my desire to read and then *sing* the hymns was closely tied to my father's great love for music. He was an accomplished organist and frequently gave recitals. He brought the idea of a male chorus into the church, something still very prominent in Lutheran churches in Nebraska today. Since a male chorus was something new, my father often had to arrange the music for male voices. With his commitment to music, it was no wonder that when the church in Snyder built a new church, my father made sure it included a new pipe organ. Nor can I forget the influence on me from my mother's side of the family. Her father (my grandfather Julius) was well respected as the leading tenor in the church choir. And my mother's sister, my aunt Selma, was a concert pianist for visiting artists who performed in the San Francisco area. (By the way, she was married to Rev. Theodore Brohm, the president of Synod's prep school in Oakland, California, across the bay from San Francisco.)

Although we left Snyder when I was only seven years old, I am still proud to claim Snyder as my birthplace. Those first seven years were important years in my life. I still wonder if my parents were not right when they called it the garden spot of the earth.

SPRINGFIELD, ILLINOIS

My love for learning and for the ministry continued to be fed when the family moved in 1921 to Concordia Seminary in Springfield, Illinois, where my father became professor of symbolics (confessions of the church). Not that anything major there influenced me; rather, the experience reinforced in my grade-school eyes the importance of an educated clergy for the church.

As I look back on those years in Springfield, I may have been as impressed with the state capitol as I was with the seminary. One of my friends and schoolmates those years was Harold Olson, whose father was assistant secretary of agriculture for the state. Since they lived on the state fairgrounds, Harold and I did a lot of bike riding there.

For my parents, though, the four years in Springfield were less enjoyable. My father liked teaching at the seminary, and I am told he was a very good professor, but back in those days the Springfield seminary had experienced some tough going. Members of the board were so afraid the Synod would close the seminary that they never asked for anything. That meant that salaries were low and teaching conditions were not the best. And our house ...!

When we first moved to Springfield, we were housed temporarily in the seminary president's house on the campus, because the presidency was vacant at the time. Alas, that lasted only three months. When Rev. Dr. H. A. Klein accepted the seminary presidency, we had to move to an old house on Tenth Street—a pitiful place, held together with chewing gum, *literally.* Before we moved in, the walls had cracked, and the former occupants had used chewing gum to fill the fractures. One day the whole ceiling in the kitchen fell down. Fortunately no one was sitting there at the time.

CHICAGO, ILLINOIS

God works in mysterious ways, the hymn says, but I know He frequently works through people. I've seen that time and time again while working with the LLL and "The Lutheran Hour." Our move to Chicago, however, may have been the first time I saw it in my own life. Two of my mother's brothers were living in Chicago at the time. Uncle Louis Seidel was pastor of St. James Lutheran Church, and Uncle Al Seidel was chief of staff at Walther Memorial Hospital.

We moved in 1925, when my father accepted a call to be pastor of St. Luke Lutheran Church, on Belmont Avenue in Chicago (with 3,300 souls, perhaps the largest congregation in Synod at the time). The parsonage was just behind the church, on Melrose Avenue. The home was so spacious that the second floor held the church offices as well as our bedrooms.

Of all the things I learned at St. Luke's parochial school, two lessons stand out the most, both learned at the same time. First: people in authority—even church leaders!—can be wrong. Second: recognize when to back away from confrontation. Before I describe the event, I need to tell you about my teacher there, Mr. William Burhop.

Mr. Burhop was about 80 years old—honestly—and a rather old 80 too! There were about 40 students in my class. Mr. Burhop had one method of disciplining his students. He would stand up and rise on his toes to order somebody out into the hallway. Then he would take a leather whip that he had bought at the state fair in Springfield and whip the recalcitrant across his lower legs. One of the students was Bill Bohnsack, Mr. Burhop's own grandson. He probably gave his grandfather more of a bad time than any other student in the class. I never got a whipping while I was there, but I knew that if I did, I would probably get another one when I got home.

Anyway, I challenged Mr. Burhop one day. He said the spelling of the word meaning the name of a capital city included an *o*. Here I was, having been schooled in Springfield, the capital of Illinois, where our school was kitty-cornered from the state capitol building. One thing we were taught there was that the city is spelled with an *a* and the building with an *o*. How could a teacher be wrong? Perhaps he just made a slip. I held up my hand and corrected Mr. Burhop: "No, it's the other way around." He rose on his toes and said, "Don't contradict me!" I learned both my lessons immediately!

Music, of course, continued to be an important part of my life. In the eighth grade, I had the joy of singing at Orchestra Hall in the spring concert of the Chicago Bach Chorus, directed by Wilhelm Boeppler. Included in the concert that year was a Bach cantata that went up so high the sopranos could not really sing it. To support them, he recruited 75 boys whose voices had not yet changed.

That experience included a somewhat embarrassing moment. The cantata was "Es erhub Sich ein Streit," which concludes with the great chorale "Let Your Angel Ride with Me on Elijah's Wagon Red." My mother had trained my brother and me to keep on singing through the entire last phrase of the cantata, but Boeppler wanted to have the choir halt briefly before the last note in order to create a smashingly big finish. In rehearsal, he cut us off, but I went right on singing. *"Hoffmann!"* he cried out, looking at me. Yes, I was embarrassed, but at least he knew my name!

I still remember the night of that concert. Ted Lams, who was only 19 at the time and who later married my cousin Hildegarde, was our piano accompanist. The organist was Paul Boester. But I was more impressed that we were accompanied by the whole Chicago Symphony Orchestra.

Boeppler gave us the signal, and we stood up. When we began to sing, the whole audience gasped; and before it was over, the audience was standing and shouting. When we finished, Boeppler took his bows and then tapped his baton on his music stand. "We'll do that last chorale over again," he announced. We did, and that time the audience could hear us sing. It was magnificent!

After I finished eighth grade at St. Luke Lutheran School, I spent the next two years at Luther Institute, the only Lutheran high school in Chicago at that time. One extracurricular activity provided excellent training for this future preacher, helping me to think on my feet. That was the formation of the Debating Club. One debate with another school was on the question "Should Mussolini's Governmental Principles Be Endorsed?" The club was good training in how to keep track of and logically use information in a discussion with another person, no matter what the subject matter.

To get to school, I would take the El or sometimes the streetcar to school. The El was cheaper, so usually I would take that, even though that meant I had to go all the way downtown and then go out on the Lake Street El to the school. To get to the El, I had a good four- or five-block walk from my house to the Ravenswood El station near Wrigley Field. (Naturally, I became a dedicated Cubs fan.)

The community on West Wood Street where Luther Institute was located was getting to be a little rough. After a basketball game or other activities, it was arranged that the boys would escort the girls over to the El station. What was rather ironic about all of this was that I had wanted to go to high school at Concordia-Milwaukee to begin studying for the ministry. My mother did not think I was old enough to do that. So here I was, at age 12, taking the El to school through one of the roughest neighborhoods in Chicago instead!

The worst thing I suffered once, though, was a great embarrassment to my young ego. I was standing in the rush-hour crowded train car holding onto the strap with one hand and my books in the other hand, when I felt this terrific sneeze coming on. There was nothing I could do but let it come—without a handkerchief! "Didn't your mother ever teach you anything?" a lady sitting in front of me asked. That really embarrassed me, because my mother was a very proper lady who had taught us quite well how we were to behave.

Chicago was also where I had my first experience with organized sports (along with my first contact with politicians). I played on a Little League baseball team sponsored by Alderman Feigenbush. Mr. Feigenbush gave us uniforms. They were nice uniforms too, but the name "Feigenbush" covered the whole front of the uniform from one armpit to the other! In that league, each team came to a game with a new ball, and the winning team took both balls home. My parents were seriously disturbed about that, because it seemed to them like gambling; but I played anyway.

Alderman Feigenbush was one of Mayor "Big Bill" Thompson's men. I heard "Big Bill" Thompson speak on street corners several times. He won election after election campaigning against George III of England. He'd say, "We're not going to have George III around here!" I assumed he meant that just as the American Revolution established home rule, so Chicago would not be dictated to by politicians in Washington. The German people, the Italian people, and the Polish people around our part of Chicago sided with him on that.

The other sports events in which I participated in Chicago were the track meets that my brother Kenny, my two cousins, and I ran Saturday afternoons in Lincoln Park. The cousins were Albert and Gerry, the sons of Uncle Al and Aunt Lottie Seidel. Gerry, the youngest of all of us, would organize these track meets. He would be my partner, and his brother Albert and my brother Kenny would be partners. We would run around the lake, which was maybe a quarter of a mile, and even do hurdles and all kinds of track events. Then we would total up the scores to see who had won. The scores were always very close.

I also played on the varsity basketball team at Luther Institute. I was only 12 years old that first year, but nobody knew that at the time. Luther Institute had only 10 basketball jerseys. That meant that only 10 boys could make the team. I was one of the five who scrimmaged against the first team. The first team played the games until we would be far enough ahead or behind that it did not make any difference, then we would get into the game for a few minutes. Our team had a 10 and 5 record that year—not bad for a school with only a few more than 100 students!

Years later when I spoke at a Reformation service in Des Moines, Iowa, a fellow came up to me and said, "My father is dying of cancer here in a hospital. I'd like you to come up and see him. He says he went to high school with you."

"What's your name?" I asked him.

He said, "Wageman."

I said, "Is your father 'Wags' Wageman?"

He said, "Yes, he is."

"Of course, I'll go and see him," I said. "He was on the basketball team with me at Luther Institute."

About 10:30 that night, I walked into the room where "Wags" was dying of cancer. He sat up and embraced me. Before I left, he was up and walking around the halls with me. The nurses were surprised at how much better he seemed to be doing. I introduced him as a star basketball player, and he said, "You weren't bad either."

I said, "Did you know that I was only 12 years old?"

He said, "Go on!" He was probably 17 or 18 at the time.

Remembering that incident leads me to reflect on how often little events early in life may be more important than they seem at the time. For example, I wonder how much of my love for spreading God's Word to the nations was nurtured because of a good friend and classmate at St. Luke's grade school and Luther Institute, Lydia Doederlein. She was a niece of Dr. Theodore Doederlein, who had started our Synod's medical mission in India at Ambur. He too was a member of our congregation. Lydia and I were part of the group that started the German Society at Luther Institute to foster learning and speaking the German language. She was elected secretary that first year.

And that family was the reason I first met a president of The Lutheran Church—Missouri Synod, and did so without being awestruck by the man's office. The occasion was Dr. Doederlein's funeral. My father, as the parish pastor, preached the sermon; but Rev. Dr. Frederick Pfotenhauer, the president of Synod, was there to give a little talk. Just before they went to the cemetery, my father called me into the sacristy. Instead of trying to impress me with the president's personage, my father told me to take Dr. Pfotenhauer to the house and show him where the bathroom was. That was my introduction to church presidents, whom I have been serving ever since.

Two other unusual events occurred while I was in high school, living in Chicago. I doubt they were omens, but they certainly were coincidental.

The first was the 1926 arrival of a new teacher at Luther Institute the same fall that I entered my freshman year: Louis "Swede" Menking, who eventually became Luther Institute's principal and then superintendent of all Lutheran high schools in Chicago. Swede was president of the Lutheran Laymen's League when I was called by the League in 1955 to be the permanent Lutheran Hour speaker.

The second event took place the following summer, in 1927. I "attended" my first Lutheran Laymen's League convention, which was being held at my father's church, St. Luke Lutheran. At that convention, E. H. Faster was elected to a second term as LLL president. I remember this group of people bursting in through the kitchen door at our house in order to go up to my father's office to write Faster's acceptance speech. Among the group was O. P. Kretzmann, later president of Valparaiso University.

To repeat myself, I do not claim these events as anything more than coincidences. But they do illustrate that many events in life come together in ways we could never imagine when we put ourselves at the disposal of our Lord. He holds all things in His hands, even the coincidences.

3

SCHOOLING FOR MINISTRY

F INALLY, AFTER MY SOPHOMORE YEAR IN HIGH SCHOOL, MY FOLKS decided that at age 14 I was old enough to go away to prep school to begin studying for the ministry. At the time (1928), the Synod operated 10 such schools around the United States: high school plus the first two years of college. Those pre-ministerial students who were graduated were expected to continue their education for three years at Concordia Seminary in St. Louis, Missouri. Students who took an alternate route were directed to the seminary in Springfield, Illinois. Seminary graduates received a theological diploma, but they had the option of writing a thesis in order to be graduated with a Bachelor of Arts degree also.

The prep school I first attended was Concordia College in Milwaukee, Wisconsin. I started as a junior in high school, and the next year my younger brother Kenny came in as a freshman. I had assumed we would both finish there. When I was a freshman in college, however, my father accepted a call to the Twin Cities, to Trinity First Lutheran Church in Minneapolis. Since the Synod had another prep school in St. Paul, my father had Kenny and me transfer there so that we could live at home and save the cost of boarding. We made the move at Christmastime, 1930.

After being graduated from Concordia-St. Paul in 1932, I entered the seminary in St. Louis, expecting to be graduated in the normal three years. However, I had not taken into account the Depression. Since congregations were not extending calls, the seminary added a year "off campus" in order to delay graduations a year. Eventually the Synod made that year into a year of internship under the mentoring of a pastor in office. However, when I was there, the school did not care much what a student did during the vicarage year. As a result, I was not graduated from the seminary until 1936 (at age 22).

OUR MODEL T

As I reminisce on those school years, I still get a bit giddy when I think of my first car. My father bought it for me and Kenny when we moved to Minneapolis—an old Model T that we drove back and forth to school every day, even in the winter when it was 30 below zero. Since our first class started at 7:30 A.M., we often started out from the house at 6:30.

We soon learned how to start a Model T in cold weather. We had put an electric starter on the car, and we used both the crank and the starter in order to get it going. Also, we would jack up one of the rear wheels to serve as a flywheel. If the car still did not start, we would look at what passed for a carburetor and wipe it of any moisture, or, if necessary, get a tea kettle of hot water to pour on it in order to melt the ice. After that, the car always started. We would let it run for 10 minutes. Then that Model T would run and go through ice, snow, or anything else. By the way, people called the transmission on that car the "metaphysical transmission," because nobody knew how it worked! It was the forerunner of the modern hydramatic.

One time my brother Ken got into serious trouble with my father because of that car. At about age 15, Ken and some of the Junior Walther Leaguers (the church youth group) went to a party at one of the homes. They finished up with some food at about midnight, and then they decided to play some more games. They finally stopped at about 2:00 in the morning. It was snowing, and by that time the snow was about a foot deep.

I had gone to bed, but I could hear my father pacing up and down on the floor below. I went to sleep, but I woke up at about 2 A.M. and could hear him still pacing. So I got up and said to him, "I tell you what. I'll get your car out and go look for Ken."

I had just opened the garage door and was ready to get in the car when here came that Model T, chugging around the corner down on Franklin Avenue near where we lived. It came right through the snow into our yard. When my brother got out of the car, he asked me, "What are you doing up at this time of the night?" I told him that I was up to warn him about what was going to face him when he got into the house. My father grounded him for six weeks. That never happened to me; I was a good boy! Well …

Actually, somebody had to drive that car to school. If I would have been grounded for something, my father would have had to take us and pick us up after school. That would have taken far too much time out of his busy day as a parish pastor. I was never grounded.

I have driven a number of Model Ts since that time. Once when I was in Iowa for some event, a collector of old cars came to pick me up in a Model T. I asked him to let me drive, but he said, "You aren't able to drive this car."

"Why not?" I asked. "I drove one back and forth to school in Minnesota."

He let me drive, and after a while he said, "You drive this car better than I do!"

Oh, those old Model Ts were fun to drive, with pedals for the gears and two hand levers for the "spark" and for the accelerator.

THE LOVE OF EDUCATION

Those eight years between entering Concordia-Milwaukee and graduation from the seminary were not merely fun years, they were highly significant for me. They were the years when the seeds planted earlier came to bud.

High school in Chicago was enjoyable, but I was thrilled when I was allowed to enter prep school. Most of the Synod's prep schools (including Milwaukee and St. Paul) were patterned after the classical education of the German *gymnasium,* complete with Latin names for the classes: *Sexta* ("Sixth") for lowest class (high school freshman) on up though *Prima* ("First") for the college sophomore class. We studied the subjects that public schools normally require (math, science, history, etc.) plus German (the mother tongue of Lutheran history), Latin (the language of classical rhetoric and early church history), and Greek (the original language of many classics, including the New Testament)—plus various courses in religion and the Bible.

The seminary classes were structured around four disciplines: exegetical, homiletical, historical, and practical theology. The exegetical part meant that we also had to learn Hebrew in order to study the Old Testament in its original language.

I relished the classics—especially Greek! Although I had already started to learn the language in Milwaukee under Dr. Victor Bartling (a gentle man and a wonderful teacher), it was Professor Moenkemoeller, in St. Paul, who really got me interested. He was a small man, very demanding, and he put the fear of God into his students. In some ways, he was very hard on his students, but we learned the language. I learned Greek well enough that during my last year at St. Paul, I met with some classmates before first hour in order to help them prepare for Moenkemoeller's class that day.

41

Then, two years later, during that year "off campus" from the seminary, I was accepted into graduate school at the University of Minnesota to study linguistics and classical languages (even though I had no undergraduate degree at the time). The head of the linguistics department was Dr. Marbury B. Ogle, who had just come from being the head of the classical school in Rome. The first class I had with him was a seminar on Cicero. He came into the classroom and threw about 15 copies of Cicero's letters on the table. He expected us to read it at sight! I found out then that a person could do that, but you had to put your mind to it. Later on, when I was teaching classical languages, I used that method too. There were all kinds of people in that seminar, including teachers and scholars from other departments, because they wanted to study with this great man.

At the University I also had the good fortune to study under a professor from Germany, Dr. Reichardt, who taught Sanskrit, Old Norse, and other languages. As a result, I was able to get my master's degree in classical languages *and* linguistics. I went back to finish my final year at the seminary with a master's degree from the University of Minnesota, even though I still did not have my bachelor's degree!

The thesis I wrote for my bachelor's degree was on the difference between Plato and Paul in the understanding of immortality. In those days, scholars were saying in an offhand manner that St. Paul got his idea of immortality from Plato. Nothing could be farther from the truth! Paul made a big point of the fact that immortality for Christians, the resurrection of both body and soul, was something which all Platonists deny. (My thesis, an original study and more like a master's thesis, is still in the library at the St. Louis seminary today.)

I can scarcely talk about this love for education without mentioning the many fine professors I've had. In prep school, part of our affection for them was expressed through nicknames—even though not all those were literally complimentary. Professor Moenkemoeller at St. Paul was "Monkey"—never to his face, of course. Other nicknames I remember from Concordia-Milwaukee are "Pope" (Paul) Zanow, "Heinz" Gienapp, and President Dr. G. Christian Barth, "the old man." Bill Ackmann was the athletic director, a position he had held, I think, since the flood! I remember that he would kick you in a certain part of your anatomy if you did not do things right. But we liked him, and we played hard for him.

I particularly remember "Tab" (Prof. Edward) Jenne. He was my English teacher in my first year at Milwaukee. Fifty-four years later, in the summer of 1993, I visited with him for the last time. I was in Milwaukee at the German Fest, preaching to an audience of over 4,000 people. I spoke in German, but they asked me to sprinkle my sermon with English, because many of those present could not understand German anymore. After that service, Rev. Elmer Neitzel, who had been in the class ahead of me at Concordia-Milwaukee, took me over to visit Tab. That was about six months before he died.

The most provocative teacher of all at Concordia-St. Paul was Professor Lorenz Blankenbuehler. He had the whole *Cambridge History of English Literature* at his fingertips—literally *on* his fingertips! He would have a stack of cards in his hand and would have rubber bands around them in all kinds of ways. He would unroll them and roll them up again and use them to give his class lectures. When he could not get his point across to us, he would talk to the radiator and say, "You poor radiator. You sit there so dumb like that. But you're still brighter than the ones who are sitting here!"

Professor Blankenbuehler, who later became editor of the *Lutheran Witness,* also became our good friend. When we moved to St. Louis, we would invite him to our home together with Pastor Elmer Foelber and Pastor Arthur Kuehnert from Ebenezer

Church in St. Louis. Those fellows were all in school with my father. Both Professor Foelber and Pastor Kuehnert were in my parents' wedding party.

LIFELONG FRIENDSHIPS

The close-knit community of the prep-school-through-seminary system built lasting friendships. Elmer Eggold, a roommate in Milwaukee when I was a senior, later became superintendent of Lutheran high schools in Milwaukee. Two friends I left behind when I had to transfer from Concordia-Milwaukee to Concordia-St. Paul were Bill Buege, a "swift," which meant he lived at home in the city, and Ozzie Waech, who came from Crete, Illinois, and lived in the dormitory. We did not get back together again until a year and a half later when we entered Concordia Seminary in St. Louis. There we became very close friends.

We did not have much money in those days—it was still the Depression and we were students—so we looked for inexpensive things to do for fun. Bill Buege, Ozzie Waech, and I would take long walks to a sandwich shop in Richmond Heights (a St. Louis suburb near the seminary) for roast beef sandwiches. Bill Buege, who later went on to be the pastor of large churches in Minneapolis and St. Louis, and Dean of the Chapel at Valparaiso University, tells me that he still remembers with fondness those walks.

At the seminary, they called me "Big Oz," and they called Ozzie Waech "Little Oz." Among our classmates those names have stuck ever since. Little Oz and I were roommates during our second and third years at the sem. He was a great roommate, a good student, and in his last year at the seminary president of the student chorus. He was even friend enough to go with me to a Cubs-Cardinals baseball game at Sportsman's Park. Of course, we had to wait until the day's classes were finished, but we at least got there.

As I remember it, the Cubs were in contention with the Cardinals for the pennant that year (1936), and the Cubs won that day—their 19th win in a row, I believe.

In those days we were not allowed to have radios in our rooms, but Ozzie Waech had a little box radio that he brought into our room and put into one of the desk drawers. He especially liked to listen to "Sugar Blues" by Clyde McCoy. Almost every noon he would listen to that.

One time Ozzie Waech got sick and was in bed in our room. For some reason, Dean Fritz came up to the room to visit him. I happened to be there at the time, and we had the radio on. When the dean entered our room, I slid over to where that radio was playing and pushed the drawer shut. Dean Fritz pretended that he never heard that radio at all!

God used Ozzie Waech in remarkable ways. He served The Lutheran Church—Missouri Synod as Director of Evangelism for many years. I preached at many evangelism rallies and other gatherings that he put together.

THE LOVE OF SPORTS

The love of sports awakened in me while we lived in Chicago continued to grow throughout my school years. I remember one particular game during my first year in Milwaukee (my *Quarta* [junior] year in high school). President Barth's son, Wally, was on the softball team of the class ahead of us with Elmer Neitzel and my roommate Ollie Eggerding. At a crucial moment in one game we played against them, Luther Kleinhans hit a hard line drive about knee high off to my right. I lurched for the ball, caught it on the fly, and doubled the runner off first base. The old man was watching the game and rooting for his son's team. He just waved his hands in disgust and left.

Our *Quarta* softball team was very good. We won the championship that year for intramural softball, something almost unheard of. That meant that we beat out the teams from the three classes ahead of us, including two college classes!

I made Concordia-Milwaukee's All-Star softball team each year—even as a high-school junior. Each year when the alumni team from the St. Louis seminary came up to play in the annual game, I was the shortstop on the Milwaukee team.

My sports days didn't end when I entered the seminary. I played first base the year after the graduation of Dick Siebert, who later played for Philadelphia under Connie Mack. We played some good teams, like Piney Woods College. They had a black pitcher who, I think, must have been Don Newcombe. He only allowed us two hits—and I had one of them! I took second on the throw home, which was beaten to the plate by the man who was on second base, and a round of applause rippled through the crowd. But nobody brought me home, and we lost 2 to 1!

I sometimes wonder if it was my combined love for sports as well as for education that helped me get elected student body president during my final year at the seminary, even though I was still the youngest student in my class. Of course, I had gone to school at both Concordia-Milwaukee and Concordia-St. Paul, the two biggest preministerial schools in our synodical system at that time, so I had a pretty good constituency!

My opponent in that election was Bill Kennell, at whose wedding I met my wife, Marcia, a few years later. He lost the election, but we made him manager of the stationery store. That was the most lucrative position on campus at that time, because the manager got to keep a percentage of the profits—very important for those of us paying our own way through school! Those of us who served in student government were not paid anything.

We officers (including Roland Wiederanders, vice-president; Ed Runge, secretary) met over lunch each day in the alcove of the dining hall. We always had a chair there for any faculty member who wanted to sit in on those luncheons. We must have done all right as officers. On one occasion, Professor "Gus" Polack made the observation that there were no "undercurrents among the students this year"—which, by the way, had not been true the year before.

A LOVE FOR MUSIC

Music has always been an important part of my life, especially during my days at the seminary. In addition to singing in the seminary chorus (directed during my first year by parochial school teacher Walter Wismar), I also sang with the St. Louis A Cappella Choir and got involved with three other students in forming the Schubert Quartet.

My special thanks go to Dr. William B. Heyne, the director of the St. Louis A Cappella Choir, for he first got me involved in music at the seminary. He was a cousin of some of my cousins and, with his brother Walter and my cousin Ted Brohm, had played in a string trio on the very first broadcast from Lutheran radio station KFUO in 1923. At the time KFUO was located in an attic studio of the old Concordia Seminary on Jefferson Avenue in south St. Louis.

Bill Heyne insisted that I sing in his St. Louis A Cappella Choir (which I did for all three of my years at the seminary). The choir, well-known in St. Louis, sang to packed houses at many concerts in the Sheldon Auditorium. We also sang at the dedication of the city's Kiel Auditorium, with the mayor sitting right in the front row. I was one of three people in the second bass section. We rehearsed three times a week, either at the St. Louis Conservatory of Music on Olive Street or at St. Peter Lutheran Church on Kingshighway. Financially, singing in that choir was a losing proposition, because we had to pay our own streetcar fare to get to and from rehearsals!

I owe a great debt of gratitude to Bill Heyne. He gave me invaluable training in the use of my voice. He taught me how to use it naturally, the way it is supposed to be used, without ever becoming hoarse. Anyone who learns how to do that can talk all day long without ever feeling it. Once in a while, if I have to yell because there is no microphone, my voice may get tired, but otherwise, thanks to him, I never have any problems with my voice.

I believe a lot of pastors could learn from that. If the only thing a person knows how to do is yell, there is something wrong with the use of his voice. For example, many pastors sing/yell at the top of their voice—and for the most part off-key. That is what happens when you yell. If they would just sing in their natural voice, they would sound much better.

Anyway, Bill Heyne's training paid off handsomely when four of us formed the Schubert Quartet, the singing group I remember most fondly from my seminary days. We practiced a lot—about 22 hours each week. By the time we went on tour, William Heyne said we were the best rehearsed quartet he had ever heard. We sang 90 concerts in churches throughout the Midwest during the summers of my first and second years at the sem.

In addition to myself singing bass, the members of the quartet were Vic Meyer, first tenor; Ozzie Waech, second tenor; and Ed Runge, baritone. Our accompanist that first year was Ken Runge. The second year, I served as the accompanist as well. I played piano and organ, and would accompany Vic Meyer on his solos and play Bach chorales while the others took the offering. Ed Runge was our treasurer, and he kept very good books.

We (the quartet) purchased a Model A Ford, which served as transportation for our group. We were not allowed to have cars on campus in those days, but the dean permitted us to keep it in a nearby garage if we would not use it unauthorized. We carried our programs, our music, and other material around with us in a trailer that had been lent to us by two sisters and a brother whose name was Bopp. Their residence was on Kingshighway right near St. Peter Lutheran Church.

One summer (I forget which) our car was not running very smoothly. While we rehearsed at Ozzie Waech's home in Crete, Illinois, where his father was pastor, and gave concerts in the area in the evenings, we tore down the car's engine and put in new piston rings. I knew how to do that, because I had done it with our Model T. After three days, we had the engine put back together, but when we went to start the car, it wouldn't work. Then I realized we had to open the carburetor, and when we did that, it started right away.

Little Oz was the one who usually arranged our summer tours by sending letters to pastors and congregations. Unfortunately, one of the first concerts he arranged for us never happened. We were to sing at a church in Washington, Missouri. There was no bridge across the Missouri River at that time, and we all forgot that the ferry stopped running at seven o'clock. There we were, with no way to get across the river in time for our concert. That was the only time we missed a concert date!

We had some very interesting experiences on those concert tours. We sang candlelight concerts, and in some places, the churches were so dark that people actually brought flashlights in order to see. I also remember one concert in Minnesota where the mosquitoes kept flying into our mouths. We swallowed them and just kept on singing!

Nevertheless those concert tours were enjoyable, and they were profitable for us too. Because we stayed in people's homes, our only expenses were food and gas. We saved our money and did not spend it foolishly. The result was that those Schubert Quartet tours paid our way through the seminary.

During my last year at the seminary, because of the extra time required of me as president of the student body, I had planned to curtail my involvement in the various musical groups. But by this time Bill Heyne was director of the seminary chorus, and he would not take no for an answer. I continued to sing in the seminary chorus and in the St. Louis A Cappella Choir, as well as practice with the Schubert Quartet.

DR. WALTER A. MAIER

I could have mentioned Dr. Maier earlier under those professors who meant a lot to me. He nurtured our love for learning, especially languages. His impact on me, however, requires more than a passing reference.

"There were giants in those days." Between the two World Wars, the Synod was struggling to become a truly American church instead of a branch of German Lutheranism, yet not lose its unique and pure doctrine. What would that mean for how we worship, how we preach, how we reach out to the unchurched, how we formulate in English the beliefs we hold so dear? Space does not permit mentioning everyone who should be remembered, but certainly the roster includes President and Professor Ludwig Fuerbringer, Professors Theodore Graebner, J. T. Mueller, William Arndt, John H. C. Fritz, W. G. Polack—and especially that giant Walter A. Maier, affectionately known as WAM.

Although "The Lutheran Hour" had been only a one-year affair when I arrived at the seminary in 1932 and would not return to the air until 1935 (during my vicarage), WAM was not idle. He was still writing for and editing the national *Walther League Messenger;* speaking twice a week over radio KFUO; preaching on a regular basis; addressing large gatherings (such as, in 1932, Detroit's 200th anniversary of George Washington's birth), rallies, and Luther anniversary celebrations; serving as faculty advisor to the seminary Students' Missionary Society; helping out as time permitted at the congregation he and the Students' Missionary Society founded, St. Stephen's; and doing a host of other things so numerous that the *St. Louis Globe-Democrat Sunday Magazine* wrote of him on September 4, 1932, "Dr. Maier cannot possibly keep up the mad pace he has set for himself in the first thirty-eight years of his life ..."

I took all of WAM's classes: Psalms, Minor Prophets, Hebrew, and all of his electives. We had his class in Psalms on Monday mornings at 7:30. I still remember him during my final year at the sem, standing against the blackboard, lecturing after his long train ride back from Detroit the night before. "The Lutheran Hour" was being broadcast again live from Epiphany Lutheran Church there. He had to take the overnight train back to St. Louis because some in Synod—including some at the seminary—did not support his Lutheran Hour activities. That did not include Dr. Arndt, who read all of his Lutheran Hour sermons before they were broadcast and later on read all of mine too. Dr. Arndt was a fine man. He would often write me a personal note after he read my sermon that would say, "I got so much out of that sermon," or something like that.

I graded papers for Dr. Maier during my middle year at the sem. He would always grade my paper first, and would find some way to mark something off. I had memorized the material and knew it was perfect, but he would hand the paper back to me marked 99½ percent or something like that. Then he would laugh!

We did not get paid for grading papers, but I would be invited to his house now and then for dinner. I would sit at the table in his house on "faculty row" with him, his wife, Hulda, and his two sons, Paul and Walter, Jr., who were young boys at the time. When dinner was over, we would sing a hymn. When I was there, we usually sang one in German marked "auf eigener melodie" (to its own melody), and I would have to figure out how to sing that

51

whole long stanza in German. Dr. Maier would sing in his brassy voice, and all the rest of us would sing along.

Dr. Maier was the one who got us students to make calls on people in "Hooverville," the shantytown down by the Mississippi River. We would call on the people who lived there and ask them to come to our services on Sunday morning. They all said they would come, and maybe 15 or 20 would show up. That experience taught me to keep on inviting someone who had said no the first time.

I remember another time when members of Dr. Maier's Students' Missionary Society canvassed in the Soulard neighborhood in south St. Louis. One time I came to a certain house where a number of ladies were sitting in the next room. I went through the series of questions we normally asked, and when I came to the question "Are there any children here to be baptized?" I heard a few giggles from the next room. It finally dawned on me that this was a house of prostitution!

Dr. Maier was a special person and a great man. It was a great loss to the church when he died so young. When his wife, Hulda, died on December 27, 1986, her funeral was held in the Christ of All Nations Chapel at LLL headquarters in St. Louis. Dr. Paul Spitz, president of the Missouri District of The Lutheran Church—Missouri Synod, preached the sermon. He had been a pastor at St. Stephen's Lutheran Church in St. Louis, which had been founded by Dr. Maier, and to which he and his whole family belonged during the time he was professor at the seminary. I had the honor of giving a talk at the end of her funeral service.

If anything, I would have to say that WAM's influence on me was greatest in instilling in me a love for missions and evangelism. Yes, education and linguistics were a love for both of us, but not nearly as great a love as getting out to others the Good News of what God has done for us in Jesus, our Savior.

SEMINARY GRADUATION

At the end of that school year in 1936, I received my bachelor's degree from the seminary, but there were few calls. Only two graduates out of the 160 in my class received a call into the parish ministry. I was not one of the two, but I did receive an offer of employment as a professional church worker. Before my graduation, Rev. John Molstad, chairman of the board of Bethany College in Mankato, Minnesota, had come down to the seminary and offered me a position as chairman of the English department and dean of men at the college. I asked seminary President Ludwig Fuerbringer what I should do, since the school was part of another church body: the Norwegian Evangelical Lutheran Synod. He said, "That might be a good thing for you to do. But you have to understand that those Norwegians are somewhat peculiar, and you'll just have to get used to them!"

My father, however, gave me the most important advice. He said, "Don't get mixed up in the politics of the 'Little Norwegian Synod.' "

I found out that he knew what he was talking about. It seemed, at least at that time, that many of the pastors in that Synod were mixed up in the politics of their church body in some way. I took my father's advice and stayed out of it, and I have tried to stay out of church politics ever since that time.

I did accept the offer to teach at Bethany. You know, I have never turned down a position in the church, and I have never applied for one either. I think a person should do the best he or she can to serve the Lord where He has placed us. When the time comes that He wants us to do something else, He will let us know. That's the way it has been for me, and He has surprised me in some remarkable ways!

One more story about church politics. In the 1960s and '70s, I almost was pulled into the fray. In those years I was nominated several times for president of The Lutheran Church—Missouri Synod. I did not run for that office; others nominated me. The last time I was nominated was in 1978. That year synodical officials told me that if I wanted to let my name stand as a candidate for president, I would have to agree beforehand to serve if I were elected. I did not agree to that, because I believe it violates the doctrine of the divine call. According to that doctrine, you have a divine call to the position in which you are serving, and when you are called to another position, you seek the guidance of the Holy Spirit to determine which position God is calling you to at that time. For that reason I did not let my name stand, and said I would write a letter to the pastors of our church body explaining my position. The synodical Public Relations Department asked me not to write that letter. They promised to make my reason for declining the nomination known, but they never did.

Ach! Politics!

SHADOWS ON THE HORIZON

In the early morning light, objects at a great distance are obscured, in part because of their distance and in part by the shadows they cast. And because they are so far away, we don't know whether they have any import for us or not. Only later in the day do we see things more clearly. As I look back on my school years, two of those then-distant shadows had greater importance than I could have imagined: radio (obviously) and laymen.

To a certain extent, radio and I grew up together. By the time I entered prep school in Milwaukee in 1928, the first regular broadcasting station (KDKA, Pittsburgh) was almost eight years old; baseball had been broadcast since the 1921 World Series in New York; RCA was eight years old and NBC was almost two; the first coast-to-coast broadcast, the 1927 Rose Bowl game, had occurred 20 months earlier; and Chicago station WMAQ had just begun broadcasting "Amos 'n' Andy." The seminary in St. Louis had established station KFUO only four years earlier, and its new campus in 1926 even housed KFUO's own building, complete with broadcasting tower. The Lutheran Laymen's League assisted in paying for the building.

Looking back, it seems only natural that in 1930 my father accepted the call to be pastor of Trinity First Lutheran Church in Minneapolis, primarily because they were broadcasting their services over WCCO radio, one of the most powerful radio stations in the Midwest at the time. They continued to do that for several years, until the Depression became so deep that they could not get the money even to pay for the telephone lines to carry the broadcast, which was all they were paying for at the time.

As a teenager, I was caught up in the excitement of it all, just as everyone else was. But because of my father's enthusiasm for spreading the Gospel over the radio, and because of the rousing articles by the editor of the magazine for the Synod's youth, *The Walther League Messenger* (the editor being "that young prof in St. Louis," Walter A. Maier), I had some appreciation for the first nine-month attempt to start "The Lutheran Hour" (October 1930–June 1931). What a thrill, then, in 1935 that I was able to return to the sem from my "year away" to study once again under WAM, who had restarted "The Lutheran Hour" earlier that year.

I mention these things because I see in them God's hand, preparing my heart for the future. To be sure, I was not the only person excited about the opportunity to spread the Gospel via radio waves. Still, I can't envision God calling someone as speaker for "The Lutheran Hour" who considered radio frivolous at best or a tool of Satan at worst.

In this connection, I also see God's hand in my love for learning as well as in the personal relationship that developed between Professor Maier and me as his student. Every pastor needs to be educated, but speaking over radio to an audience around the world and doing that week after week requires a lot of hard preparation. And my training in classical rhetoric didn't hurt, either. I wonder, though, if I would have accepted the call to "The Lutheran Hour" if I had held WAM in such awe that I could not follow in his footsteps. Instead, when the call came to me in 1955 to be the speaker for "The Lutheran Hour," I could almost imagine WAM saying to me, "Go ahead; it's okay."

The second shadow on the horizon to which I call your attention is my early appreciation and respect for the laymen of the church. How could I not love my grandfathers, both of whom were laymen? How could I as a child not be grateful for—and impressed by—the kindness of Harvey Seebeck, the auto dealer in Snyder, Nebraska, who loaned our family a car when ours broke down?

One layman, Ernest Rubbert, was largely responsible for paying for my father's broadcast of worship services over WCCO in Minneapolis. When things got difficult for him, he even borrowed money against his insurance policies to pay for the broadcasts! This early member of the Lutheran Laymen's League also was paying for scholarships for 10 seminary students. (By the way, my brother Kenny later married Rubbert's granddaughter Violet.)

I also think that of those in my seminary graduation class, only two students at the time received calls into the ministry. Yet most of those who went into secular employment still served the church in one capacity or another. I think particularly of Frank Thiede, one of my classmates at Milwaukee, who earned a top management position with Sears. After a Lutheran Hour rally one time he came up to me and said that he probably should have gone into the ministry. I told him that he was serving the church as a dedicated layman probably better than he would have as a pastor—which surprised and then gratified him!

My good friend Dr. John Behnken, president of The Lutheran Church—Missouri Synod, under whose leadership I served for 15 years as public relations director of the Synod, was accustomed to saying that "the ministry is the highest profession." I disagreed with him—and told him so. (Happily, our disagreement never disturbed our close relationship.) I feel, as Martin Luther did, that every worthy vocation is an opportunity to serve God. A call into the ministry offers special opportunity to witness to the grace of God in Jesus Christ, the Son whom He sent to be the Savior of the world. The vocation itself, however, does not need to be defended by downgrading other professions. I have always been repelled by such attempts. The highest status is that of the order of priests to which all Christians belong through their faith in Jesus Christ. Although I've always believed that, each year with the Lutheran Laymen's League has steeled that conviction within me.

As I reminisce, I certainly do not believe that I was the only nor automatically the best person to be chosen to be the speaker for "The Lutheran Hour." At the same time, I certainly can see in retrospect God's hand at work in my life preparing me for the call when it came. The glory is His alone!

4

GETTING ESTABLISHED
1936–41

T HE SUMMER OF 1936 TURNED OUT TO BE ONE OF THE MOST significant times in my life. That is when I first met my wife-to-be, Marcia. As I mentioned, we met in connection with the wedding of my classmate Bill Kennell.

Thinking about weddings: People today may think it strange that back then, students at the St. Louis seminary were not allowed to be engaged, much less married. What was even stranger was the number of new graduates who seemingly started dating, fell in love, got engaged, made plans for the ceremony, and then actually got married—all within the space of a month or two after graduation! Bill Kennell's wedding wasn't until the following January or February, but he and I (as the best man) met that summer in Minneapolis to make plans with the bride, Marjorie Ekblad, and her best friend and bridesmaid, Marcia Linnell. To be honest, I have to admit I do not really remember much about that meeting. My heart, mind, and energies were on my forthcoming years at Bethany College, Mankato, Minnesota, and its student body of just under 100.

The school was originally built by the Wisconsin Synod as Mary and Martha finishing school for girls. When it became coeducational, the faculty suggested that it be renamed Bethany, keeping at least a reference to the biblical sisters—and their brother, Lazarus—by renaming the school after their hometown. Somehow at some point in time, the school went bankrupt, and the Wisconsin Synod hoped to buy it back at a bankruptcy sale. Before they could do that, however, the Norwegian Synod bought it out from under them. That caused a lot of hard feelings between the Norwegian Lutheran Church and the Wisconsin Synod, a tension that lasted for many years. I had good friends in both bodies and refused to let antipathies affect my relationships with any of them. As my father said, "Stay out of their politics."

As a side comment, I'm constantly amazed by the people connections that pop up in life, especially in the church. In chapter 2 I told you about my Springfield, Illinois, grade-school friend Harold Olson, whose father was the state's assistant secretary of agriculture. Well, Harold's uncle was the first president of Bethany after the Norwegian Synod bought it.

And years later, when I was asked to preach at a building dedication for the church I had attended in Springfield (Trinity Lutheran), Harold was the one who introduced all the guests, from the mayor on down to the lowest dogcatcher. It was a very hot day, about 107 degrees in the shade, and the introductions took a solid hour. Before we started the service, Pres. Walter Baepler of the Springfield seminary leaned over to me and said, "If you would just get up there and say, 'God bless you all. Amen,' that would be the most sensational sermon you ever delivered in your life!" I did not feel I could do that, because they had brought me all the way from New York to preach there. I preached the sermon I had planned. After I was finished, Baepler said, "They didn't listen to a word you said!"

Those details had nothing to do with my decision to accept the offer to teach at Bethany after graduation from the seminary. Rather, I was pleased to be able to serve our Savior in a capacity for which I had been preparing for a long time. Beginning when

I helped my classmates at Concordia-St. Paul study for Greek, through my language classes at the seminary and while getting my master's degree at the U of M, I knew I wanted to teach linguistics. I was thrilled when I had the offer from Bethany to be head of the English department as well as dean of men. (At the time, Bethany was like most Lutheran prep schools: a high school plus two years of college.)

With my master's degree I was qualified to teach in the college, but the state of Minnesota required specific education courses for teachers to be certified to teach high school courses. That meant another summer back at the University of Minnesota. The first half of that summer (1936) I took Education 101, 102, and 103. I was most grateful when Dean Miller, head of the graduate school, allowed me to finish my teacher requirements on the graduate level.

One of my professors and my advisor for that summer session was Professor Sorenson, who later became the first president of the University of Minnesota at Duluth. He was considered by the students to be the resident left-of-center radical, as he sat in his suspenders to teach class. In spite of his politics, he was smart; he wrote our textbook on statistics.

Another class I took was taught by Dean Miller. What I learned in that class has been important to me over the years. He called the course "Individual Differences." His thesis was that while all people have similarities, we all—even identical twins—have our own identities and differences too. He emphasized that when we deal with people, we have to respect their differences. I really believe that class has helped me to deal with people individually and personally over the years.

Another thing Dr. Miller emphasized to budding teachers was that they cannot prevent anyone from being educated to the limit of his or her capabilities. Later on, my brother-in-law Ray Class was named manager of Amtrak from St. Paul, Minnesota, to Seattle,

Washington. He was required to take a CEO graduate course at the University of Pittsburgh. He came to me and said, "I never even finished high school. How can I take a course like that?"

Recalling my experience with Dr. Miller, I said, "You may be more educated than many of the other CEOs who will be there from steel companies and other great corporations."

As it turned out, when he returned from taking that graduate course, he told me that he had a grand time with presidents of America's great corporations, and that he felt right at home with them.

TEACHING AT BETHANY COLLEGE

Those four years when I was teaching at Bethany were very busy years. I had come there to be the head of the English department and dean of men, but just before I got there, Dr. Walter Buszin, who had been head of the music department, accepted a call to Concordia College in Fort Wayne, Indiana. They asked me to serve as head of the music department as well, which I agreed to do.

Also I was given the job of recruiting Missouri Synod students for Bethany throughout the Midwest during the summers. That was very important, because there were not enough students in the Norwegian Synod to support the school. After I had done my recruitment, about half of the students there were Missouri Synod.

I coached the basketball team in my last year at Bethany. We took second among the junior colleges in all of Southern Minnesota that year. One of the players on the team was Paul Ylvisaker, who became the dean of the Graduate School of Higher Education at Harvard. He had diabetes, and he would often have to suck on a lemon or an orange during a break in the action in order to continue to play.

I think I enjoyed working with Bethany's music program the most. One of the fun challenges was teaching the music appreciation class, which I had never had myself. I bought a big phonograph, and some of the boys from the class would carry it back and forth from my room to the classroom. I also bought records of both traditional, classical music and more modern music, and we would listen to those records and talk about them. Both the students and I learned a lot!

I also directed the choir—and a very good one it was! We rehearsed every noon. Sometimes the whole choir would rehearse, sometimes we would have sectional rehearsals, and sometimes I would rehearse just one voice. There were 50 members in that choir from freshmen in high school through sophomores in college—more than half the student body! It got to be as attractive to be in the choir as on the basketball team. As one student, Norman Schuett, wrote years later in a 1989 newsletter, "In his [Hoffmann's] rehearsals he always encouraged us to higher standards. With him the hard work of rehearsal was a joy ..."

The crowning experience with the choir came when we developed the largest choir that I have ever directed in my life: 700 voices. Here's how it came about.

We organized a music festival at Mankato. Bethany choir would participate, but as the core of a mass choir assembled from throughout southern Minnesota and northern Iowa. The hard work of recruiting and organizing the off-campus groups fell to student Joel Ingebritson, who was the son of the president of the Norwegian Synod. He arranged for regional rehearsals in 31 different locations, all of which I traveled to at least once for regional rehearsal.

When all 700 voices sang together the night of the concert, it was magnificent. The Armory in Mankato was packed with 1,500 people, which was all the building would hold. The local newspaper reported at the time that the concert was "impressively executed and impressively staged under the able baton of Oswald Hoffmann."

How grateful I was for the work of Joel Ingebritson. Years later, after World War II had begun, he stopped by our house for dinner, and we spent the evening together. He was a sergeant in charge of about 200 men. They were on a mission so secret that he could not even tell me what it was. That was the last time I saw him.

As a classroom teacher, I was really hard on my students—perhaps too much so. Years later, when I would see former students, they would say, "I remember that test in humanities that you and Carl S. Meyer put together and then knocked out all the easy questions and gave us the hardest ones you could think of." Further conversation usually showed that they viewed our tests as an obstacle course to get through before they could get out of the school. They looked at that as one of the great achievements of their lives! (Carl Meyer was the academic dean at the time and went on to become a professor at our St. Louis seminary.)

ENGLISH LUTHERAN CHURCH, COTTONWOOD, MINNESOTA

The last year I taught at Bethany, I also served as pastor of English Lutheran Church in Cottonwood, Minnesota, about 100 miles away. With their call, I was ordained and installed at that church in 1939. My ordination was into the little Norwegian Synod of which that church was a member. My father came from Minneapolis to preach the sermon.

I would go to Cottonwood every other Sunday to preach and sometimes during the week for special occasions such as weddings or funerals. I clearly remember one funeral I had there. A certain well-known man in town claimed to be an agnostic. His two sons came to church, but he never did. Later on, when he was in bed at his home dying of cancer, I would visit him every time I was in Cottonwood. His sons told me that when I would leave, he would underline a passage in his Bible and say, "Hoffmann talked about that."

Before he died, he confessed his faith in Jesus Christ as his Savior. The big Lutheran congregation in town offered us their large building for his funeral, but we had it in our little church. The place was packed, because everybody knew that he had been not just unchurched but agnostic. I have seen his sons a few times since then in different places, and they still come up to me with tears in their eyes.

I put a lot of miles on my car those four years, recruiting in the summers, going to all those regional choir rehearsals that one year, driving back and forth between Mankato and English Lutheran Church in Cottonwood, and between Mankato and St. Paul, where Marcia was (itself a trip of over 80 miles one way).

My car was a 1931 Model A Ford roadster with a rumble seat. My father had bought it for me for $200. We had to replace the cloth top, but otherwise the car was in excellent condition. It was a handsome car. Marcia insists she married me because of that car!

During that fourth year at Bethany (1939–40), I had resolved to complete the residency requirements for my Ph.D. at the University of Minnesota. Accordingly, I made plans for a one-year leave of absence from Bethany, the school year to begin the fall of 1940. I also resigned from my call as pastor of English Lutheran Church in Cottonwood.

MARCIA AND MARRIAGE

Although I first met Marcia when the four of us were planning Bill Kennell and Marjorie Ekblad's wedding the summer of '36, I really did not pay much attention to Marcia until the wedding itself early in 1937.

I had been to Chicago to attend the funeral of my uncle, Rev. Louis Seidel. I caught a terrible cold, then had to rush to my parents' home in Minneapolis for the wedding. Dr. Gerald Koepke, a well-known eye, ear, nose, and throat specialist and a member of my father's congregation, came to the house and put something up my nose with toothpicks. The mucus drained all the way to the floor. That cleared my sinuses, and I felt good for the wedding a day or so later.

I was the best man for the wedding, and Marcia was a bridesmaid. None of us had any money at the time to do anything really special. After the wedding, the whole wedding party simply went to Marcia's house. I guess that's when I really first noticed her.

Marcia's maiden name was Linnell. Her father died when she was nine years old, and her mother had moved from Osceola, Wisconsin, first to Luverne, Minnesota, then to St. Paul, where her mother's sister owned a dress shop. There she met Marcia's stepfather, Henry Doeren, a Missouri Synod man. Originally he was a member of the Wisconsin Synod, but his mother wanted him to go to a church where they worshiped in the English language. He went to a budding young church called Redeemer, started by Dr. Oscar C. Kreinheder, who later became president of Valparaiso University. Pastor and Mrs. Paul Lindemann were at Redeemer when Marcia was growing up. They became good friends to Marcia, and would take her along on some of their summer vacations at Lutherland camp in the Poconos of Pennsylvania or Camp Arcadia in Michigan. If I remember rightly, it was while Marcia and Marjorie were working at one of those camps that Marjorie first met Bill Kennell.

Marcia's stepfather had been in the electrical business, but during the Depression, the family lost everything. Because of that, they could not financially help Marcia attend college. However, she received a scholarship to the Minneapolis Institute of Art, and by the time I met her, Marcia had been graduated.

In searching for a job, Marcia went to a friend of her mother in the clothing manufacturing business. She wanted to find out whether she should go to Chicago to the *commercial* art school there for a little while. This female executive asked Marcia whether she had ever done any fashion designing, and Marcia said no.

"Well, do some," the woman said.

Over the weekend Marcia went home and did some fashion designs. When she went back and showed them to the woman, she gave Marcia a job "drawing the line," as they say in the dress business, providing jobbers with some idea of how a dress will look after it has been produced.

Shortly after she began, the people she was working for moved their offices to Cleveland. To keep her job, she would go by train to be in Cleveland during the week, and then come back to Minneapolis on the weekends.

I was very busy during these years, and Marcia was home only on weekends. We did not see each very often. Maybe we would go to a concert together once in a while or something like that. As a result, our relationship developed gradually over the next few years.

Marcia says that what attracted her to me was that I was so interested in everything. "He'd go to see someone off on the train," she says, "and pretty soon he'd be in the cabin of the locomotive asking the engineer how the train worked."

There was definitely a mutual attraction there! It's lasted through all the years, and developed some in the meantime!

My last year at Bethany, 1939–40, was the year I proposed to Marcia. I put the ring on her finger and asked her to marry me. I proposed to her on the scenic heights above the Minnesota River across from what is now the Minneapolis-St. Paul International Airport. We have flown right across there many times since then. I'll say to Marcia, "See that place down there? That's where I put the ring on your finger!"

After I proposed to her that night, we went to see her parents, and they were both delighted.

I was on a weeklong choir trip at the end of the school year just before our wedding. Marcia had to go and get the marriage license. When she got on the elevator, the operator realized the purpose for her presence and called out loudly, "This elevator to the marriage license bureau!" Then when the elevator got to the fourth floor, the man again called out, "Fourth floor! Marriage license bureau down the hall to the right!" Marcia told me later that she was very embarrassed, because she was sure that some of the people on the elevator knew her!

We were married at Redeemer Lutheran Church in St. Paul, Minnesota, on a rainy Sunday afternoon, June 23, 1940. Rev. Herbert Lindemann preached the sermon, and my father performed the wedding. My best man was my brother Kenny, and Marcia's matron of honor was her sister Evelyn. The congregation's regular organist, Olinda Rast, played for our service. For our honeymoon we drove to St. Cloud and spent the first night in a hotel there. Then we went up to Rutger's Lodge, near Brainerd, where we spent four days. I think that cost us something like $24 with all meals included—not per day, but for all four days we were there!

After our honeymoon, we went back to begin our married life in an apartment we had rented on Portland Avenue in Minneapolis. Of course, when we were married Marcia quit her job. That's the way you did things in those days. If she had continued to work, my mother, as a pastor's wife, probably would have disowned Marcia for not being the "proper" stay-at-home pastor's wife.

TEACHING FOR A YEAR AT THE UNIVERSITY

My salary at Bethany had been $900 a year plus room and board. Fortunately, during the year of residency for my Ph.D. (and our first year of marriage), my salary was better. I was asked to take over the graduate courses at the University of Minnesota for my former professor Dr. Marbury B. Ogle during his sabbatical year—at a salary of $2,500. That was pretty good in those days! I even traded in my Model A Ford and bought a new car. We were not living in luxury, but we did all right.

Because I had a master's degree in both linguistics and classical languages, I was invited to teach all of Ogle's graduate courses. I taught classes in Greek lyric poetry and in the historians Herodotus and Thucydides. I also taught a number of Dr. Ogle's Latin courses, including Advanced Latin Composition, in which students learned to write Latin in the style of Cicero.

Norman Gienapp, who became a teacher of Greek at St. Paul's College, Concordia, Missouri, was there studying for his master's degree at the time. He was older than I was but took almost all of his classes from me. As a future cousin by marriage, he also lived with Marcia and me during that year. I could not serve on his examination committee, however, because a teacher had to be a full professor to do that.

That was the year three students—the daughter of the treasurer of The Lutheran Church—Missouri Synod, Virginia Streator, and two others—invited me to start Missouri Synod services on the campus. They got permission to use the Continuation Center on campus, which had a chapel in it. The Catholics were having services there four times each Sunday morning. I went to the Jesuit priest who was conducting those services to see whether we could arrange a time to have our services. "Well," he said, "let's see. It takes me about 30 minutes to do the mass, and if I have a 10-minute homily, that's 40 minutes. Maybe you could use the chapel between 9:20 and 10 A.M."

Unknown to me, Dr. Walter Huchthausen, a well-respected professor in the school of architecture at the university (who also happened to be the son of my father's predecessor at Trinity First Lutheran Church in Minneapolis), went to the president of the university, Guy Stanton Ford, and arranged for us Lutherans to have our services at 11 A.M. Professor Huchthausen took the point of view that Lutheran students cannot be expected to come out for a service at 9:20 in the morning!

Two days later, I got a bitter phone call from that Jesuit priest. "If I'd known you wanted 11 o'clock, I would have let you have it!"

The students took care of all the arrangements for those services, including the financial arrangements. I preached every Sunday, or if I had to be away or could not be there for some reason, Norman Gienapp preached. We had an average attendance of 100 to 110 students each week. After that year the district built a student center with a chapel off campus, and Missouri Synod services have since been held there.

I suppose, strictly speaking, conducting those services was a violation of my contract with the university, because I had agreed that I would do nothing but teach. However, President Ford did not care. Later on that year, I met him at a reception, and he asked me, "Are you having a good time?" He knew all along what I was doing.

By the time that year was over, I had fulfilled all my residency requirements to work on my doctoral dissertation on English writers and their use of the Latin text of the Bible. I was planning to go back to Bethany to teach and write my dissertation—in fact, Marcia and I were just getting ready to move to Mankato—when at the end of July I received the call to be professor of Greek and Latin at Concordia Collegiate Institute in Bronxville, New York. Although I had known since February that I was one of 16 nominees to the position, I assumed the call would go to someone else. That it came to me was quite a surprise!

I had no formal call to Bethany College, because only pastors of the Norwegian Synod were called there at the time. And even though later I was ordained and installed into the Norwegian Synod so that I could be pastor of the church in Cottonwood, everyone "knew" that I was a Missouri Synod Lutheran at heart, so I still wasn't given a call to Bethany. As a result, when I got the call to Bronxville, I was surprised that a board member of Bethany said, "Oh, you shouldn't care about not having a call. You have the highest position of anyone here!"

I said, "I thank you very much for that, but I feel this is a call from God, and I should accept it."

When pastors have to decide whether a call to serve in the church is from God or not, they use prayer mixed with common sense, self-assessment, and counsel from other pastors and advisors. Almost all the input I received from others and from my own heart concluded that the call from Bronxville was, indeed, a call from God. Pastors *do* care about having a divine call, and I was happy to receive one from my own denomination. Second, teaching Greek and Latin would use my talents better (and be more fun for me) than teaching English. Third, as a husband and soon-to-be father, I had a larger responsibility than the salary at Bethany could handle. They had been paying me (as a single person) $900 a year plus room and board; Bronxville was offering $1,800 a year plus housing (but no board, of course). The U of M had paid $2,500 for the year, but I had to pay for my own housing out of that—and the agreement was that it would last only the one year.

On the negative side, leaving Bethany meant leaving the choir. I knew I would keep my hand in music somehow—I loved it too much not to be involved—but I wondered if ever again I would have as much fun as when I directed that 700-voice choir. In spite of that, I was convinced God wanted me to be in Bronxville in the fall of 1941.

5

CONCORDIA COLLEGIATE INSTITUTE BRONXVILLE, NEW YORK 1941–48

WHEN I ACCEPTED THE CALL IN 1941 TO TEACH CLASSICAL languages at Concordia-Bronxville, I truly felt that God had put me where I belonged and that I would stay there for the rest of my ministry, teaching in our Synod's educational program for future pastors. The only "step up" that I could have imagined would have been a call to the seminary itself. But even if that would never happen, perhaps I could be an inspiration to other boys first starting Greek as Professor Moenkemoeller had been to me at Concordia-St. Paul.

As a Christian committed to getting the Gospel into every nation, I knew that my work at the University of Minnesota the previous year would never compare to this call. Here I had the opportunity for personal involvement in the students' education on the basis of a shared faith in Jesus Christ. True, although bigger than Bethany, Concordia was small that first year I was there: 171 students; 91 in the high school and 80 in the college (only 27 of them women). But when I was installed as professor at the

September 14 opening service of the school's 61st year, I thought I was close to heaven on earth.

I had been called to Concordia-Bronxville to teach Greek and Latin, replacing Dr. Henry Stein, who was in his 80s. But since he had no pension plan, he continued for a few more years to teach the college classes, and I taught in the high school. (When he fully retired, I taught on both levels.) I also did things for Dr. Stein around his house. The last thing I remember doing for him was taking out his Christmas tree—at Easter time! He passed away about the same year that I left Concordia.

After about two years of teaching at Bronxville, Professor Alfred Bichsel, the head of the school's music department, left to teach at Valparaiso University (and later the Eastman School of Music in Rochester, New York). Although my time was already more than full, I was thrilled to be asked to take over. I developed the department the way we had it at Bethany. I brought in an M.A. from New York University, Mrs. Ellen Anderson, to teach piano, and I hired a band director who also gave instrumental music lessons. The school had a store of instruments, because Professor Bichsel had been a great instrumentalist, as well as being a very good choral director. The students were able to use these instruments and to take piano or organ lessons for their own private pleasure or for professional service later on.

Sad to say, I never had the opportunity to organize a mass choir similar to the one I directed at Bethany. At Bronxville, I directed the choirs when they sang for special occasions on campus, however we did not go on any concert tours. I simply was too busy teaching 25 hours a week, working with the music department, and serving as the school's public relations director.

One year I served as temporary registrar of the high school. In preparation for the school year, I tried to lay out the program in such a way that any student could take any course he wanted. That was before the time of computers, and it was not easy! I remember being down on the floor of our house with all these cards trying to work it out.

One student for whom I had a lot of difficulty working out a program was Chester Edelmann, a Christian Jew (and today a leading pediatrician in New York City). Although not a preministerial student, he wanted to take Greek, an option my scheduling hadn't considered. I was able to accommodate him, though. I remember this incident in part because the request was so uncommon. More unusual was his sister's wedding, which she had asked me to perform (and which I did, in the living room of my home). His sister, Meta, also a Christian Jew, was marrying an Orthodox Jew. The groom's mother refused to come to the wedding, because it was a Christian ceremony. Interestingly, after a year or so, the groom joined St. Mark Lutheran Church in Yonkers.

Chester's father was treasurer of the H. L. Green Company and also of St. Matthew Lutheran Church, the oldest Lutheran church in the western world. I remember one time I was leading a Bible class, and the Edelmanns mentioned casually that they had given up a friend's violin concert in order to be in the class that evening. Their friend was the world-renowned violinist Jascha Heifetz! That shows how devoted many of those Jewish members were!

A SHIFT IN EMPHASIS

I began teaching at Concordia-Bronxville in the fall of 1941, the year the United States entered World War II. I still remember that December 7, when the Japanese bombed Pearl Harbor. I had accepted a side job directing the choir at Pastor Adolf Meyer's church, St. Mark's in Yonkers. I took that job because I loved music too much not to be involved somehow, but also because I needed the money. My supposed salary of $150 a month from the school was cut 10 percent to $135 before I even started. They did provide our housing, but that was still not a lot of money—not with our first child on the way!

Anyhow, that afternoon of December 7, I was directing the choir in an Advent hymn sing. When it came time for the benediction, Pastor Meyer stood up and announced that the country was at war.

Concordia knew immediately that it would lose most of its male students to military service. All across America, young men of college age were being drafted, even though the armed services of the U.S. had been building for well over a year. Seven months earlier, on Mother's Day, the Synod had had a special collection for its chaplaincy work, resolving that "they shall not march alone." Within about a year, over 60,000 young men from the Synod as a whole were in the military. Concordia-Bronxville put even its president, Arthur J. Doege, on loan to the chaplaincy.

On behalf of the school, I was put on the road almost immediately to recruit new students for the college department—students we needed to keep the college afloat during those years. Having done recruitment for Bethany, I was the only logical choice. By using every spare day I had to recruit girls and more preministerial students, we managed to keep the enrollment pretty much what it had been. Because of the pressures of time, however, I had to give up the idea of writing my doctoral dissertation. A person is allowed only a certain time period in which to complete the written requirements for a doctorate. That did not mean I quit learning in life; that I could never do. I was disappointed, though, that I was unable to take that final earned degree as a way to say to God, "I have tried to be faithful in using the talents You have given to me. Thank You, Lord." Of course, I could not know then that our Savior was preparing me for an entirely different type of service to the Gospel.

When I did the recruitment for the college, I realized they needed someone to do much more than try merely to recruit students. What they really needed was someone to explain and represent the school—someone to say in and to the community, "Concordia is much more than the insular and rigidly Germanic school you may assume; we are a thoroughly American school that offers the very best in education under God—and you will be proud of your sons and daughters who graduate from here."

The school officials agreed that we needed a public relations program, and they made me the director—expecting me, of course, to continue to teach a full load in the classroom. As a "bonus," I was provided my own office and a secretary. (Only one other professor had his own secretary.) I also had a mimeograph machine and an addressograph machine—the most advanced technology of that time!

One reason we needed public relations in the community so badly was that a former member of the faculty, a Professor Koch, had come to the United States from Germany and was a vocal Nazi sympathizer. He went around giving speeches supporting the Nazis. Consequently our school had the reputation with many people of being Nazi.

An interesting story about Koch was told to me by Louis Lochner, a Pulitzer prize-winning Associated Press correspondent who was stationed in Berlin during World War II. He was a Lutheran and a good friend of mine. His first wife had died, and while he was in Germany he had married a German woman whose husband had also died. They were extremely happy about finding each other, and had been married by Pastor Koch, who was then a Lutheran Free Church pastor in Berlin.

I was chairman of the Lyceum Committee at the college one year, responsible for special student programs. After Lochner returned from Berlin, Acting President Albert Meyer and I invited him to be the speaker on the first of our programs.

"You couldn't even pay my agent's fee," he said to me, "but we'll work it out." We agreed that we would pay him, and he would donate the money back to the college.

On the night before the program, Al Meyer and I were having dinner together with Louis Lochner and his wife. "You had our pastor as a professor here at your college," Lochner said.

"Yes," Al Meyer said, "but he didn't understand boys very well."

Lochner's wife replied, "He didn't understand boys. He didn't understand girls. He didn't understand men. He didn't understand women."

Louis laughed and told us what had happened. Koch had performed their wedding ceremony, and in the wedding address he spoke on the subject "Life is full of trouble and sorrow."

After the ceremony there was a big wedding reception at the Adlon Hotel, one of the finest hotels in Berlin at the time, attended by about a thousand people. Those attending included the head of the diplomatic corps and many other prominent people, including the future Pope Pius XII. It was decided to give Pastor Koch another chance to speak at the reception, thinking that maybe he would have something more appropriate to say. He again spoke on the subject "Life is full of trouble and sorrow."

Professor Koch's Nazi sympathies embodied the school's desperate need for the public relations program I began. Sadly, his words fueled sentiments such as those expressed in the extreme by *The Sign, National Catholic Magazine,* January 1943, which carried a political cartoon naming "Hitler, the spiritual successor of Luther." To be fair, though, one would have to say that a country that would intern some of its citizens because of their ethnic background (Japanese) would also view other citizens suspiciously because of theirs (German). Who was it, after all, who provided spiritual services for German prisoners of war interred on Ellis Island if not the German Lutherans, as we were popularly known?

(The pastor for the Ellis Island Christmas Day service one year after Pearl Harbor was Dr. Arthur Brunn, pastor of St. Peter Lutheran Church in Brooklyn, and fourth vice-president of the Synod.)

We today tend to forget (or have never known) that when the war began, great social pressure was exerted on every person as well as every business and every agency to set aside petty differences in order to get behind the war effort. Clearly, if our little German-background school was to survive, the people of New York needed to know not only that we existed but that we were thoroughly American as we offered an education second to none. Heading up the school's Public Relations Department was at least as important as teaching Greek and Latin. I was grateful to be included.

As a side topic, I again call attention to people connections and the opportunities God provides through them. The public relations efforts at the college were supported largely by the Lutheran Education Society, of which Dr. Irene Koenig and I were the membership committee. Dr. Koenig, a medical doctor, was the daughter of Rev. Dr. Francis Pieper and the wife of Rev. Dr. George Koenig, president of the Atlantic District of The Lutheran Church—Missouri Synod.

Pieper's son-in-law, Rev. Dr. George Koenig, was a schoolmate of Walter A. Maier through Concordia-Bronxville and the sem. When WAM passed away, Koenig preached at his memorial service on the Bronxville campus. At that service (which I attended), Dr. Koenig talked about living and dying, ending up with one sentence: "Whether the time is long or short, what difference does that really make?" When Dr. Koenig died, I was privileged to have the sermon. I began it by quoting Dr. Koenig's own sentence: "Whether the time is long or short, what difference does that really make?" What a good theme to live by! People who have the

Lord Jesus in their hearts don't have to worry about times or seasons. It is a good way to live!

One other story that illustrates the usefulness of people connections comes from the life of Louis Lochner. Sometime between 1930 and 1932, when Heinrich Bruening was chancellor of Germany (before Hitler's time), Lochner and Bruening were on the same train, going from Berlin to Rome. Knowing ahead of time that Bruening would be making the trip, Lochner, as head of the Associated Press Bureau in Berlin, got a compartment reservation in the same car as Bruening. During the trip, Lochner made sure that the chancellor had ample chance to invite Lochner in to visit over a bottle of Chianti.

When they got to Rome, Lochner did what Europeans did back then: he immediately went to the Vatican, left his business card, and went back to his hotel. Not more than a half hour later, the Vatican called to invite him to visit with Pope Pius XII. During their lengthy chat, Lochner told the pope about the trip, about meeting Bruening, and their arrival in Rome.

On the way back to Berlin, Bruening and Lochner again were in compartments in the same car, and again they visited. As they sat and talked, Bruening said, "You know, the Vatican has the most comprehensive spy system in the world. When I went in to visit the pope, he told me that I had a bottle of Chianti on the table in my compartment on the trip down!"

STRIVING FOR EFFECTIVE OUTREACH WITH THE GOSPEL

As I hinted above, Lutherans in the U.S. were not viewed as a significant religious force. Many factors contributed to that perception, including our fragmentation. One hundred years earlier, in the 1840s, Lutheran clergy and Lutheran congregations in various parts of the country (at that time, from the East Coast to the

Midwest) had formed Synods in their locales—New York, Pennsylvania, Michigan, Indiana, Ohio, Missouri, etc. The founders of the Evangelical Lutheran Synod of Missouri, Ohio, and Other States had hoped to bring together all new-world Lutherans into one denomination—one that was unified in doctrine and practice. Although that did not happen, the leaders of the church kept doing what they could to bring it about.

Two major contributions seemed to promise the most hope. First was the establishment of the Synodical Conference in 1872, a loose association of Lutheran denominations that were unified in doctrine and practice but that did not look for organic union into one super-church. Membership varied according to the prevailing doctrinal controversies. In 1940 the group included the Missouri, Wisconsin, Slovak, and Norwegian Synods. (By the way, I for one benefited from the Conference, for it enabled me to be ordained in the Norwegian Synod, yet accept a call to the Missouri Synod without any problems.)

The year 1938 saw the second major contribution toward hope: the development of documents by both the Missouri Synod and the large American Lutheran Church that people on both sides expected would lead to pulpit and altar fellowship based on unanimity of faith. Again, the goal was not the glory of a super-church but the more effective spread of the Gospel. The outbreak of World War II along with the anti-Lutheran biases that surfaced in the U.S. highlighted how important those goals were.

The fact that fellowship was not realized by the end of the war frustrated many. Some felt that the problem was the lack of doctrinal purity of the American Lutheran Church. Others felt that the problem was the over zealousness to doctrinal jots and tittles of some in the Missouri Synod. Perhaps the latter is the reason why, in May 1945, St. Louis Professor William F. Arndt published former President Schwan's theses on "Evangelical Practice." Schwan originally presented these to the Central District in 1862. (Schwan was president of the Synod from 1878 to 1899.) Arndt's reissuance of those theses were understood by many as an attack on their concern for pure doctrine—an attack that caused a furor in the Synod and brought Arndt and a number of other seminary professors under counterattack.

On September 6-7, 1945, a group of pastors and professors of The Lutheran Church—Missouri Synod met at the Palmer House Hotel in Chicago. The group met to discuss how it might stimulate the Missouri Synod to reexamine its theological heritage, to reinvigorate its evangelical spirit, and to exert a restraining force on the legalistic tendencies that seemed to be in the ascendancy at the time. I was the youngest member of that group.

The result of that meeting was a paper containing 12 theses, which was called "A Statement," and which was later referred to as "The Statement of the Forty-four." That document and a covering letter from Rev. E. J. Friedrich, president of the Colorado District at the time, who chaired the meeting of "the 44," was sent to every pastor in Synod. This was done because it was felt that simply presenting our concerns through official channels of Synod would not be altogether effective.

This document caused a lot of controversy. A regional conference of the Northern Illinois District requested that the five signers from the St. Louis seminary resign. Finally, meetings were scheduled with the signers and the Praesidium of Synod and the district presidents. Papers were prepared to explain each of the individual theses.

Because I had been schooled in Greek and Latin, I was assigned to write on Thesis 5: "We affirm our conviction that sound exegetical procedure is the basis for sound Lutheran theology." This thesis deplored the fact that Romans 16:17-18 had become for some a Scripture passage prohibiting people from praying with anyone who did not agree with us in every point of Christian doctrine. Based on sound exegetical and hermeneutical principles, this thesis also pointed out the misuse of 1 Thessalonians 5:22 in the King James Version translation that we are to avoid "all appearance of evil." This text would be better understood in its true meaning: "avoid evil in every form."

In my paper, I pointed out that the phrase "contrary to the doctrine which ye have learned" (Romans 16:17) is adverbial rather than adjectival. The normal linguistic translation of the passage should be "Mark those who, contrary to the doctrine which you have learned, cause divisions and offenses and avoid them." Prepositional phrases were understood as being adverbial in both Greek and Latin. All of these theses were then published in a book entitled *Speaking the Truth in Love*.

As the 1947 convention of the Synod drew near, "the 44" could see that "A Statement" had divided people rather than helped them and that tensions were running so high that faithful pastors and congregations were concerned. Therefore, representatives of "the 44" withdrew "A Statement" as a basis of discussion, with the promise by the Praesidium of the Synod (its officers and the presidents of the districts) that they would consider the issues that had been raised. In a reconciling move, the convention passed the following:

> WHEREAS, "A Statement" as such no longer is a basis for discussion according to the "Agreement" reported by the President; and
>
> WHEREAS, The issues raised by "A Statement" and by memorials referring to "A Statement" are being submitted for study to pastors and congregations on the basis of materials supplied by direction of the President; and
>
> WHEREAS, The subject matter is such as to call for time and patience, so that all pastors and laymen may have an opportunity to study the same in a quiet, earnest, and faithful manner (a course which the Church should always follow); and

WHEREAS, It is imperative that we continue on the foundation of God's Word, and God's Word alone; therefore be it

Resolved, That the President continue to submit to pastors and congregations material for the Scriptural study of the questions at issue.

If anything, the experience reinforced what I started to learn firsthand at Bethany: stay out of church politics. Although the issues may be important, politicizing them may interfere at times with proclaiming the Gospel to the world. At the same time, a pastor—especially one in public relations—has to be a "people person." I guess I've always been that. The approach served me personally when it helped me be elected student body president at the seminary, but it benefited the outreach of Jesus Christ as I served in recruitment and public relations at both Bethany and Concordia-Bronxville. How significant that attitude would be throughout my life, I had no way of knowing at the time.

SOME FAMILY MEMORIES
FROM THE BRONXVILLE YEARS

We lived on Midland Avenue in Tuckahoe in a house the college owned. Concordia-Bronxville owns many faculty houses there now, but at the time they owned only two off-campus homes. We had been told that this would be temporary for us until housing became available on campus, but we lived there all seven years I was on the faculty.

Robert Glad, the engineer at the college, and his wife were our next-door neighbors. Proud of having come from Sweden, they displayed on their living room wall a picture of King Gustav, the king of Sweden at the time. We Hoffmanns—especially my Swedish Marcia—were grateful that they invited us over every Christmas Eve for a traditional Swedish dinner.

Our two oldest sons were born while I was at Concordia-Bronxville—Peter in 1942 and Paul in 1945. They were born at Lawrence Hospital in Bronxville, a hospital with a very fine reputation. (Kate was born there too, but after I left teaching.) Marcia says she originally chose that hospital because I was gone so much and the hospital was close enough for her to get there on her own, if necessary.

We attended Village Lutheran Church, right across the street from the college. Our children will tell you that that church was always very much a part of our family life. So much so, in fact, that one of the things Paul remembers from his early childhood is a time when he made a fuss about not wanting to go to church and I had to discipline him appropriately.

One other family memory is of a rather disastrous train trip during the summer of 1943. We were going to visit our parents in Minnesota for about a month. Marcia went ahead of me, because I still had some work to do at the college. (By the way, because of the war, gasoline and tires were drastically rationed, and air travel was not as accessible or as affordable as today. Going by train was the transportation of choice for most people. However, except for 1943, Marcia and I were able to amass enough gas rationing coupons to drive to Minnesota every summer.)

Marcia had spent many hours knitting a baptismal shawl for Peter during the year before he was born. She had done the beautiful work she always did. She put that shawl and all our clothes in a trunk. She also took along extra shoes, because they too were rationed and unavailable unless you first got the required coupon, which a person couldn't do very well on a trip away from home. As a result, if one expected to need something on a trip, it couldn't be bought then; it had to be taken along.

Anyway, we booked a roomette on the train for Marcia and Peter, but there was no room in there for that big trunk. We checked the trunk as baggage. On the trip home we checked the trunk again, and they put it on a different train from the one we were on.

When we got back to Bronxville, we waited for three or four weeks for that trunk to arrive, but it did not show up. Finally we learned that there had been a fire in Bucyrus, Ohio, in the baggage car of the train our trunk was on. Our trunk and everything in it had been completely destroyed in that fire. They sent us a check for something like $300. That did not nearly cover the cost of what we had lost, nor did it compensate for all the hard work Marcia had put into that beautiful baptismal shawl. We applied for more money, but there was no sign that we would get it.

A few months later, Marcia received a telegram informing her that her stepfather in St. Paul, Minnesota, had died. I was teaching a class at the time, and she called the college and asked them to give me the message. Professor Louis Heinrichsmeyer came into my classroom, and in a very somber mood whispered to me that Marcia had died. He had got the message wrong!

I rushed right down to the house. There was Marcia, very much alive but completely broken up. She wanted to go to the funeral, but we had no money for the train fare. I was preparing to go up to the school to ask for an advance on my salary, something I had never done before in my life, so that she and Peter could take the train to go to the funeral.

Just before I was ready to leave the house, the mail came—and included a second check from the railroad for the loss of our trunk. We used that money for Marcia and Peter to go to her stepfather's funeral.

We found out later how that happened. A Roman Catholic neighbor named Walsh worked for the Burlington Railroad. He had talked to some people, and as a result of that we got the second check. It came at just the time we needed it most! God's surprises often come at the most opportune moments!

I did not go to the funeral with Marcia, because by that time we had an accelerated program at the college as a result of the war. This meant that we had a full schedule of classes all year round, with the high school and the college having summer vacations at different times. Since I had students in both levels, I got no extended summer vacation. We did manage, though, to work in a trip each summer to Minnesota to visit our parents.

An automobile trip from New York to Minnesota was a very long drive in those days. There were no interstates back then and almost no four-lane highways. I used to make up little stories for the boys as we went along. There would be these two characters in the stories, "Poder and Pool," who were quite obviously Peter and Paul.

We did not have air-conditioning in our car, and it was a very hot trip. When Paul was about a year and a half old, he had chicken pox and was running a fever when we took the trip. He would not sleep unless Marcia held him on her lap in the backseat. Babies act like little heaters!

The only other trip we took during those years was a trip to Williamsburg, Virginia, over one Thanksgiving vacation, because I had a few days off at that time.

That's the way it was during those seven years in Bronxville. They were good years, and I enjoyed them very much. Looking back, I can see the hand of the Lord also helping me focus on what our church is all about, the Gospel of Jesus Christ, and getting that message beyond the confines of just our Synod—lessons that would become extremely important for the rest of my life. How that would happen changed drastically in 1948 when I was elected to be public relations director of the Missouri Synod— another one of God's surprises in my life.

6

THE CREATION OF SYNOD'S PUBLIC RELATIONS DEPARTMENT

I N 1948, I ACCEPTED THE POSITION AS PUBLIC RELATIONS DIRECTOR OF The Lutheran Church—Missouri Synod. The process to get to that point, though, was more involved than the statement suggests.

In the years after World War I, the Synod worked with the American Lutheran Publicity Bureau (ALPB) in New York City in getting out tracts, press releases, *The American Lutheran* magazine (Rev. Adolf F. "Ade" Meyer, managing editor), and any other public relations materials. Realizing that this was not enough, the temporary press committee at the 1926 Synodical Convention successfully petitioned for the establishment of a full, ongoing synodical Press Committee. Of interest, three Missouri Synod members from the ALPB staff were on that pro tem committee at the '26 convention: Rev. "Ade" Meyer, Rev. F. H. Lindemann, and Mr. J. F. E. Nickelsburg. The board-staff of that first official committee were Ade as chairman, Nickelsburg as treasurer, and George C. Koenig. Except for an occasional switch between Meyer and Lindemann as chairman, Meyer and Nickelsburg served on the Press Committee for its entire life of about 21 years—and maintained their involvement in the ALPB.

World War II forced another look at how our Synod's Gospel outreach was being received. What we found was that the forces shaping my public relations work at Concordia-Bronxville were playing also against the Synod as a whole. Some of these included

- the prejudice against German Lutherans;
- the difficulty in maintaining our church's definition of ministers over against the government's definition;
- the problems in helping the military understand that Lutherans are not the same as other Protestants and that *Lutheran* chaplains are needed in addition to Protestant ones;
- the constant need to keep the government aware of the proper separation of church and state as it pertains to public schools and the kinds of financial support the government can give to students in parochial schools.

The Synod did what it could at the time. We had a productive (even if volunteer) Press Committee; we supported and benefited from the American Publicity Bureau; our Army and Navy Commission supplied pastors for the chaplaincy as well as maintained contact with the government; and we were thankful for the promotion given to Lutheranism by "The Lutheran Hour." But those involved knew this wasn't enough.

One small action our Synod took was to change its official name. Not that the action had a large public relations impact, yet I mention it here because it parallels other public relations efforts. Already at the 1944 convention of the Synod, a motion was made to help define our body as a *church,* because some Americans seemed not to know the meaning of the word *Synod.* That convention opted for the name "The Lutheran Church, Missouri Synod." Although it was rejected by over ⅓ of the congregations after the convention, the variant "The Lutheran Church—Missouri Synod" was upheld following the 1947 convention, when the denomination was 100 years old.

What made the difference between 1944 and 1947? I would have to say, the end of the war. As long as our country was at war and our churches were suffering from the lack of manpower as well as money, many in the denomination tended to look inward. But when the war ended and we could see that the country was booming instead of retrenching, expectations grew. There is no doubt that the psychology of the church changed.

The same thing happened with the Synod's approach to publicity and public relations. Synod's Press Committee members had long known that its scope was too narrow and its budget of $2,500 was too limited to accomplish what truly needed to be done. Therefore, at the 1944 convention, the committee proposed that Synod establish a Department of Public Relations. (The Press Committee at that time still included, among others, Ade Meyer and J. F. E. Nickelsburg.) The convention resolved

> 1. That the *Praesidium* in conjunction with the Board of Directors be instructed, and are hereby instructed and empowered, to cause a survey to be made to determine the exact requirements, location, and personnel of a public relations service for our church;
>
> 2. That the *Praesidium* in conjunction with the Board of Directors be instructed, and are hereby instructed and empowered, to effect the establishment of such a service when expedient.

When the next convention (1947) was drawing near and the Press Committee still hadn't heard anything official, they again memorialized Synod for the creation of a Department of Public Relations. But in case that wouldn't pass, the Press Committee let the Synod know that $2,500 wouldn't do the job anymore; at least double that amount would be required. (I was at that convention at the Palmer House in Chicago, serving on Ade's press staff. At the time I was also on the Board of the ALPB, chairman of its Tract Committee, and a staff editor for its magazine, *The American*

Lutheran. Chicago, by the way, was where the constituting convention of the Synod had been held 100 years earlier.)

The Praesidium and the Board of Directors of Synod, however, had done their job. Their report to the convention shows that the process took longer than expected and brought out widely varying views—with the result that a Department of Public Relations could not be established between conventions.

Therefore, Committee 13, "Publicity" (Rev. Henry Rische, chairman and two years later the first editor of Synod's family magazine *This Day*), acting on various memorials and in consultation with Synod's Board of Directors and others, did recommend that a Department of Public Relations be established, that Synod's Board of Directors appoint a separate Board to oversee the department and to appoint a director, and that the office be located "in one of the nation's principal cities" as determined by the new Public Relations Board and Synod's Board of Directors. The original resolution by the Press Committee had shown that the office should be located in New York City because (quoting the resolution),

> All national news agencies such as the Associated Press, the United Press, International News Service, Religious News Service, the leading national magazines and all national radio chains have their headquarters in New York City; generally, all prominent church bodies also have their news headquarters in New York City; [and] direct contact with aforenamed groups seems essential for effective work.

Evidently, Committee 13 at the 1947 convention did not want the floor to argue the benefits of New York against, for example, Washington, D.C.; hence the resolution wording to leave the location up to the appropriate boards. (The final decision was to have the main office in New York with branch offices in Washington, D.C., and St. Louis.)

The resolution passed unanimously. At the time, other denominations had publicity departments that measured success by column inches in the newspapers. We were the first religious organization of any kind to have a full-fledged public relations department. A year later, in 1948, all the preliminary work was done for the new Board (Ade Meyer, again chairman) to hire its first director (me) and to open its main office in New York City. The fact that I was hired was not a total surprise, given my public relations work for Concordia-Bronxville as well as my work with and for the American Lutheran Publicity Bureau and Synod's Press Committee. Yet when I was participating in those previous positions, I had no inkling that the Lord was preparing me for something else in life.

In addition to Ade as the chairman, the board included as secretary Dr. Albert Huegli (who later served as president of Valparaiso University), as treasurer Mr. Fred Strodel (vice-president for advertising of the Fair Store, Chicago), Mr. John W. Boehne, Jr. (a member of Synod's Board of Directors), Mr. George A. Halter, and Rev. Manfred E. Reinke (St. John Lutheran Church, La Porte, Indiana). Others who were on the board in those early years included Dr. Herman Gockel, who became the scriptwriter and producer for Synod's "This Is the Life" television series, and Dr. Arvin Hahn, who became president of Bethany College, Lindsborg, Kansas.

As an aside, I need to add that the public relations position became attached to a call to St. Matthew Lutheran Church in Manhattan, where I was known because I had been teaching Bible classes there while on the faculty at Bronxville. That's how it happened that I could accept the position of Director of Public Relations and at the same time be a preaching assistant pastor at St. Matthew Lutheran Church on Manhattan Island in New York City. I was installed at St. Matthew and inducted into the office of the public relations director at the same service on October 17, 1948.

And one more aside, this one illustrating that God prepares us even when we are not aware. In order to allow Dr. Walter A.

Maier some time off during the summers, temporary fill-in speakers for "The Lutheran Hour" were used. During the summer of 1948, I was that person.

And a final aside—more than anyone else, Ade Meyer was responsible for the public relations outlook of the Synod. Barely three years out of the seminary and already editor for the ALPB's *The American Lutheran* magazine, he was a leader in the temporary press committee at the 1926 convention of the Synod. That committee convinced Synod to establish a permanent committee, and Ade was promptly appointed its chairman. He served on that committee for 21 years, fighting for its replacement by a full public relations department in the Synod—a dream that finally came true during the 1947 convention. When that happened, Ade again was appointed chairman, overseeing that department. He kept serving on that committee until the 1965 convention, just five years before his retirement.

Ade died on July 6, 1988, driving to pick me up at the airport. I was going to preach that evening for the 65th anniversary of his ordination.

THE PURPOSE OF THE DEPARTMENT OF PUBLIC RELATIONS

I think there was no church body at that time that needed public relations more than the Missouri Synod. We were greatly misunderstood by many outside our church body. Far too many saw us as an isolationist body and as a German church.

At first, some in the church thought that our purpose was to do newspaper (and maybe some radio) advertising so that people in every town and city could find a Lutheran church in which to worship on Sunday mornings. One of those who felt at first that our primary purpose should be advertising was our own board member Fred Strodel. With his background in retail sales at the

Fair Store, I suppose that was understandable. We had to convince him of our greater purpose.

We set up a principle for public relations that was published in every convention proceedings book after that: "Our purpose is to identify ourselves in the public mind with Jesus Christ." We always advocated that Synod do things in such a way that people would understand that our devotion was first and foremost to Jesus Christ. If for some reason that did not seem to be the case with whatever people were doing, we would emphasize that our church body needs to represent Jesus Christ. We did not believe that we were the only ones who represented Him, but our position was that if no one else was there to represent Him, we would be there.

The bylaws of the Synod tried to walk a middle road between both camps: true public relations and just advertising. The functions and duties assigned in the 1949 printing of the bylaws were as follows:

a. The [Public Relations] Board shall correlate the work of the District Press Committees and otherwise provide for the dissemination of news through press and radio;

b. present the Lutheran viewpoint on issues of the day;

c. answer attacks against our Church;

d. keep abreast of legislative developments with a view to preserving our constitutional guarantees of the separation of Church and State and maintain contact with the State Department in the interest of Synod's missionary and educational program.

THE PUBLIC RELATIONS OFFICES

Because school years begin for teachers well before the students appear, I resigned from Concordia-Bronxville as of August 1, 1948, in order to make room for a replacement. Doing so allowed me also to help Ade Meyer get everything for the office in place for an official opening on September 1. Unfortunately, I was no longer being paid by Concordia-Bronxville because I had resigned my position there, and my position as public relations director of Synod did not begin until September 1. In addition to working the entire month of August without a salary, I had to wait until the end of September to get paid by Synod—with the result that I actually went two whole months without salary. I suppose if I had been a little more savvy, I would have asked about that. I did not, however, and no one else ever inquired about it either. On the other hand, there wasn't much money for an extra month or two worth of salary. Our entire annual budget for the Public Relations Department was only $29,000—for three locations, staff salaries, and program besides—and still there were those who believed that was too much!

Our first New York office was in the same building as the American Lutheran Publicity Bureau (ALPB) at 1819 Broadway, at the triangle where Central Park West and Broadway meet. The building was owned by Manufacturer's Trust, whose president was Mr. Henry von Elm, a member of St. Peter Lutheran Church in Brooklyn. He rented us office space there at a very reasonable rate. Later on, after the Manufacturer's Trust Building was torn down at Columbus Circle to make way for the Coliseum, the Atlantic District of the LCMS and our Public Relations Department along with the ALPB rented space in the Central Savings Bank Building. Everyone called that building "The Rock of Gibraltar," because it was built out of big chunks of granite. Our Lutheran offices were on the fifth floor. I served on the board of ALPB and on the staff of *The American Lutheran,* a magazine published by them, but that was my only connection with them. The synodical office for public relations was completely separate from ALPB, although we did coordinate our publicity efforts.

I was in charge of our office in New York; Paul Schulze, who later became a pastor on the West Coast, was in charge of the St. Louis office; and Olinda Roettger was our public relations person in Washington, D.C.

Lest the reader assume we started everything from ground zero, I should tell you the background of our Washington office. During World War II, a tremendous number of human needs thrust themselves on every church, needs far too great for any one church alone to meet. Whenever the LCMS could, it joined with not only the Synodical Conference but also with the National Lutheran Council in meeting some of those needs.

One such project was the establishment of Lutheran Service Centers. In the U.S. these centers served as focal points for Lutheran servicemen and other workers passing through, meaning that the centers not only provided recreational facilities but sometimes dormitories too. The 29th service center we jointly opened was in Washington, D.C. The building purchased was at 736 Jackson Place, N.W., across the street from the White House and around the corner from Blair House. On the main floor was a large reception room with tables and chairs; the basement was for recreation; the third and fourth floors were men's dormitories, and the second floor was for offices—administration of the Service Center, two pastors serving as military chaplains (one LCMS and one National Lutheran Council [NLC]), and offices for two women (again, LCMS and NLC) who would reach out to the many thousands of young women moving in and out of Washington to work for the government, most of whom lived in government housing areas. Olinda Roettger, who had worked for Lorrie Meyer (President Behnken's right-hand man), was the LCMS woman.

Dedication of the Center was on Sunday, March 26, 1944. The event obviously was of importance in the capital. Among the 2,000 people attending the ceremony were the Crown Prince of Norway, his wife, and three children; ambassadors/ministers/dignitaries from Norway, Czechoslovakia, Sweden, Latvia, Iceland, Denmark, and Estonia; as well as congressmen and senators from around the U.S.

Keeping all that in mind, jump ahead four years to 1948. The war is over. The vast number of military personnel and government employees passing through Washington is down—with the result that the need for so much space in a Lutheran Service Center is also down. The LCMS, at its 1947 convention, has established not only a new Department of Public Relations but also a new Armed Services Commission—and both of us are looking for quarters in Washington, D.C. Heading up the National Lutheran Council end of things at the Lutheran Center is Lutheran Church in America pastor Dr. Paul Empie. Chaplain Kenneth Ahl is the head of the Armed Services Commission.

Everything came together that summer as plans were made to renovate the Center for new use: The NLC (owners of the building) occupying the first and second floors, Public Relations and the Armed Services Commission the third and fourth floors. I was installed on October 17, with my primary office in New York. On November 14, the Lutheran Center in D.C. was dedicated, and a week later Ahl was installed in Washington. Olinda Roettger, however, was always on the job, making a smooth transition from the Center's work on behalf of working women in D.C. to our public relations person there.

Olinda was the natural choice to assist us, because she knew so many people in government positions. For example, she was a personal friend of Clark Clifford, at that time an influential government official. She often got us appointments with people that we would not otherwise have been able to see personally. In spite of her talents and proven track record, some people in Synod questioned whether a woman should be in charge of our Washington office. Pastor Rudy Ressmeyer, president of the Southeastern District of The Lutheran Church—Missouri Synod (and, therefore, pastorally responsible for the Washington, D.C., area), defended Olinda's abilities, and she continued in her position.

When we opened our offices, the president of Synod, Dr. John W. Behnken, requested me to come and see him at his home and office in Oak Park, Illinois. He wanted to talk with me not only about what my duties would be, but also about my relationship with him. He asked me at the time to respect confidentiality in all our relationships and conversations. He said, "If you disagree with me about anything, I want to hear it from you and not from someone else." Our relationship soon came to a very mature level. I understood Dr. Behnken, and he understood me.

Early on, I also told Dr. Behnken that I needed to attend the meetings of the Board of Directors of Synod. Dr. Behnken agreed immediately, but he told me that if anyone objected, I would have to leave. That was quite a bold step at the time, because even Dr. Lawrence (Lorrie) Meyer, Dr. Behnken's right-hand man who administered the Synod on his behalf, was not allowed to attend those meetings. (Dr. Meyer had official job titles through the years, but they meant little. His real job was to serve the president.)

I went into the first Board of Directors meeting after my request and stood at the end of the table opposite Dr. Behnken. Sitting at that end of the table was "Pope" (Dr. Paul) Schultz, the chair of the Board's subcommittee on Synod's educational system. He looked up when I entered the room and said, "Osvald!" pronounced in his German way. Then he opened his notes and showed me what was on the agenda. A few moments later I looked up at Dr. Behnken, and he had a big smile on his face. It turned out that Dr. Schultz was the one he was afraid might ask me to leave. I did not really share his concern, because Schultz had been my childhood pastor when our family was in Springfield, and he was a friend of my father.

Dr. Behnken became my very good friend. Whenever he came to New York—for example, for an appearance on television—he always stayed at our home. One time when he was in New York, I took him to visit Dr. Arthur Brunn, first vice-president of the LCMS, who was dying of cancer. I did not go with him into the house, because I felt that their conversation would be much freer if they were alone together. When Dr. Behnken came out of the house, he said to me that the cancer which Dr. Brunn had must be very embarrassing to him. Because Dr. Behnken did not offer more information, I didn't ask. I felt that if Dr. Behnken did not want to talk about something, his feelings should be respected. That shows the kind of relationship he and I had. When Behnken died on February 23, 1968, all but one of his pallbearers were chosen because of their position in the church. The family was asked to choose the other one. I was very honored that they chose me.

OUR 350 "SATELLITE OFFICES"

Not all of our public relations work was done through our offices. We were able to set up, with the cooperation of Synod, a volunteer organization of 350 men and women throughout the districts of Synod. Janet Pries, who was in charge of the Synod's news service, would write the news for Synod, then send it out to these 350 people, who would put a local twist on it and see that it was placed in their local newspapers. (Janet worked in the St. Louis office after Paul Schulze left.) We probably had more coverage of Synod at that time than at any other time before or since.

This volunteer corps of public relations people from around the country would meet annually, usually in St. Louis. In those annual meetings, which usually lasted two or three days, I would train them in all aspects of public relations work. Our volunteers were some of the most wonderful people I have ever worked with! All of them did everything at their own expense.

After 1955, when I took on the additional duties of Lutheran Hour Speaker, I was ably assisted in the conduct of our public relations offices and of the volunteer organization by Rev. Norman Temme, who had been chairman of the Public Relations Department in the Nebraska District and pastor of First Lutheran Church in Omaha, Nebraska.

One of our volunteers was Martha (Fritz) Baepler, the daughter of Dean John Fritz of the St. Louis seminary. She had married Dr. Walter Baepler, who became president of the seminary in Springfield. She was our public relations director in the Central Illinois District—and did a great job there! Later on, I visited her in the Home for the Aging in Valparaiso, Indiana, where she spent the last years of her life. She was still the same talkative, vibrant person that a public relations person gets to be. She knew that when you are talking to people, you have to let them know who you are. "I'm a follower of Jesus Christ," is the first thing you can say, and then the other stuff comes along after that. That's what takes you from here to there, from earth to heaven. An identification of who you are should always be the first thing!

I organized the volunteer public relations organization through the synodical districts, some of which were not too convinced that the districts should be involved in public relations. One of these was Andrew Zeile, president of the Michigan District, who appointed his district vice-president, Walter Schoedel (father of Rev. Walter Schoedel, who served as pastor of my home congregation, Concordia–Kirkwood, for many years until his retirement in 1992), to the position of public relations director of Michigan to keep an eye on things. As time went on, Andy Zeile became one of our greatest friends. He attended every meeting of the Board of Public Relations. I guess he became convinced that our efforts were worthwhile.

Having shared with you how the Public Relations Department came about and how we organized it, I will share in the next chapter some of the things we were able to accomplish.

7

THE WORK OF THE PUBLIC RELATIONS OFFICE

The following article of mine appeared in the April 18, 1950, issue of *The Lutheran Witness.*

PUBLIC RELATIONS FOR SYNOD

By the Rev. Oswald C. J. Hoffmann
Director of Public Relations
New York, N.Y.

Little over a Year Old

Synod established its Department of Public Relations through action of the Chicago Convention of our Church in 1947. It was not until September, 1948, that the New York headquarters of the department were opened at 1819 Broadway. One month later the department opened its Washington office at 736 Jackson Place, N.W., on the fourth floor of the Lutheran Center, overlooking Lafayette Park and the White House.

Today, after little more than a year's existence, the department is firmly established and has proved its worth as an interpreter of the Missouri Synod to uninformed, misinformed, or misguided public opinion.

Interpretation

The essential task of the Department of Public Relations is interpretation. It would be difficult to enumerate all the groups and agencies of our country which, through the interpretive program of public relations, have become aware of, and some appreciative of, the Christian mission of faith and love being carried on energetically by the Missouri Synod. They include the press, radio, and other sections of the communications industry, many governmental agencies, colleges and college students seeking information, welfare groups (especially those interested in legislation), other religious groups, bodies, and individuals.

Positive Emphasis

The Missouri Synod is conducting a large-scale positive mission for Jesus Christ. Public Relations has consistently attempted to promote a positive understanding of Synod's purpose and program. On several occasions it has issued statements by our president, Dr. John W. Behnken, setting forth the Church's positive views on issues of the day, some of them highly controversial. One such statement severely criticized sponsors of legislation to legalize euthanasia, or mercy killing. It may be that the Church will have to speak again on this question, which presents a clean-cut issue of God's Law to the American public as well as to the medical profession. This was one case in which the Missouri Synod and the Roman Catholic Church expressed identical opinions. Ours was the only Protestant body, to our knowledge, which issued a forthright statement of its views based upon Scripture. Dr. Behnken's statement was widely quoted in the public press.

Federal Aid

The American people evidently are not accustomed to hearing from the Missouri Synod. As a result they know too little about our Church.

It came as a great surprise to newspaper editors, the day that Mrs. Franklin D. Roosevelt published her famous reply to Francis Cardinal Spellman, that the Missouri Synod had a great interest in the controversy, because it operates the largest system of parish elementary schools in American Protestantism. As a result, newspapers and radio stations all over the country carried Dr. Behnken's statement outlining the views of our Church on this explosive issue. *Time* magazine "wrapped up" its story on the controversy with Dr. Behnken's pronouncement, which took issue with both Cardinal Spellman and Mrs. Roosevelt on the basis of our traditional adherence to the principle of separation of Church and State (correctly understood, of course).

Organization

Much of the credit for what has been achieved in this short time must go to the public relations representatives who represent the Districts and circuits of Synod. These men, both laymen and pastors, give of their time voluntarily to promote good relations between our Church and the local communities where it is working.

These men are listening posts to sense pubic opinion and, at the same time, outlets for the kind of free and full information which will correctly and fairly interpret our Church to those who do not yet know us well.

If our members, especially in certain areas, see the name of the Missouri Synod a little oftener in public print than they did formerly, in all likelihood these District and circuit representatives are most responsible for that development.

The District organizations operate, of course, under the direction of Synod's Department of Public Relations.

Public Relations, Not Publicity

The Department of Public Relations is not so much interested in getting the name of the Church into the papers, as it is in building understanding. We cannot expect everyone to agree with the Missouri Synod, but we are justified in hoping to develop some understanding of who we are in the Missouri Synod and what we are about.

Identifying Ourselves with Jesus Christ

We do not claim that there is no salvation outside the Lutheran Church. Our whole history is a protest against that monstrous claim.

On the other hand, we do lay claim to the whole heritage of evangelical Christianity as embodied in Jesus Christ and the Scriptures. We plan to let the world know that we are for Jesus Christ, and for Him alone. In all its work the department proposes to follow closely the principles of Martin Luther, who was devoted to Jesus Christ in exactly the same way.

Naturally we shall meet problems, as we have met some difficult ones already in the last months. Some call for stern and even sharp action if the cause of the Church is to be defended and promoted properly. Others call for kindness and understanding on our part. We pray often, and we hope all our members will pray with us, that God will make the department of public relations a blessing to our Church and to the cause of our Lord Jesus Christ.

Looking back, I'm still convinced that I was right when I wrote in the article, "The essential task of the Department of Public Relations is interpretation" and "We plan to let the world know that we are for Jesus Christ, and for Him alone." In order to carry out those goals, we had to work with the government as well as with the press.

RELATIONSHIP WITH THE MEDIA

As one can determine from the above, our actual work varied greatly. Our primary focus, though, was on public relations outside the Synod. Consequently, our primary relationship was with the public media. As a result I became acquainted with George Cornell, religion editor of the Associated Press; George Dugan, religion editor of the *New York Times;* Dave Runge, religion editor of the *Milwaukee Journal;* Bill Thorkelson, religion editor of the *Minneapolis Star-Tribune;* and many others throughout the country. One especially good friend of our public relations office was Lillian Block. She was a Jewish woman who was the head of Religious News Service (RNS). RNS was sponsored by the National Conference of Christians and Jews (NCCJ). Each day RNS would produce and distribute a batch of 50 to 60 pages of news releases. The Lutheran journalist Eric Modean got his start working under Lillian Block at RNS, as did many other Lutheran journalists.

One thing I did almost immediately when I became public relations director was to send out notices to the various media telling them that we were now establishing our office. I also went to introduce myself to some of them in person. I remember going to visit George Crothers, who was head of the CBS public affairs office. I asked him, "What can we do for you?" He said, "There's nothing you can do for us!"

Later George Crothers became one of my best friends. Once when he had a big problem on one of the CBS "Look Up and Live" programs with William Sloane Coffin (then president of Union Theological Seminary), Crothers asked me to take over the program. I suggested that he should work it out with Coffin instead. That is what he did.

One year the LCMS produced a film in St. Louis on the historical facts of Lutheranism in the United States. When we premiered that film at the Museum of Modern Art in New York, I invited George Crothers to come. Not only did he come with his wife, but he also brought his father and mother with him. They had been missionaries in a foreign land and were glad to be there.

Pamela Ilott, who worked under George Crothers in the public affairs department and was in charge of all religious programming for CBS, also became a very good friend. She had come to this country from England. She was Anglican, but her first job after coming here was to write "Lutheran Hour News" for Pan-American Broadcasting Company, the agency that did media placement abroad for "The Lutheran Hour."

I also became good friends with Doris Ann, who was in charge of religious programming at NBC. Her full name was Doris Ann Schartenberg, but nobody ever used her last name. She was a Roman Catholic, but she was always interested in our Lutheran perspective on things.

RELIGIOUS PUBLIC RELATIONS COUNCIL

As public relations director for the Missouri Synod, I also became involved in an organization at that time called the National Religious Publicity Council (now called the Religious Public Relations Council). The National Religious Publicity Council had been initiated by three laypeople: Mr. DeRose, whom I did not know; Mr. Hinkhaus, who was a printer; and Mr. J. F. E. Nickelsburg, who was from the American Lutheran Publicity Bureau and had been on the previous Press Committee of the LCMS.

The NRPC began very small, but its purpose was very well stated. It was "to give professional status to the people working in the area of public relations for the church." If they were not professionals, the organization's goal was to help them become professionals, so that they could hold their own with professionals in any other area of public relations and do a good job.

I was chairman of the Awards Committee of the Religious Publicity Council. Up until that time, they had given three awards which they kind of joked about, because they always went to the religion editors of large metropolitan newspapers. To the great surprise of those reporters, when they received these awards, they all got raises!

As chairman of the Awards Committee, I suggested that people who had been nominated for an award submit a sample of their work. One of the newspapers that won the award was the community paper in New Braunfels, Texas, which turned out to my surprise to be a thoroughly Lutheran community. One of our synodical public relations directors nominated this paper, the newspaper submitted material showing how well it covered the field of religion, and the awards committee recognized for the first time that news about religion is not confined to the larger metropolitan areas of the country!

The newspaper that won sent someone to New York to accept the award. They were grateful to receive it, because no paper outside the metropolitan areas had ever been recognized in those days.

I then was elected to a one-year term as president of the Religious Publicity Council. I served three terms as president. It was during that time that we went from being a publicity organization to being a public relations organization.

While I was president, we organized new chapters in several communities. We had had chapters in New York and Philadelphia, but during my presidency, chapters were started in St. Louis, Chicago, and several other places.

PUBLIC RELATIONS WORK
AND THE GOVERNMENT

I once had an interesting conversation with Hubert Humphrey, a Democrat, when we were coming back from Minnesota on an airplane. He talked about how politics really works in Washington, D.C.

"We make fists at one another 10 percent of the time," he said, "but the other 90 percent of the time we have to work together because we have legislation to pass.

"I just spoke at a meeting up in Minnesota," he continued, "and I praised Senator William Knowland. [At that time Senator Knowland, publisher of the *Oakland Tribune* was the Republican Senate leader.] A fellow came up to me after that and asked, 'Whose side are you on?'

"I had to tell him how things operate in Washington," Humphrey concluded. "We do fight 10 percent of the time; but ever since I've known Senator Knowland, when he tells you he'll do something, you don't have to write it on a piece of paper. What he tells you he will do, he will do."

We need to thank God for people like that—public servants, on opposite sides, who worked together for the common good.

As public relations director of Synod, I always let people in government know that I was not acting in a partisan capacity. I was willing to be friends with anybody. I was willing to help anybody too, and I looked to anybody for help who could possibly give it, if it would advance the interests of the church. We were not in politics, but when it was in the interest of the church, I would personally go to people and say, "It's time now to make a decision, and I'd like to see the decision made this way."

The point is that over the years we have been able to have some small influence on government—not by trying to influence their position, but by honestly telling them what we believe is right based on God's Word. That's what we did as a public relations department, and that's what I did later as Lutheran Hour speaker.

The synodical resolution that authorized the department told us to (1) establish and work with district press committees; (2) present the Lutheran viewpoint on current issues; (3) answer attacks against the LCMS; and (4) do what we could to work with the government on Synod's behalf.

Fulfilling the first task was easy in a way; we simply coordinated our work with existing structures. Most of the time that meant preparing press releases (often mats for pouring hot lead type) and photoprints that the district representatives as well as parish pastors could submit to local newspapers. In addition, we held public relations workshops for the district representatives and in general encouraged a professionalism among them. And, as soon as possible we began to set up a churchwide organization of Lutherans in public relations work.

Items 2 through 4 of the resolution allow no easy categorization of our work. The Eleanor Roosevelt-Cardinal Spellman event mentioned in the article at the beginning of this chapter illustrates what I mean. At the time, congress was considering a federal aid-to-schools bill, and Cardinal Spellman, assuming to speak for Roman Catholics, thought that the bill should mandate spending for children in parochial schools as well. Mrs. Roosevelt, widowed out of the White House only four years previously and certainly not a quiet bystander in politics, publicly lambasted Cardinal Spellman and the Catholic Church for trying to wipe out the First Amendment's separation of church and state. She said that parochial schools should get no tax money for anything. He countered that she was a bigot and un-American.

Keep in mind that this was 1949. When the press wanted to know "the church's" position on anything, it almost always turned to the Roman Catholic Church. Who in the press even knew that the Lutherans ran the largest non-Catholic parochial school system in the world? And how many in the press would even connect the cardinal's statements with a previous situation in New Mexico in which 143 priests, nuns, and brothers were teaching in 28 *public* schools, requiring everyone to pray the "Hail, Mary" four times a day and to go to confession? The practice was halted by the state, but not until enough Protestant parents brought suit. Of course, every time our church reported such matters, the Catholics attacked us too for being bigoted. Clearly, when the Spellman-Roosevelt comments aired, some sort of public response/involvement on behalf of the LCMS was warranted.

In addition to getting out the word about Lutheran schools and our Synod's official position on state aid (that it's okay for human services such as transportation, but even then we should be wary), I wrote a press release for President Behnken that included the following statements:

> Lutherans ... regret the attack made by Cardinal Spellman on Mrs. Roosevelt. Particularly do Lutherans deplore the cardinal's implied attack on the principle of separation of Church and State. ... If Mrs. Roosevelt's discussion of federal aid to education were really anti-Catholic, as the cardinal charges, it would be anti-Lutheran, too. ... Careful reading of Mrs. Roosevelt's statements ... convinces us that they were not hostile to religion or to any individual church (quoted in *The Lutheran Witness,* August 23, 1949).

One of my important tasks was to help our synodical president, Dr. John W. Behnken, prepare public statements for the press. When the church needed to make a statement about something, more often than not it would happen on a weekend when no one was available. I would write his statement, then call him up in St. Louis and read it to him over the phone. He was always very appreciative of what I did. He also participated fully in the process. He would listen to what I had written, then chew around on it for awhile and make changes to make the statement his own.

He always listened respectfully to what I had to say and often used the statement I had written with very few changes.

Federal aid to education was one of the burning issues in those days, but there were many other important issues we dealt with as well. In January of 1949, we issued a press release in which Dr. Behnken stated his opposition to a petition by 379 clergymen asking the New York legislature to pass a bill permitting voluntary euthanasia (a statement used by the Associated Press to conclude its summary of the debate).

Other news releases from our office included one in October 1951, that contained a statement by Dr. Behnken in which he strongly objected to President Truman's appointment of an ambassador to the Vatican.

Another item calling for a reaction was the arrest and imprisonment of Cardinal Mindszenty of Hungary. Although Lutherans often argued with and about Roman Catholics, and although Cardinal Mindszenty may or may not have gone too far in meddling with Hungarian politics, his arrest and imprisonment by the Communist officials was seen as a direct attack against Christianity as such and not merely against a Catholic bishop. We saw it as no different from the Hungarian conviction of Lutheran Bishop Lajos Ordass. (Sad to say, the U.S. press barely noticed the arrest of a Lutheran bishop; Mindszenty's arrest, though, brought howls of protest from U.S. Secretary of State Dean Acheson.)

Some items during those days could have been serious if they were not so farfetched. Yet even in such matters we made our voice heard. One of those was the proposed "Christian Amendment" to the Constitution introduced to the 81st Congress by Albert M. Cole of Kansas. It proposed that as a Christian nation, the U.S. recognize the authority and law of Jesus Christ. Similar to prayer amendments today, it was well-intentioned but misguided. God needs no such government approval and/or permission, and the government needs no such intrusion into its affairs by first one and then a myriad of religions.

ON BEHALF OF GERMAN DISPLACED PERSONS

Some public issues required only press releases, but other matters needed a whole lot more work in order to accomplish what needed to be done, even if the task was not specifically related to one of the four responsibilities outlined in the Synod's resolution of 1947. One such task related to the *Volksdeutsche,* German refugees and expellees who had no country to call home. These were people of German ancestry who had lived for generations outside of Germany—for example, in Russia, Poland, Hungary, Yugoslavia, Estonia, Latvia—but who, because of World War II, were pushed from their homes.

I went to meetings on that subject in New York. In one meeting, a Jewish representative was delivering a speech in which he opposed granting the Germans official Displaced Persons status. The International Relief Organization (which was helping to bring stability to Europe after the war) said that these refugees of German ethnic origin, these *Volksdeutsche,* were not their concern. The Canadian Christian Council for Resettlement of Refugees did what it could to help. And a lot of German Lutherans in the U.S. supported that Canadian effort. What an embarrassment that our own government was not doing anything!

Olinda, from our Washington, D.C., office, helped change that. Along with the National Lutheran Council (our co-tenants in the D.C. Lutheran Center) and the National Catholic Welfare Conference, our department testified before the Senate Committee considering the subject of defining refugee status in the laws of the United States. Senator William Langley of North Dakota asked whether any other country was recognizing these *Volksdeutsche* refugees. Our department representative replied that Canada was far ahead of the United States in this respect. Senator Langley pretended not to have any knowledge of this. "Do you mean that somebody else is being more generous to refugees than we are?" he asked.

"That is exactly the situation!" our representative replied.

After that, the laws were changed, and the *Volksdeutsche* were recognized as legitimate refugees.

I should add that our church was concerned for more people than just German DPs and expellees. Following the war our Emergency Planning Council office worked quite closely with the International Relief Organization to assist as many DPs of any nationality as we could who wanted to settle in the U.S.

DRAFT DEFERMENTS

I do not know if the synodical resolution establishing the Department of Public Relations had in mind that we would handle draft deferments from military service, but we did (at least beginning with the Korean War and the period following). In a way, we were in a natural position to do so, with our office in the Lutheran Center alongside Synod's Armed Services Commission.

As far as military deferments were concerned, we worked on the principle that after having gone to the heads of all the departments involved in granting deferments, we would work with the people who were actually making the decisions in Selective Service. We found out who they were and established a good relationship with them. They trusted us because they knew we would not ask for deferments if we were not absolutely convinced that the request was a legitimate one. In others words, the person to be deferred under the law had to be either a minister of the Gospel or one who was engaged in work equivalent to that of a minister of the Gospel. We went to bat for people who were under the obligation of accepting a call and having to ask for permission from the congregation to accept another call. This included only our pastors, male teachers, and those who had declared themselves to be studying for those positions. As a result of our total integrity about this, we had a very good relationship with Selective Service and its directors.

ADDITIONAL WORK IN WASHINGTON, D.C.

In some respects, Olinda Roettger in our Washington, D.C., office had a harder job than I did. As listed in the December 28, 1948, issue of *The Lutheran Witness,* her assignment included

> making contacts with key government offices as occasion may demand, attend conferences of government agencies, with representatives of other national organizations whom the government often calls upon for consultation regarding educational, social, and kindred problems. It will also be her job to watch legislation, attend congressional hearings, and scan the *Congressional Record* for items of interest to the church, such as federal education, foreign relief, displaced persons, public housing, to act as a clearinghouse for information about our church, supplying the Federal government, the press, and other public agencies with authentic information and official pronouncements.

One of the items Olinda helped set up in cooperation with the National Lutheran Council were annual "Washington Churchmen's Seminars" for Lutherans active in government at all levels. We usually brought the participants out to the Lutheran seminary campus at Gettysburg, Pennsylvania (about a two-hour car trip) for these in-depth seminars, during which we discussed ethical concerns for Lutherans in government. Congressmen Al Quie and Walter Moeller were among those who played an active role in these seminars.

Olinda also helped to set up our "Lutheran Student Washington Seminars" sponsored by our department and a similar department in the National Lutheran Council. Each year about 35 Lutheran college students from all over the country would come to Washington, D.C. Olinda would make arrangements for them to sit in on a session of Congress, visit the Supreme Court, and in general get them acquainted with what goes on in Washington. I would often go with the group, explaining some of what was going on, and speaking to them about Christian concerns related to government. They would be in Washington from Monday through Thursday, then on Friday about 20 of them would usually take an optional trip to New York to visit the United Nations.

For many years, I organized "Church-State Consultations" four times a year in Washington, D.C. They included the major denominations of every description. I attended most meetings, along with representatives of other groups like the National Council of Churches and the National Association of Evangelicals. The National Council of Churches was represented by people like Eugene Carson Blake. The evangelicals were represented by outstanding leaders like Carl Henry and Clyde Taylor, General Secretary of the National Association of Evangelicals.

PUBLIC RELATIONS AND PRESIDENTS OF THE UNITED STATES

President Dwight D. Eisenhower

I met Eisenhower in 1958. I was still Director of Synod's public relations office while being "The Lutheran Hour" speaker. That was at the time when things were heating up in Lebanon, and we had just sent in the Marines. I had written some prayers and sermonettes that we called "Prayers for Peace." Concordia Publishing House had put them in book form, NBC had recorded them, and we sent them to our Lutheran Hour stations.

John W. Boehne, a member of Synod's Board of Directors, and I went to the White House to present a book and record of those prayers to Eisenhower. NBC had provided a special gold record, and Concordia Publishing House had prepared a beautiful Red Morocco leather bound book especially for our presentation.

We were the only appointment on President Eisenhower's calendar that day; but when we got to the White House, we were kept waiting for two hours. This was on a Monday, and Eisenhower was in conference with his secretary of state, John Foster Dulles, about the speech the president was to make at the United Nations on Wednesday. After they had finished, Dulles went to his car, which had been parked in back of the White House so that no one would know he was there.

When we entered the Oval Office, Eisenhower said, "I have a few Lebanons on my mind this morning."

"I can appreciate that," I said. After that, we made our presentation, and then we started talking, and it became a social occasion.

It was about lunch time, and President Eisenhower picked up the gold record to take it up to the living quarters of the White House where he would meet his wife for lunch. "We're going to play this record at lunch," he said. "The only trouble is that the recording machine up in the White House living quarters doesn't work too well!"

I still think it strange that the president of the United States did not have the best equipment available!

President John F. Kennedy

In 1960, Walter Moeller, a Lutheran pastor from Ohio who had been elected to the U.S. House of Representatives, asked me to meet with presidential candidate John F. Kennedy in Congressman Moeller's office to discuss Kennedy's position on the separation of church and state.

I spent 45 minutes alone with Kennedy that day in Moeller's office. It was the day before the Wisconsin primary. While we were talking, people kept poking their heads in the door and saying, "Senator, we have to go to the plane for the primary," but Kennedy kept right on talking about his position.

I had taken Jaroslav Pelikan's book *The Riddle of Roman Catholicism* to the meeting. "Oh, that's a book from another day," Kennedy said. "I am for separation of church and state." Then he added, "Of course, I have every bishop in the country against me."

As it turned out, not all the bishops were against him. Two churchmen who supported him were Father John Courtney Murray and Richard Cardinal Cushing.

At one point in our conversation, Kennedy said, "When I get into the presidency, you are not going to find priests running up and down the halls in the White House."

I asked Kennedy about the traditional position of the Roman Catholic Church, which at that time regarded the corporate church-state relationship as found in Portugal to be the ideal situation. He assured me that this is America, 1960, and stated his opinion that his own church had fared much better here than in Portugal.

I told him that I thought he would have to state publicly his position on church and state. He responded that Al Smith had tried to do that, and that his own advisors were telling him not to get into that area at all.

As it turned out, Kennedy succeeded in avoiding the subject during the nomination campaign, but probably won the election with a straight out-and-out separation of church and state statement at a large meeting with Baptist pastors in Texas about a week or so before the election. His opponent, Richard M. Nixon, waffled on the subject. Nixon probably lost the election because he did not come out squarely for a separation of church and state that would preserve the freedom of religion in a country and at the same time allow suitable cooperation between church and government that would not violate the principle that allows people to have complete freedom not only in their faith, but also in the propagation of their faith.

President Lyndon B. Johnson

I met Lyndon Johnson (while he was still a senator) through Senator Magnuson. I did not really know Senator Magnuson very well, but I knew some of his staff. He would let me use his office whenever I was in Washington and had to be at the capitol building. That was very helpful, because then I did not have to go all the way back to our public relations office on Lafayette Square.

Every year, Senator Magnuson would invite me to lunch on May 17, *Sittende Mai,* which was Norwegian Independence Day. A small group of senators were invited for lunch in the office of the Clerk of the Senate that day. One year the group included Hubert Humphrey, Everett Dirksen, Lyndon Baines Johnson, majority leader, and Theodore F. Greene, chairman of the Foreign Relations Committee, who was already about 90 years old.

During the course of the luncheon, Johnson asked me, "What do you think of radio and of our government's use of it?" I told him that I thought they were doing very well with it, but that "The Lutheran Hour" would never use government radio, because we wanted to remain independent.

"We're going to cut every other department's budget except radio," Johnson said, "because radio can get across borders without interference."

"That's exactly why we use radio," I said.

Johnson was quite an operator. Magnuson was chairman of the Senate Commerce Committee. After lunch that day, Johnson said, "Say, Maggy, I've got a little bill I need your help with. It's just a little one … something like seven and a half million dollars. Do you think you could get your committee to take that up?"

Magnuson smiled and said yes, he thought he could do that. That was the price he had to pay for getting Lyndon Johnson to attend that lunch.

President Richard M. Nixon

Another president I met with was Richard Nixon, although that was in 1971, when I was no longer with the Public Relations Department. I found Nixon to be a most personable man.

"Now, don't sit down when you go in to see him," they told me. "He has a full schedule of appointments for today, and he can't see you for more than 10 minutes."

When I went into his office, he said, "Sit down." I did, and we talked for 45 minutes.

This was after I had been to Vietnam for the second time to observe Christmas with the troops. President Nixon had asked me to come to the White House to report on my visits to Vietnam and Korea. We talked about his concern regarding drug abuse among U.S. military personnel. As a result of that, I was among 71 clergy and lay church leaders invited to the White House by President Nixon to discuss the problem of drug abuse.

"Do you ever talk about drugs on your program?" he asked me.

"We sure do," I said. "We were talking about drugs before you people knew it was a problem."

ANOTHER MISCELLANEOUS DUTY FOR THE LCMS

Since at that time New York City was the main point of entry for those flying into the United States, our New York office—as an unofficial extension of the synodical office in St. Louis—was in charge of welcoming foreign visitors who were coming to our synodical headquarters in St. Louis for meetings with synodical officials or for other reasons. Marcia will verify that many of those visitors ended up at our house for dinner—often on very short notice.

Marcia was good at making meals stretch to accommodate however many visitors might be there at the time. She would begin the meal with black bean soup served with lemon. She says she served the black bean soup because it matched her dishes and our upholstery—and because it helped fill up our dinner guests before the main course, which sometimes would be a little thin depending on the number of guests I brought home.

Marcia bought Crosse and Blackwell black bean soup in large cans from a small grocery store near our house. One summer when we returned from a trip to Minnesota to visit our parents, she went to the store to buy her black bean soup and there was none on the shelf. When she asked the grocer about this, he said, "Well, there were only two of you who bought that soup. You were gone so long, I didn't think you were coming back, and the other lady committed suicide!"

Not only did those visitors eat with us, often they stayed at our house. One of Marcia's favorite guests was Bishop Bo Giertz of Sweden. She was proud of him because he was a Swede like her. He had had more theological books translated into other languages than any other Lutheran, and he was still such a congenial man. Marcia liked him because when he was at our house, he made himself at home. Our German visitors were often more stiff and formal, but he was not like that. If you had a bowl of apples out on the table, he would think nothing of helping himself to one.

One of the German visitors we hosted was Bishop Hans Meiser, bishop of the Lutheran Church in Bavaria. Lorrie Meyer was to have hosted him, but I had to take over his tour here because Lorrie Meyer had a heart attack. Bishop Meiser and his wife stayed with us at our home in New York. One day he said to me, "My grandchildren would not be alive today if it had not been for the Missouri Synod program of CARE packages sent to Europe."

Lorrie Meyer instituted the CARE package program that we operated after World War II. He was that kind of a man. He did things that had not been done before. He was not an elected official of the Synod, but he was Dr. Behnken's assistant, and he often accomplished things that otherwise would not have happened.

Other travelers through New York City whom we hosted were those going to the mission field and missionaries returning home. Those returning missionaries would sometimes be very ill, and we would have to make special arrangements for their care. A couple of missionaries came back so ill that we had to make arrangements for an ambulance to meet them at the airport, then house them at an international hotel nearby until hospital care could be provided.

Sometimes we had to save seminary students going to the mission field from their own naivete. I remember when Gene Bunkowske, now director of the missiology program at Concordia Seminary, Fort Wayne, and a synodical vice-president, came to New York on his way to Nigeria with his new bride, Bernice. They came into our office with their sleeping bags and told us that they had found this delightful place to camp out in Central Park while they spent a week sightseeing in New York. We had to convince them that was not a good idea, and we made arrangements for them to sleep in the gym of St. Luke Lutheran Church just off Times Square during the time they were there.

We met many people there in New York in those days, and had many of them at our house. So many people came through our house that we could not remember them all. When we got to St. Louis, sometimes we would meet someone and think that we were meeting for the first time. "Oh, we met you before," they would say. "We had dinner at your house in New York!"

It's interesting when I look back to realize how varied our duties were in those days. We were very busy, but somehow we accomplished what needed to be done. One thing that helped me maintain my rigorous schedule was my ability to take five- or ten-minute catnaps. I would put my head down on the desk, go sound asleep for a few minutes, then wake up refreshed and ready to go. Over the years I have been pretty much able to do that, especially on airplanes during extensive travel.

The credit for all that we got done through our public relations office needs to be shared with many people, including our two secretaries, Ruth Adams and Marie Maier. Ruth supplied a lot of the savvy for the ongoing program, including travel and things that had to be done. Marie was responsible for the physical setup of the pressrooms at the synodical conventions and other conferences. That is probably the way the pressrooms are still being set up today.

Many times we had meetings over lunch in my office. The girls would go across the street to the Jewish delicatessen to bring in something for lunch. Our favorite was matzo ball soup. Many decisions were made in my office over those matzo ball soup lunches!

8

PUBLIC RELATIONS, TELEVISION, AND THE MOVIES

OMETIME AFTER I BECAME LUTHERAN HOUR SPEAKER, I WAS ATTENDING a meeting at which was discussed the use of radio and television. The National Council of Churches representative had long maintained—and was still saying it at this meeting—that radio and television programs could only be "bell ringers," pure advertising for the churches. Finally, Dr. Alexander of the Presbyterian Church of the South spoke up. "I don't understand what you're talking about," he said. "If Dr. Graham and Dr. Hoffmann can use radio as a pulpit, why in the world can't you?"

That use of the media—to preach the Gospel—was my goal from the very first day on the job at the Public Relations Department of the Synod. As I mentioned in a previous chapter, I had been caught up in the excitement of radio ever since I could remember, including its use as a tool for evangelism. That's why my father had taken the call in 1930 to Minneapolis. Also, on New Year's Day of 1948, when KSD-TV in St. Louis experimented with a telecast of "The Lutheran Hour," I was allowed as a fill-in to have the thrill of being the speaker. In addition, almost everyone in the media across America assumed that TV would mean the eventual death of radio. Therefore, when later in 1948 I was offered the position of public relations director for the Synod, I knew I was not going to limit myself to press releases advertising Sunday mornings; radio and now TV would shout the Good News from the rooftops and the mountaintops. In my mind, the "PR" of my job would stand for "Proclaiming the Redeemer."

RADIO AND TELEVISION

The Lutheran Church—Missouri Synod recognized early the value of radio and television for getting out the Gospel message. Already in 1935, the Synod had established a radio committee, primarily to assist congregations in their outreach. That same year, "The Lutheran Hour" restarted permanent broadcasting, with its magnificent and eloquent speaker, Dr. Walter A. Maier. During the 1940s, the American Lutheran Publicity Bureau also developed some materials that congregations could use over radio. And when the Public Relations Department of Synod got into full swing in 1949, it too (in cooperation with the Radio Committee and the ALPB) began to provide materials.

In the late 1940s, no department in Synod was officially given the assignment to produce *network* radio and television programming. However, we in the public relations office ended up doing it anyway, primarily because of our contacts with the media. That included CBS Radio's "Church of the Air," one or two television programs a year on CBS's "Lamp Unto My Feet" (which always began with a skit), one or two TV programs annually on NBC's "Frontiers of Faith," and occasional television programs on ABC. I usually did not appear on these programs, but I did schedule all the guests. I often would ask Dr. Behnken, the president of the seminary, or some other synodical official to be on the program.

I remember one of those "Lamp Unto My Feet" programs we did with the Armed Services Commission of our church. It began with a skit about a young man in the Army down at one of the southern military installations. He got into trouble and was beaten up. The army tried to get us to change that because they did not feel it was a good advertisement for the military, but CBS refused to change it.

Rev. Kenneth Ahl, head of the Armed Services Commission, was on the program, and the moderator was Lyman Bryson. George Crothers was sitting in the control room with me. He was telling me about a previous program during which the moderator had asked a leading question and the fellow being interviewed answered by saying yes. That answer, of course, is deadly on an interview program, often leaving the moderator with nowhere to go.

At the end of the skit on our program, with the young soldier in bandages, Lyman Bryson, who was a very fine moderator, turned to Chaplain Ahl and asked, "Whose fault was it that this boy got into trouble?"

Kenny Ahl answered that question beautifully. "First of all it was his fault. And then again it may be our fault too, in that we don't provide facilities in the way we should to keep these young men occupied when they're off duty all weekend."

Then Bryson asked, "Is it true that your church, probably more than any other church, provides facilities like that and has programs for people who are in the Armed Services?"

And Kenny said yes.

In the control room, there were great guffaws of laughter. George Crothers said that the previous time producers and directors had gone off the wall, but this time they just laughed uproariously.

Kenny had six pages of stuff with him that had been prepared for him by Rev. Lambert Brose, who at that time was serving as a writer for the Armed Services Commission. It was probably good stuff too, because Brose was a good writer. I had told Kenny to forget about that stuff and just answer the moderator's questions, but he brought Brose's material into the studio with him anyhow. He was so occupied with this material, that when that question came, he froze. Bryson quickly recovered and went on to something else. It turned out to be a very good interview.

Many of our network TV programs originated from Trinity Lutheran Church on Long Island. The pastor there was Dr. Jack Rippe, the Atlantic District president. The crew liked to go out there because Rippe's wife, Helen, would provide a wonderful feast for them. Once in a while she also served as organist for the telecast.

My First TV Appearance

I remember very well the first time I appeared on television. It too was on WPIX in New York on a Sunday evening at 6:30. It was to have been a half-hour program, and I was to deliver a 12-minute sermon. The program immediately followed a hockey game, and the hockey game ran over. They came to me and said, "You'll have to cut your sermon to six minutes."

I had worked very hard on that sermon and had cut it to what I thought was the bare minimum, but right there in front of the cameras, I had to cut it in half. After the broadcast, the program director came up to me and said: "That's the best 12-minute sermon in 6 minutes I've ever heard!" Then he said, "Maybe that's a sign. Maybe it's better to have a 12-minute sermon delivered in 6 minutes than a 6-minute sermon delivered in 12 minutes!"

Another time, NBC insisted that I appear on one of their network TV programs for Easter. I remember that I preached on that great text in Acts in which St. Paul says to King Agrippa, "Why should it be thought incredible with you that God should raise the dead?"

I also remember being interviewed on "The Betty Furness Show." The subject was sex and morality. I was defending the traditional Christian position, and the fellow I was debating, a disciple of Havelock Ellis, was advocating a completely materialistic view of sex. Candice Bergen was also being interviewed. When Betty Furness asked her what her thoughts were on the matter, she said, "Oh, Dr. Hoffmann is right. I agree with him."

"Face the Nation"

There was one other television program I appeared on that I remember very well. It was the CBS program "Face the Nation." Here's how that happened.

In 1961 Francis Cardinal Spellman gave the Roman Catholic response to a recommendation by President Kennedy's task force on education. The Cardinal said that tax money for education should be allocated to parochial schools as well as to public schools, and he claimed this was the position of "the church." (One would think that the trouble he caused in 1949 [mentioned in chapter 7] would have been enough to teach him that he did not and could not speak for all denominations. Evidently, he forgot the lesson by 1961.) As the Religious News Service reported,

> "It is imperative," the prelate declared, "that our nation provide every child with the teachings necessary to develop his moral and intellectual abilities to their highest potential. The requirements of national defense as well as the general welfare of our country demand that ... no child be treated as a second-class citizen."

> Lashing out at the recommendations, Cardinal Spellman said, "It is unthinkable that any American child be denied the federal funds allotted to other children which are necessary for his mental development because his parents choose for him a God-centered education."

> He emphasized it was his belief that the task force proposal was "unfair to most parents of the nation's 6,800,000 parochial and private school children." (In his address, the prelate specifically mentioned Lutheran and Baptist schools in addition to Roman Catholic.)

"Let Cardinal Spellman speak for himself," I responded on behalf of the Synod. Somehow that statement caught on and was very heavily publicized.

As a result of that, I was asked to appear on "Face the Nation" in a debate with Monsignor Frederick G. Hochwalt, with Howard K. Smith serving as moderator. When we tried to find a suitable time for doing the program, the only time we could find was while Monsignor Hochwalt was at the convention of the National Catholic Welfare Association in Atlantic City. We did the program in a penthouse suite in a hotel there where they set up a studio. Fred Friendly, who became the president of CBS, was the producer.

We had very little time to plan the program. We went out to dinner that evening surrounded by hundreds of nuns, the teaching force of the Roman Catholic Church throughout the country. All the nuns were eating chocolate sundaes that night, which they probably were not served too often in the convents of those days.

At that time, of course, all nuns wore habits representative of their order. I asked Monsignor Hochwalt, who was the head of the whole educational program for the Roman Catholic Church in the United States, which order some of them sitting near us were from. He said, "I don't know which order they're from. There are so many of them!"

On "Face the Nation," I disagreed with the positions of Cardinal Spellman. I took the position that we would not accept any support for our parochial schools that violated the policy of separation of church and state, a policy designed to protect the principle in our Constitution of freedom of religion. At the same time, I saw no reason why parochial schools should not be treated equitably and fairly in receiving funds given by the government for all schools to provide services not directly related to the instructional program.

Later on, Monsignor Hochwalt told me that his mother, who lived in Cleveland and who had been watching the program, had wired him with two pieces of advice: quit criticizing the president (John F. Kennedy), and comb your hair!

Other Interviews and Programs

June 12, 1955: "Success Story, U.S.A.," an interview by Hardy Burt; the Mutual Broadcasting System

July 27, 1963: An interview by Ray Scherer

November 24, 1963: An address to the nation in memoriam of President John F. Kennedy; the Mutual Broadcasting Company

February 2, 1971: "The Today Show," an interview by Joe Garagiola; NBC

July 11, 1976: "A Conversation with Dr. Hoffmann," a special with Richard Hunt; NBC News

January 2, 1977: "Lamp Unto My Feet," a special with George Crothers; CBS News

The TV Series "This Is the Life"

In the early years of television, I had many conversations with William Paley of CBS and other television executives about how Lutheranism might get on television. Time and again the conclusion was that anyone's programs had to be attractive and at least somewhat entertaining and that they had to be professional.

As a result of those conversations, our church's "This Is the Life" television series (a dramatic format) was born in my office. My basic idea was that we would do a series of stories focused on one family, similar to successful radio shows such as "One Man's Family." The Lutherans would fund the project, but we would "allow" the National Council of Churches to distribute it under their auspices at no cost to us or the stations. (Remember, this was about 1950, and stations assumed that they might have to actually buy religious programs in order to keep their licenses.) This was a good arrangement for us, because it meant that our only cost was the production of the program and the Council of Churches would

127

have no control at all over the content of the program. It was also good for them because, as the official Protestant group paralleling the Roman Catholic Church and the Jewish faith, the Council of Churches needed some good programming at that time.

I made the proposal to the Synod by taking it to the college of presidents (all the district presidents plus the officers of Synod). Others had told me that this group would "chew my head off" when I got there. Instead, they gave the proposal a unanimous vote in favor of doing a program.

I let the college of presidents know that this large undertaking could not be done by our office unless we had more staff. Nor could it be done by the Synod's Radio Committee, because it did not have a focus on television nor a full-time staff person. Both the Public Relations Department and the Radio Committee had petitioned the 1950 convention to rectify this absence of official leadership for entry into television work. The convention's decision was to rename the committee the Radio *and Television* Committee and to authorize it to hire a full-time director, but this was halted because of lack of funds.

Clearly, a leadership void existed. The Lutheran Laymen's League had hoped to fill that void in 1950. Already that summer they prepared a pilot TV program for their summer convention: a Lutheran Hour for television. (They had hoped to feature Dr. Walter A. Maier, but he had died that January. Curiously, they featured me instead as a fill-in.) And on Thanksgiving Day of that year, the LLL launched a brief series over ABC with LCMS President Behnken as the speaker.

Synod's Board of Directors, however, wanted to keep our foray into TV identified with the denomination as a whole rather than with one of its auxiliary agencies. Near the end of 1950, the Board of Directors appointed a Television Advisory Committee to study the whole area of television and Christian proclamation of the Gospel. The dean of students of the St. Louis seminary, Dr.

Oswald Carl Julius Hoffmann, age 3, Snyder, Nebraska.

In 1921, Oswald's father accepted a call to teach at Concordia Seminary, Springfield, Illinois. Shown here are Rev. Carl J. Hoffmann and his wife, Bertha, Oswald (age 7), and brother Kenny (age 4).

In 1963, the Ossie Hoffmann family moved to St. Louis. The family consists of *(left to right)* John, Paul, Katharine, Marcia, Dr. Hoffmann, and Peter.

In 1956, Dr. Hoffmann and LLL President Harry Barr review an article about "The Lutheran Hour" in the February issue of the secular *Coronet* magazine. The article was titled "The Word in 56 Languages."

Dr. Hoffmann's presence before radio microphones began with the formation of Synod's Public Relations Department in 1948 and stretched through his service with "The Lutheran Hour"—a total of 40 years.

When Ossie became Lutheran Hour speaker, he began circling the globe as part of his mission to preach the Gospel to all the world—sometimes in person.

Writing his report on his observations at the Second Vatican Council, Dr. Hoffmann here checks some of the Latin documents for reference.

Dr. Hoffmann interviewed Marion Anderson as part of the 1960 special Lutheran Hour Christmas program. All of these specials were exceptionally well received.

Dr. Hoffmann visits with Richard Cardinal Cushing in the latter's home in Boston. The visit occurred during the 1965 LLL convention in that city.

The first "Christmas in …" program, December 1968, featured an interview with Haile Selassie I, emperor of Ethiopia. The country had been Christian since the fourth century.

Marcia and Ossie Hoffmann examine a gift bracelet that Emperor Haile Selassie I sent to Marcia at the conclusion of the 1968 interview. She had a chance to thank the emperor personally when they saw him again in 1974 at a reception for the United Bible Societies, which was meeting in Addis Ababa.

In 1970, in connection with a trip to Vietnam to visit the troops during the Christmas season, Dr. Hoffmann stopped in the Philippines to do an interview with President Ferdinand and Imelda Marcos.

Dr. Hoffmann interviewed the governor general of Jamaica, Sir Clifford Campbell, as part of the 1972 Lutheran Hour special, "Christmas in the Caribbean."

During their 1979 visit to Taiwan, Mrs. and Dr. Hoffmann had the chance to talk with President Chiang Ching-kuo, the son of General Chiang Kai-shek.

In 1960, Marcia joined her husband for a mini-vacation upon his return from Moscow and Warsaw, where he met with religious leaders to discuss Lutheran Hour expansion. The picture is in front of Windsor Castle, London.

Leonard Wuerffel, was appointed chairman. (In January 1951, the Synod asked the LLL not to compete with the Synod's TV ministry. In part, that was to improve the likelihood that Synod's initial investment of $750,000 on a one-year try would not be wasted.)

By the time of the committee's third meeting (May 18, 1951), it recommended the series I originally proposed: 28 30-minute shows. The Synod's Board of Directors agreed enough to establish a Lutheran Television Productions Committee, Dr. E. R. Bertermann (of the LLL), chairman. By the fall of that year, Rev. Herman W. Gockel was hired as the religious advisor for the series, and two pilot shows were completed. About the same time, Mr. Melvin Schlake was hired as the business executive.

I went out to Hollywood in order to help cast the first programs, originally called "This Is the Life," featuring the Fisher family and their minister, Pastor Martin. Years later, the focus on the Fisher family was dropped, because Herman Gockel insisted that he could not produce enough sufficiently original "Fisher Family" programs. That is when the program took on the anthology format, which it followed until production stopped in 1981.

Sam Hirsch was the producer of most of those programs. You did not need a written contract to do business with Sam Hirsch; all you needed was a handshake. Although he was a Jew, some people wondered whether he actually was a Lutheran. He would always ask, "Where's the sin and grace in this program?" Every time I would preach in the area he was always there, and he would drop a $100 bill in the collection plate.

Thanks to people like Sam Hirsch, Herman Gockel, and others, our Synod has been in the forefront in television throughout the years. We Lutherans were highly respected by everyone, because we had the most effective television program that was produced by any church body.

After the series was a year old, I wrote the following for *The Lutheran Witness* (October 13, 1953):

When "This Is the Life" began a little over a year ago, no one dreamed that a year later it would be televised on 115 stations all over the country, with foreign television services offering to use it, too. (135 stations on October 1.)

"This Is the Life" constituted a new departure in the use of mass communication for the spread of the Gospel.

The Missouri Synod has shown itself to be a true 20th-century descendant of Martin Luther by its willingness to use every avenue for the proclamation of the Gospel.

THE MOVIES

The *Martin Luther* Film

What I wrote above about "This Is the Life" held true also for our feature-length film *Martin Luther.* In the early 1950s, plans began to be formulated for production of a feature film about the life of Martin Luther. The Lutheran Church—Missouri Synod participated in that project largely because of Lorrie Meyer's involvement in the planning process.

After meetings with the National Lutheran Council and executives of the other Lutheran bodies, it was decided that a separate organization would be formed to be responsible for the Martin Luther film. This was beneficial from both a public relations and a financial stance. The organization was called Lutheran Church Productions. Paul Empie, director of the National Lutheran Council, was elected president, and I was elected secretary.

The board included a wide range of people. Among the board members were Rev. Karl Maier, Virginia, the brother of Dr. Walter A. Maier and very interested in audiovisuals; Dr. Franklin Clark Fry, president of the ULCA; Lorrie Meyer (who at that point had the title of Planning Counselor of The Lutheran Church—Missouri

Synod); Dr. Otto Dorn, president of Concordia Publishing House; and Mr. Melvin Schlake (of the "This Is the Life" board).

We went about doing all the things needed to produce a major film. Louis de Rochemont had just finished his work on "The March of Time," and had become interested in producing feature films. We hired his company, Louis de Rochemont Associates, as our production company. Lothar Wolff became our producer, and Alan Sloane was our writer.

Irving Pichel became our director. He had directed *Santa Fe* and many other good films.

Sloane worked on the script for 15 months. When he was finished it was approved by all the church bodies except the Missouri Synod. We said his script was fine as a television script, but that we wanted this to be a major motion picture. The fact that the Missouri Synod rejected the script, it seemed, confirmed the suspicions of others that the Missouri Synod had only entered the project to kill it.

I did not think that was true, but I do remember Lorrie Meyer coming to my office and saying that he thought it might be a good idea if we withdrew from the project. I told him in no uncertain terms what I thought about that. I knew what withdrawal would do to the standing and reputation of the Missouri Synod as a trustworthy organization. I told Lorrie that we were not going to do that, and if he persisted in that he would soon find out that was the wrong way to go.

I said it with a rather strident tone of voice, I guess. When we went out of the office, the two or three secretaries were sitting with their hands on their desks, not able to move. As we went out the door, I said something to them like, "Get on with the day!"

We did tell the other Lutheran bodies, however, that the film script needed work. To back up our words, the LCMS contributed $100,000 above what we were going to contribute. The other two bodies had to contribute another $100,000 too. Otherwise they would have lost some of their voting rights in the corporation.

We had $500,000 in all to produce the film. We got by on that only because we were filming in Germany in 1952, and the exchange rate in those days was five to one in our favor. We got that because we were not going to take anything out of the German economy or country but would only contribute.

We hired people from UFA, the former production company in Germany, as our technical people. Our camera people and other technical people were the top people in their fields.

Henry Endress, who was stewardship secretary of the LCA, served as business manager of the project. He signed all the wage receipts and everything else that had to be signed. In Germany that was a big job. For every person there were 13 copies of everything, each one of which had to be individually stamped.

A lot of the fellows who worked for us had been members of the German military during World War II. They said, "Boy, we're sure glad you won the war! You saved us from being suffocated by all the paperwork!"

Thinking of those former German soldiers, I talked to many of them about their faith. I remember asking one in particular which church he belonged to.

He said, "I'm Lutheran."

I asked him, "Do you go to church?"

"No."

I said, "Why not?"

He said, "You were never on the Eastern front" [against the Russians].

I said, "I don't quite understand what that means."

"Well," he said, "on the Eastern front, quarter was neither asked nor given. It was dog eat dog. It was sheer brutality. Life didn't mean anything."

These men had become nihilists, and they had to be won back from that. I do not know how you do that except with the Gospel. That's what I gave them. " 'In Christ, God was reconciling the world to Himself [2 Corinthians 5:19],' " I told them, "and by the way, that's true for you guys too. Whatever sins you've committed, if you confess them, they will be forgiven. That's the way it is. 'If we confess our sins, [God] is faithful and just to forgive us our sins' [1 John 1:9 KJV]. We don't have to make that true. It is true. It's all been done by God. You accept Him and the power of the resurrection of Jesus Christ and you have a new life."

They listened to me. I can only hope that the Spirit worked in their hearts.

I was over there for the three and a half months it took to complete that film. I was never paid a cent, except for the per diem to cover our meals and our hotel bills, and other miscellaneous expenses.

On June 23 of that summer, our 12th wedding anniversary, the crew gave me the gift of a telephone call home to Marcia. That was the only phone call home I made during the whole time I was there. In those days people did not make long-distance telephone calls; we kept in touch by mail.

We would begin almost every day by rewriting the script. We knew we were doing that almost at the peril of our lives, because this was the script that had been approved by all three Lutheran bodies. But we also knew that to make a good feature film this had to be done. We went ahead and did it! Most of that was under my supervision.

Lothar Wolff, our producer, was a refugee from Germany. He knew how to treat our German crew. They worked very hard, but every two weeks or so they had to prove that they were there by making some demand. Lothar knew how to handle that, and it would usually end up with everybody sharing a great big laugh,

133

and the crew getting down on their knees and saying, "Thank *you,* Mr. Wolff!"

Niall MacGinnis

The main actor in the film was Niall MacGinnis. He was an Irish Catholic who was not very active in his church. He was also a medical doctor. He would spend six months as an actor, then would serve for six months as a ship's doctor on a British cruiser or freighter.

I was at the casting call in London. Our casting director was a wonderfully competent woman by the name of Maude Spector. She provided some very talented actors for us to choose from.

Niall MacGinnis read for the part of Karlstadt. We did not have any really good candidates for the part of Luther. Finally I suggested that we use Niall to portray Martin Luther. That turned out to be an almost tragic mistake.

While we were on location in Germany it was not unusual to have a glass of wine in the evening after we had finished shooting. But Niall would take one glass of wine, and he would become a completely different person. He had been a medical student in London during World War II and had had to minister to people who had been injured in the bombing raids. After one glass of wine, his hatred for the Germans would come out vehemently.

After about a week, the Germans on our crew came to us and said, "You get rid of that fellow, or we'll put him in the hospital."

Irving Pichel, our director, Lothar Wolff, and I got together and decided we would have to get another actor to play Luther. That meant we would have to forget about the first week of shooting. That would have been expensive because we had been on location with horses, wagons, and all kinds of other things.

134

We had already picked out the actor whom we were going to engage to replace MacGinnis. Then Niall asked to meet with me. He said to me, "If you go with me, I'll go with you."

I said, "All right, I'll go with you. But that means you won't touch another drop until the end of the picture."

I recommended to the others that we stay with him. We did, and Niall MacGinnis became my responsibility.

Niall was a very talented fellow. He had been in the Caribbean and learned Calypso songs. In the evening, he would play the piano and sing those songs, but he never touched another drop of wine.

Niall loved his coffee. In those days, the cost of coffee in Germany was prohibitive. I had some friends there who were chaplains, and they would go to the PX and get little bottles of Nestle's coffee, which they would give to me from time to time. I would throw a bottle of coffee to Niall at the piano. He would catch it and go on singing.

Once Niall quit drinking wine, he was able to finish the picture, and he did the best work of his whole career. He was in other films after that, but he never had a part like that again. Ironically, later on he married a German countess!

We hired Charlotte Wanamaker, the wife of actor Sam Wanamaker, as dialog director. That was necessary because we had people from so many countries working on the film. One day we were talking about our Christian faith and she said to me, "How could anything that happened 2,000 years ago be of any value today?"

Irving Pichel, our director, was standing there with me. Before I had a chance to reply, he said, "Oh, that doesn't bother me at all. The light that comes from out there in space comes from a lot longer ago than that!"

I do not know much about light-years and all that stuff, but the fact is that Christianity is not illogical. You do not have to be a fool to be a Christian!

After we were back in the United States and the initial editing had been done, we showed a rough cut of the film to a few select people, one of whom was Franklin Clark Fry. The rough cut, of course, did not have the opticals or the music or any of the special effects.

After we showed it, Fry said, "This film can't be shown anywhere except in church basements."

There was silence—I mean, dead silence. And then Mrs. Fry said, "I don't see why not."

You know what? Dr. Fry was silent, and we went ahead with production of the film.

After all the editing was finished, we were convinced that we had a good film. We had hired many extras and spent several days shooting scenes about the Peasants' War. Those were magnificent scenes. But when the film was edited, we had to cut out scenes from the Peasants' War because they made the film too long.

We hired Robert E. A. Lee to set up premieres of the film in three cities: Minneapolis, Houston, and St. Louis. *Martin Luther* premiered in 1952. It was a phenomenal success. People took the train all the way from the Dakotas to Minneapolis for the premiere there, where its 25-day run drew 98,000 viewers. After the premieres, it was shown in theaters all over the country.

Roman Catholic Opposition

One thing that helped make the film a success was the opposition encountered from some Roman Catholics. Prelates and Roman Catholic journalists tried to discredit the film in any way they possibly could. There were ways they could have legitimately done that, but they did not see those. For example, we combined two characters named Oleander into one person, because we did not want to introduce too many characters with the same name into the film. They never caught that!

136

People attacked the film even without ever having seen it. In those days any non-Roman Catholic who said anything against their church was immediately put on the chopping block. When those attacks were all in and we looked at them, we discovered that the most violent objections often came from Protestants who had joined the Roman Catholic Church.

One of those who attacked us most vehemently was one of the star reporters of the Roman Catholic Church, Lon Francis. He attacked the film in a pamphlet issued by *Our Sunday Visitor,* with the "nihil obstat" of the Roman Catholic censor. It was titled "The Martin Luther Movie, Unhistorical, Unbiblical, Unfair."

We gave Roland Bainton, professor at Yale University and a recognized Luther scholar, the responsibility for answering all those attacks. He did very well in a pamphlet that Lutheran Church Productions published. The title of that pamphlet was "Roland Bainton speaks on the Martin Luther Motion Picture, Authentic, Historical, Biblical, Fair, Informative, Inspiring."

In spite of the Roman Catholic opposition, *Martin Luther* was honored in a number of ways. It received Oscar nominations for photography and art direction. It was named First Honored Film at the Edinburgh International Film Festival in Scotland in 1953, and at the Melbourne Film Festival in Australia in 1954. It was selected as Picture of the Month in March of 1954 by the Evangelische Film-bilde in Frankfurt-am-Main, Germany; and as Picture of the Year by readers of *The Christian Herald,* an international interdenominational magazine.

Not only was the film popular and an award winner, but it made money. Our revenue was actually double the cost of the film. By the end of 1953, over 1.5 million people had paid to see the film, which was shown in some 170 theaters. We presented the profits to the participating church bodies.

Three years later, in December of 1956, we had the TV premiere scheduled for WGN-TV in Chicago. All the sponsors were lined up; everything was a "go"—when the night before the station pulled the plug. Too much pressure on the station from Roman Catholics. The Chancery Office of the archdiocese, with Cardinal Stritch as archbishop, countered that it had made no formal protest to the station. We knew, however, that Roman Catholic laity in the area had been urged to protest to the station, and had done so in large numbers.

I talked to the managing director of WGN and told him that this was a very shameful thing to do. He told me that might be so, but they were going to pay us what they had guaranteed to give us for the showing of the film. But they would not put it on WGN, he said, because they had so many Roman Catholic viewers.

Two months later (February 15, 1957), the independent Catholic weekly *The Commonweal* chastised fellow Catholics who had forced this censorship. The magazine agreed with our viewpoint (a point well established before and since then) that one denomination ought not be allowed to control the public airways according to its own beliefs. The United States is a pluralistic society in which every religion and denomination has a right to exist. Of course, this was before the Second Vatican Council. In 1956, the Roman Catholic Church still taught that it alone had the legal and moral right to exist anywhere in the world.

By March of 1957, we had 150,000 signatures on a protest to the FCC, urging action against it for giving into "sectarian pressure" when it canceled *Martin Luther.* In the end, the TV premiere was held March 8, 1957, over WISN-TV, Milwaukee.

WGN's decision not to show the film turned out to be a terrible mistake. We took the money WGN paid us and published newspaper ads about the showing of the film on Chicago's WBKB-TV in April, two days after Easter. We probably had a bigger audience than we would have had on WGN, because everybody wanted to see what this program was that the Cardinal was against. Shortly after that, Cardinal Stritch was relieved of his post and assigned to be a member of the Curia in Rome. Unfortunately, he died on the ship going over to take up his post in Rome. Inasmuch as we were able to arrange for another station in Chicago to air the movie, we dropped our action against WGN-TV.

Question 7

When Lutheran Film Associates (which Lutheran Church Productions had become) decided to produce another film, we had to ask all of the member Lutheran bodies to budget new money to finance it.

The second film in which we got involved was *Question 7*. It was produced in 1960. Bob Lee supervised the production of the film, and I was on location with him in Germany for several weeks. This is how that film came about.

We had been looking for a sequel to the Luther film and had considered doing a film on Johann Sebastian Bach. We did research on him and a number of script ideas were developed.

On one of the research trips into Bach country in East Germany, it was discovered that there was a vigorous contest between the government and the church for the souls of the young people. We looked into that and decided to have a script prepared on that subject. We had the same producer and writer who had worked on the Martin Luther film, Lothar Wolff and Al Sloane, write a script. They prepared several drafts which our board evaluated with regard to how good the story was and how interesting it would be to an audience. When we were satisfied that we had a good script, we made arrangements to produce the film.

Once again, the goal was pure "PR," meaning "proclamation." The farther away from World War II the country was getting, the more we seemed to put our trust in ourselves. The times were prosperous and peaceful. Korea was behind us, and Vietnam was mostly unknown. The post-war church attendance boom was over. People were beginning to question whether church, religion, was truly necessary or even worth the bother. But those questions could arise only in a prosperous democracy; Christians living under communism faced true struggles. We in Lutheran Film Associates knew that the answer was to be found in the Gospel, where the Christian faith leads people to struggle toward the solution of their problems on the basis of consciences formed by Christian conviction. That's why we went to Germany to film *Question 7*.

Our Mercedes 180

Before the filming began, Marcia and I made a little trip through Europe, including Sweden, the country of Marcia's ancestors. I decided to buy a car to do this. I went to a dealership in Stuttgart to buy a Mercedes 180 with a gasoline engine, but all they had were diesels. I did not particularly want a diesel, but since that was all that was available, I bought a Mercedes-Benz. I paid $2,500 for it, brand new!

When I left the agency, the man said, "Just drive it like a *Schports Kar*," which is what I did. You had to do a lot of shifting, because the engine was not very powerful. But when we went over the Alps, we found out that that car did not heat up, no matter how hard you drove it or how high you went. Then we were glad we had a diesel car. In fact, I loved that car so much that I brought it over here and drove it for 13 years. It is the most economical car I have ever driven in my life! We ended our trip in Copenhagen. I sent Marcia off to the United States, and I went with the car to Hamburg, to a little hotel on the lake, which was to be the production headquarters for the film.

Production of Question 7

The story of *Question 7* was about a boy who was the son of a pastor in East Germany. The issue was whether he could go to college and still maintain his faith. How he answered Question 7 would decide his future. The film ended with the boy running through the Brandenburg Gate, which was still open at that time.

We began shooting in Moeln in Schleswig-Holstein. In this West German town, we recreated the East German village. In a factory there, I opened the filming with a special prayer for the production.

I stayed in Germany for about two weeks as a consultant to Bob Lee, whom we had put in charge of the film. We would often sit around in a rathskeller at the hotel in Hamburg the night before a shooting rewriting the script for the next day, because sometimes when you are shooting you discover that a script you thought would work does not work at all.

Question 7 was a critical success. It won many prizes, including the St. Francis of Assisi Award for the best film of the year. Unfortunately it did not win much of an audience in the United States. People at that time did not seem to be too interested in the subject, although they became more interested later when the Brandenburg Gate was closed.

We also produced a German version of *Question 7,* which was shown throughout West Germany. Over there, the film had large audiences and made a great deal of money.

A TV Documentary

The next filmmaking I was involved in was quite a few years later, when I was no longer part of the Synod's Public Relations Department. CBS sent me to Germany to narrate a TV documentary on the Augsburg Confession on the occasion of the 450th anniversary of the Augsburg Confession in 1980. Pamela Ilott had hired Bernard Flynn as director of the film. After we had finished the shooting, while I was still in Germany, I read in the paper that he had died in Munich while editing the program. CBS put a director named Richard Siemanowski in charge of the project, but only

Flynn really knew the footage he had and how he had planned to put it together. Siemanowski did the best he could, and CBS did air the program.

My last filmmaking was in 1981 as host-narrator of *Yeshua*. I'll tell you about that later.

9

SOME FAMILY MEMORIES
FROM SEDGWICK AVENUE

A s I MENTIONED EARLIER, I ACCEPTED THE POSITION AS PUBLIC
relations director for the Synod in 1948. For several
months thereafter, we lived in a four-room apartment in
Manhattan that overlooked the Columbia University football field.
We could sit out on the fire escape and watch their games. When
they played Army, we watched the whole West Point cadet corps
come marching by.

My cousin from Chicago, Gerry Seidel, played football for
Columbia under Coach Lou Little. He scored the touchdown that
beat Army. Those were the days when Columbia went to the Rose
Bowl. It's a little bit different today!

At any rate, after some months, Charles Nehring, a board member of Concordia-Bronxville and one of the Nehring brothers who
controlled real estate in the Washington Heights area and the
Bronx, bought a house there to be the house of Synod's public
relations director. I do not know why, but Synod insisted on buying that house when it was not the custom to buy a house for
synodical employees. Synod paid $25,000 for the house on Sedg-
wick Avenue! I would have preferred that they give me a housing
allowance and let me buy the house, but they bought it. In the
long run, that worked out fine, because New York passed a law

that said a church-owned house is regarded as a parsonage, and one does not have to pay taxes on such a house.

Historic Washington Heights lies across the Harlem River from the place where the British had gun emplacements to attack George Washington's colonials at the beginning of the Revolutionary War. Washington managed to get out, but he lost 2,000 men. Our house was at British Battle Emplacement #7. There were rumors that skeletons of Revolutionary War soldiers had been found on our property, but that was never substantiated.

Our house had been built by a lawyer in 1898 on a hillside overlooking the Harlem River, right above the Fordham Bridge, not far from Fordham University. It had been quite a showplace in its time. When we had to have some repairs done in the house, workers told us there was not a plain piece of millwork in the entire house.

The house had three stories, but there were really five levels, including the basement and the subbasement. The basement had been the kitchen and the servants' quarters. By the time we moved there, the kitchen had been moved into the large butler's pantry on the first floor. We put a Ping-Pong table in the basement where the kitchen had been.

Throughout our years in that house, the children kept trying to think of creative ways to use the subbasement. One time the boys thought they might be able to grow mushrooms there and make some money. Our daughter, Kate (Katharine Ann), young at the time, thought she might be able to talk me into making it into a stable and buying her a pony. She told her mother many years later that she thought that if she could talk me into buying her a pony, she believed it would grow up to be a horse. Kate loved horses! When she spent a semester in England during her college years at Valparaiso University, she learned to ride English style.

During our early years in that house, we enjoyed sitting on the balcony off the first floor and watching the world-class Columbia

University scull crews work out on the river. Later on, that balcony became somewhat hazardous, and we had to close it off, but we had fun while it lasted.

Our house was on the same street (Sedgwick Avenue) on which Yankee Stadium is located, but about two and a half miles away. One year when the Yankees were in the World Series, I walked down to Yankee Stadium with Peter and Paul (Peter Carl and Paul George). This was when they were still very young, but they both remember it. It probably took us about 45 minutes to walk there. I do not remember whom the Yankees were playing, but it was about the sixth game of the World Series. We just went to the bleacher entrance, paid our $2 apiece, and sat down to watch a World Series game. How simple it all seems in retrospect!

OUR SON JOHN

In 1950, while we were living in that house, our son John Linnell was born. He was baptized after about a month. Shortly after that he developed a high fever and was in Children's Hospital for three weeks.

I was on my way to the synodical convention in Milwaukee at the time. It was my first convention as public relations director of Synod. The evening before the convention, I had spoken at a memorial service for Dr. Walter A. Maier in Shawano, Wisconsin. At 2:00 in the morning the phone in my motel room rang. It was Marcia and Ade Meyer calling to tell me that John was very ill. They told me to go on to the convention, because there was really nothing I could do back in New York. (Later Ade came out to the convention, and we worked in the pressroom together. I remember writing the prayer Dr. Behnken used at the convention concerning our country's entry into the Korean War.)

Son John had a high fever and had osteomyelitis in his arm near the right elbow. That was in the days when they were just

145

beginning to use antibiotics, and they were not sure what would work. He was treated at Children's Hospital with five different kinds of antibiotics. Finally, it was penicillin that worked.

My uncle, Dr. Albert Seidel, who was chief of staff at Walther Memorial Hospital in Chicago, came up to Milwaukee to the convention. I told him about John's illness and he asked, "How old is the boy?"

"He's five weeks old," I said.

Uncle Albert said, "I've never heard of anything like that. He must have been injured in the birth process."

John probably was injured at birth. We had a different doctor from the one who delivered all our other children. We did that because he was a refugee doctor who had done things for our school, and we thought it was a good idea that we use him. We were wrong. Probably if we had used our regular doctor, everything would have turned out all right, even though it was a breech birth. The full nature of the birth injury was not diagnosed until John was 14 years old and we were living in St. Louis.

Dr. Frede Mortensen, who was our doctor in St. Louis, said, "Let me take a look at that boy."

After Dr. Mortensen had examined John, he called us up and said, "The news is good. He has cerebral palsy."

I said, "That's good news?"

"Oh, yes," he said. "That happened, and he's never going to get any worse, and it won't come back; but the injury to the brain has been done."

We enrolled John in Sherwood School, a special high school with no more than 10 students in a class. Just before he was to graduate from high school, we asked the headmaster at the high school, who was one of the finest educators in the St. Louis area, what he thought John should do after high school.

"Send him to a university right around here," he advised. As a result, John went to St. Louis University, where he earned his bachelor of arts degree. He also has a master's degree in library science from the University of Missouri and a degree in theology.

John is a great fellow with a genuine wit, a wonderful sense of humor, and very bright. The muscles in his legs did not develop too well, but he used to play baseball anyway because he could hit the ball a country mile. They called him "our secret weapon." They would put him in to pinch-hit, and he could get to first base. Today John plays a great game of golf and drives his own car. We are most grateful that he is so competent and lives a happy life.

MARCIA BREAKS HER WRIST

Marcia broke her wrist while we were living in that house in New York. I had just come home from being with my father, who had had surgery, and I was bringing Marcia up-to-date on his situation. We were out in the front yard, and Marcia was kicking a beach ball back and forth to John, who was about three years old at the time. The grass was wet, and Marcia slipped and fell and fractured her wrist. The same doctor who delivered John set her wrist—wrong. Three weeks later, they had to break and reset the wrist. Instead of being without the use of her arm for about six weeks, she had her arm in a cast from her knuckles up to her shoulder for 18 months. Poor little John was always hitting his head on that cast!

They actually fastened her wrist together with a staple. She has had that staple in her wrist ever since. Once when she went in for an X ray, the orthopedic surgeon said, "It's only by the grace of God and that staple that your arm is holding together."

During that time in New York, Marcia also developed a tumor in her perotic gland, under her ear. She had surgery on that in Bronxville and two more surgeries in St. Louis when the tumor reoccurred. Dr. Ogura was the only man in St. Louis who would do the surgery the third time. The tumor has come back in recent years, but her surgeon said she will not need surgery again.

OUR DAUGHTER, KATE

Our daughter, Kate, was also born while we lived in New York—on September 5, 1955. For this birth, however, we went back to the doctor we had when we lived in Bronxville and to the hospital where Peter and Paul had been born. Even though Marcia was 42 years old when Kate was born, everything went just fine.

ST. MATTHEW LUTHERAN CHURCH

As I mentioned earlier, when I accepted the position as public relations director of Synod in 1948, I also accepted a call as assistant pastor at St. Matthew Lutheran Church in Manhattan, the oldest active Lutheran Church in the western world. It had been formally founded in 1663, when the first British governor of New York, Richard Nichols, issued two proclamations after the British fleet had taken over New York harbor from the Dutch on December 5, 1663. One proclamation was freedom of religion for the Anglican Church; the other was freedom of religion for the Lutheran Church and for St. Matthew congregation. The Anglicans have lost their document, but St. Matthew still has its proclamation. It is kept in the New York Public Library, where it can still be seen today.

St. Matthew is located today in the Inwood section of Manhattan, right across the river from where we lived. I was called primarily as a "preaching pastor." I was supposed to preach whenever I was in town—which usually happened at least once a month. Rev. Alfred Trinklein was pastor of the congregation. He was a fine man, and I enjoyed working with him for more than 15 years. Many years later I also had the privilege of working with his son, Michael, when he became manager of domestic broadcasting for the LLL, coordinator of Lutheran Hour rallies, and one of the announcers on "The Lutheran Hour."

St. Matthew had a large number of Jewish members. The first ones came from old St. Matthew church on Convent Avenue, where Rev. Adolph Wismar had been pastor. Old St. Matthew congregation joined with Messiah during the pastorate of Pastor Trinklein to form St. Matthew congregation in Inwood. The number of Jewish families increased as children were born and relatives and friends decided to join the church.

There was another reason for the large percentage of Jewish members in the congregation, which at one time numbered about 75 people. There were 3,000 people, mostly Jewish, living in the block where the church was located. They would look down from the apartment buildings and see how happy our people were when they came out of church. They said it was not that way at the synagogue, and they were impressed by that. They were also attracted by Pastor Trinklein's friendliness toward them. He would work out in the garden in front of the church, and people would stop and talk with him. He would talk with them about the garden, and then he would invite them to come to church. He would say something like, "Why don't you stop in and see us?" and sometimes they did. He was such an open fellow and could talk to anybody. I guess that is because he came from the old Lutheran Bavarian gabfest community of Frankenmuth, Michigan! (I have a Frankenmuth story I'm saving for another chapter. What a great place!)

Those Jewish members were solid members of St. Matthew. One family I especially remember was the Schwartzes. The mother was Lutheran and the father was Jewish. They had one boy, Paul, who attended St. Matthew's day school. The father was a plumber and became an official in the plumbers union. At first, Mr. Schwartz came to church only off and on, but he always made it to the annual church picnic. For three years, I always took my baseball glove along to the picnic because I knew that Mr. Schwartz liked to play catch. He looked forward to that, and he would bring his glove along too. After three years, he decided he would become a Christian, and he joined our church.

Some years later, when I was attending a play at the St. Louis seminary, a student came up to me and said, "Don't you recognize me, Pastor? I'm Paul Schwartz." Paul is now a pastor in Northern Illinois.

St. Matthew was very much a part of our family's life during those 15 years. All the children attended the parochial school. One of the teachers whom all our children had was Lillian Thegel. She and Marcia still keep in touch after all these years.

On those Sundays when I was home and preached at St. Matthew, I often would call home after the last service to tell Marcia how many people I had invited to our house for Sunday dinner. Those were some of the days when she would break out that famous black bean soup. Sometimes just being friendly to people can be an important part of bringing them to know their Savior— and in helping them to bring others to know Him. Of course, we do not do that; the Spirit of God does. He works through people, sometimes people like us!

It was in the middle of all this at St. Matthew and at the public relations office that a letter appeared on my desk from the Lutheran Laymen's League asking me to be permanent Lutheran Hour speaker.

10

THE LLL

OST LUTHERANS KNOW THAT SOME SORT OF RELATIONSHIP EXISTS between "The Lutheran Hour" and the Lutheran Laymen's League—if for no other reason than they see the LLL-Lutheran Hour float in the Rose Bowl parade. I want to ensure that *every* reader of this book knows how grateful we all should be to the League for the proclamation of the Gospel that "The Lutheran Hour" provides around the world. "The Lutheran Hour" was not the reason the League was founded. The organization did not get involved with actual broadcasting until it founded "The Lutheran Hour" at the League convention in Chicago in 1930, when the League was 13 years old. (The Rose Bowl floats, sponsored by the Southern California District of the LLL, did not start until January 1, 1951.) Before and after its involvement with "The Lutheran Hour," the League always has lived up to its motto: "To Aid Synod with Word and Deed in Business and Financial Matters."

Here's the early history, as written in *A Brief History of the International Lutheran Laymen's League*, a 12-page booklet put out by the League about 1981.

When The Lutheran Church—Missouri Synod met in convention in Milwaukee in 1917, it faced a deficit of about $100,000. A dozen laymen attending the convention met on the evening of June 22 to discuss ways and means of liquidating this debt. In the process an organization was formed and the name Lutheran Laymen's League was agreed upon. On December 3, 1917, a constitution was adopted.

As its second project the League resolved to gather an endowment fund for the support of retired professors, pastors and teachers, their widows and orphans. The goal was set at a figure of $3,000,000. The first [LLL] convention highlight was the contribution of $100,000 from the floor toward the endowment fund. The sixteenth Synodical convention [of the LCMS] received the report of the endowment fund, which by year's end totalled approximately $2,700,000.

On February 28, 1923, the League embarked on its third major project. The League resolved to assist in [but not be solely responsible for] the establishment and operation of radio station KFUO. The studios and transmitter for this pioneer Christian radio station were located in the attic of the old seminary buildings in St. Louis [kitty-corner across the street from Concordia Publishing House]. Then in 1926, when Concordia Seminary moved to its new campus in suburban Clayton, the League contributed $50,000 for KFUO's new building.

At its 1929 summer convention the League authorized the inclusion of [congregational men's] clubs in the League's membership. The first Lutheran Laymen's League club charter was [issued to] Grace Lutheran Church in Fargo, North Dakota on December 13, 1929.

...

On May 31, 1930, at its annual convention in Chicago's Palmer House, the LLL founded "The Lutheran Hour." It was a great thrill when on Thursday, October 2, 1930, at 10:00 P.M. EST, the first Lutheran Hour program was transmitted over 32 stations of the Columbia Broadcasting System. The program originated in the studios of Station WHK, Cleveland. The Cleveland Bach Chorus under the direction of Mr. F. W. Strieter provided the music. Dr. Walter A. Maier, professor of Old Testament interpretation and history at Concordia Seminary, St. Louis, delivered the first series of sermons. After 36 weeks, on June 11, 1931, "The Lutheran Hour" broadcasting was suspended. [As previously mentioned, it was back on the air permanently in 1935.]

The whole concept—that the Gospel should be preached over the air, through the church's own radio stations when necessary—

began with Rev. Dr. Walter A. Maier. It was his vision. But nothing momentous happened until the projects were taken on by the Lutheran Laymen's League.

As I mentioned in chapter 8, when the League made a pilot TV program in 1950 with me as speaker, League plans were to inaugurate Lutheran Hour *Television.* That probably would have happened had not the Synod decided to get into TV. They asked the League to step aside and started the "This Is the Life" program. I mention this again, not to criticize the decisions made back then but to emphasize the leadership provided by the laity in general, especially by the men of the church.

REV. NORMAN TEMME, AND CONTINUING THE PUBLIC RELATIONS OFFICE

I credit the men of the LLL also for allowing me to continue my work with the Synod public relations office while serving as "The Lutheran Hour" speaker. The board members for the Synod's Public Relations Department were apprehensive about my accepting the offer to be permanent Lutheran Hour speaker. Had I been called upon only to preach "The Lutheran Hour" sermons, demands on my time could have been worked out. However, being the speaker means more than a weekly sermon; it includes working on specials, speaking at the many Lutheran Hour rallies and LLL conventions, answering letters from listeners, and the like. As a result, after I had been Lutheran Hour speaker for three years, the LLL strongly requested once more that I move to St. Louis.

Again, I credit the men of the LLL for their vision. After some discussion, they and I realized that leaving the public relations office without someone trained to replace me would create such a vacuum that it might have to close. That would have been too drastic for the Synod. The better decision was to hire an assistant public relations director who would be trained to take over. So committed was the LLL to this decision that the assistant's salary would be paid for by the LLL rather than the Synod.

A list was drawn up of candidates for that position. When the list was narrowed down to two, they were two of those who had served as volunteer public relations directors in the districts: Rev. Arnold Soeldner in Iowa and Rev. Norman Temme, who was pastor with Lawrence Acker at First Lutheran Church in Omaha, Nebraska. The Public Relations Board chose Norm Temme. Ade Meyer made a personal trip to Omaha to encourage him to accept the position.

The Temmes had never been in New York before. I met them at the airport, and we went into the city. We ate at a Horn and Hardart restaurant on 57th Street. Those restaurants were coin-operated cafeterias in which all the food was in vending machines. Actually the food was pretty good. There were quite a few of those restaurants called "automats" around New York City at that time. I believe there is only one left there today.

My favorite eating place in New York was Keen's Chop House. It was located in the basement of a building on 36th Street. They had a collection of clay pipes hanging on the walls and a large fireplace. Besides serving an excellent mutton chop for $7.50, they also provided a very pleasant atmosphere. At this restaurant we met Barry Goldwater, his wife, and daughter while we were entertaining the governor of Iowa, Norman Erbe, and his wife.

When the Temmes first came to New York, they did not have a place to live. They stayed with us at our house for about a month until I was able to find an apartment for them on a temporary basis. They lived there for about five months; then they found a house.

Norm served as associate director of public relations. He was a real help to me, because I was very busy trying to do three jobs: public relations director for Synod, assisting pastor at St. Matthew, and Lutheran Hour speaker. When we moved to St. Louis in 1963, Norm became the public relations director, a position he held until 1966. That year the Synod decided to move the public relations office to St. Louis, but Norm wanted to stay in New York. He resigned as synodical public relations director and became public relations director for the American Bible Society.

LLL CONVENTIONS AND OFFICERS

The duties of "The Lutheran Hour" speaker included attending and speaking at Lutheran Hour rallies that opened the annual LLL conventions, held each year in a different city. Those conventions were important to the LLL and to me because they provided great encouragement for the laymen who furnished such dedicated support for "The Lutheran Hour."

I mentioned in chapter 2 that I have some memory of the LLL convention of 1927, when it was held at my father's church in Chicago. The next one I remember attending is the one mentioned earlier in this chapter, the 1950 convention, when the LLL used me to test the concept of Lutheran Hour Television. And, as I reported in chapter 1, I was representing the Synod at the 1951 LLL convention in Sioux City, Iowa, when I was called upon to install Dr. Oldsen as Lutheran Hour speaker.

I also attended the LLL convention in 1953 in Colorado Springs, Colorado. I had been at the LCMS convention in Houston as public relations director of Synod. That was the first time the Synod had held a convention in Texas. It was the middle of an unbearably hot summer. I remember someone at that convention saying, "Whoever decided to have this convention here must have been out of his mind!" After that convention, Dr. Behnken asked me to go to the LLL convention representing him.

I was selected as Lutheran Hour speaker just before the LLL convention in Seattle in 1955. Asked to come to the convention to speak to the LLL for five minutes or so, I went.

Those who were at that convention remember it mostly for its family night activity. On family night people went out to an island where Indians cooked a salmon dinner. Unfortunately, some of those serving the dinner stole a large amount of the salmon, and there was not nearly enough salmon to feed those who were there.

When Paul Friedrich, the LLL executive director, saw what had happened, he suggested that we go out to a restaurant to have our salmon dinner. That way there would be more salmon for the others at the family night. Five of us—Paul Friedrich, Ed Schmidt (then president of what is now Commerce Bank in St. Louis), Harry Barr (then chairman of "The Lutheran Hour" committee), and Milton Carpenter (then treasurer of Synod) went to Rossellini's Restaurant for our salmon dinner. It was a wonderful occasion!

In my 33½ years as Lutheran Hour Speaker, I attended every LLL convention except one. That was the one in San Diego, because I was in Germany for the filming of *Question 7*. I spoke at the opening Lutheran Hour rally at every one of the other LLL conventions, spoke to the LLL members on the convention floor each year, and conducted Bible studies at the conventions a number of times.

In connection with the 1961 LLL convention in Wichita, Kansas, I met again the man who was elected president first in 1934, Ernie Gallmeyer, at that time an executive of Wayne Pump Company in Fort Wayne, Indiana. He was a great fellow to know. He was always quick with words and gracious of speech. When I went out to the airport to pick up Marcia, there was Ernie. We drove him into town, and along the way we saw this replica of a big steam locomotive. Ernie remarked, "That's what we have done to the railroads!"

One might take that as a pessimistic or somewhat nostalgic remark, but a moment or two later, he said, "It's the same thing we did to the horse and buggy!" Ernie always had the forward look.

Recalling Ernie, I am reminded that I have known every president of the LLL except Theodore Lamprecht, the first president, but I did know his wife. Lamprecht was a New York businessman who was elected president of the LLL at its founding meeting in 1917 and served until 1926. His wife and her sister were members of Village Lutheran Church in Bronxville, next to the college. The sister was the wife of Dr. Henry Feth, who had been one of the first presidents of Concordia-Bronxville. The women were daughters of Pastor Sievers, who came to St. Matthew Lutheran Church from South Dakota, where the girls had been born and raised in a sod hut halfway under the ground.

When we arrived in Bronxville, Marcia was pregnant with Peter, our first child. These two ladies would take her home after church, because I was gone almost every weekend trying to recruit students for Concordia-Bronxville. After dinner, all three of them would take an afternoon nap.

The second LLL president was E. H. Faster. Although I had seen him at the convention in my father's church when I was in high school, I got to know him later when he headed the financial campaign for the addition to the present LLL building. The largest contribution to that campaign was from AAL, which contributed all the funds for my office and its furnishings along with the furnishings of my secretary's office.

These men and their successors were dedicated laymen with wonderful abilities and varied backgrounds. They provided valuable service to the church through their volunteer service in the Lutheran Laymen's League. I have always appreciated the fact that the Lutheran Laymen's League under any kind of leadership realized that its most important work was to carry the Gospel to people in its own powerful form. These dedicated Lutheran laymen were totally committed to the word-of-mouth distribution of the Gospel—which, if I read it correctly, has been the New Testament way of doing things.

Of all the people with whom I have worked at the LLL, none have been the lifelong friend that Dr. Rudy Bertermann was. We had known each other since we were boys. His father, who was a classmate of my father, was pastor of a big church in Wausau, Wisconsin. When my family lived in Chicago, we used to drive up to a summer cottage in Wisconsin to go fishing. On the way, we would stop and see the Bertermanns. Many times, the Bertermann family, including Rudy and his brother, would visit us at the cottage, and we would run along the lakeshore together.

Rudy Bertermann made a great contribution to the Lutheran Laymen's League that should be recognized. He was assistant to Dr. Maier. He did a lot of writing, for much of which he did not get personal credit. He served as executive director of the LLL from 1967 to 1970, and hired some good people during that time, including Dr. William Kniffel and Bob Garmatz. Bill Kniffel organized Lutheran Hour offices overseas and also helped to organize Lutheran Hour rallies, which were important for the support of our Lutheran Hour broadcasts.

Through all its years, "The Lutheran Hour" was the flagship program of the LLL. It was a good decision on the part of Dr. Walter A. Maier to offer the program to the laymen and for the LLL to take over that program. Many laymen's organizations in all kinds of church bodies do not have a true purpose—some exist primarily for themselves; others have a purpose that is extraneous to the life and work of their church. The LLL programs, from its very inception, have been related directly to the life and purpose of the church.

The LLL has received great encouragement from members of our church and even from others outside our church because of the mission that the LLL has: to bring Christ to the nations. The result of this has been nothing less than phenomenal. The laymen of the church have been totally responsible for "The Lutheran Hour," and people gave so generously that its budget grew from $750,000 in 1955 to over $9 million in 1989. It is a phenomenal example of how God supports things when we commit them to His hands.

11

JOINING
"THE LUTHERAN HOUR"
1955

A S I RECALL, I THINK I WOULD CHARACTERIZE 1955 AS A TIME OF great expectations. Under the presidency of World War II hero Dwight D. Eisenhower and the efforts of the United Nations (celebrating its 10th birthday), the Korean "police action" (which it was called at the time) did not escalate into WWIII. Congress raised the minimum wage from 50 cents to a dollar an hour. The Salk vaccine was discovered and put into use. Three men broke the four-minute mile. The U.S. Supreme Court outlawed segregation in public schools and, later, in parks and other public places. On the average, 1,200 people *per day* were moving to California. President Eisenhower first proposed the interstate highway system. Pan American airlines placed the first U.S. order for jet-propelled passenger planes. Although Albert Einstein died, his legacy was already pushing for space travel. And the Brooklyn Dodgers won their first World Series title—against the New York Yankees.

On the religious front, *Newsweek* magazine reported in its March 28 issue that church membership was still growing faster than the population, that the LCMS was the eighth-largest Protestant denomination in the U.S., and that the LCMS's "ultraconservative tenets and independent views still attract converts." The assumption was that God was on the move in America. As a result, when I received the letter asking me to be the LLL's permanent speaker for "The Lutheran Hour," I was thrilled to be offered this new opportunity to serve the mission of Christ. (For additional details on how I was selected, see chapter 1.)

Of course, when I received the letter, I informed the chairman of the Public Relations Board, my good friend and longtime associate Ade Meyer. I asked him what he thought I should do. He told me he thought it was a marvelous opportunity and said that I should accept it, as long as I did not leave my position at the Public Relations Department.

At the first meeting of the Public Relations Board after I had accepted the position of Lutheran Hour speaker, I was asked to leave the room. The board then proceeded to give Ade a terrific riffle for allowing me to leave. Finally they agreed that if I would stay on as public relations director, they would allow me to be Lutheran Hour Speaker for one year. The board argued that the speaker's position need not be full-time; it had not been with Dr. Walter A. Maier or the interim speakers who followed him. I readily agreed, because I was absolutely convinced of the need for and value of my public relations work for the Synod—and I was thoroughly enjoying it.

A year later the board members had another meeting. They allowed me to stay in that meeting, and they all said, "*Pater, peccavi!*" ("Father, I have sinned"). They realized then that my being Lutheran Hour speaker was a great arrangement, providing excellent public relations opportunities—on which, naturally, I was capitalizing as director of Synod's Public Relations Department.

My comments above should not suggest that the only reason I accepted the position as Lutheran Hour speaker was that Ade Meyer said I should. Actually, when the offer came, I felt that a number of themes in my life were coming together in a way I never could have imagined. These strands included

- my lifelong conviction that only the Gospel of Jesus Christ touches the sick at heart;
- my conviction that the laity of the church are the backbone of the church;
- my love of language;
- the possibilities for radio as a tool in proclaiming the Redeemer, a possibility seen firsthand in my father's work in Minneapolis;
- my seminary relationship with Walter A. Maier;
- my experiences with our Schubert Quartet being in front of an audience (which *is* different from preaching); and
- my recruitment/public relations work for Bethany and then Concordia-Bronxville, which led to the position with the Public Relations Department for Synod, including a lot of training in proclaiming the Redeemer through radio and TV.

My training had included even a three-week stint as Lutheran Hour speaker back in the summer of 1948 (when I was first elected as public relations director for Synod). Compared to 1955, the process in 1948 had been somewhat different. Back then, the broadcasts were done live in St. Louis at station KFUO on the seminary grounds, with the choir in the seminary chapel. We did a program in the morning, had brunch, and then did another live broadcast at 1:30 P.M. for another part of the country. We also recorded the morning broadcast on special 16-inch disks. Because there was no way of editing those disks, if we made a mistake, we either had to let it go or rerecord in the afternoon. By 1955, recordings were put on reel-to-reel tape. We actually had Bing Crosby to thank for that. After World War II, he brought the magnetic tape recording system back from Germany. That system was almost equal in quality to live programming.

The point is, when I received the offer to be "The Lutheran Hour" speaker, I could see that God had been sculpting me for this work. I do not mean that I was the only person in the whole world whom God could have used in that pulpit, nor was I so perfect that God had to choose me. Rather, God had prepared me so that I could accept His direction. Even my pastor brother Kenny, who had been summer Lutheran Hour speaker several times, agreed.

In addition to mentioning my certainty about accepting the position, I should also share some of my apprehension. In 1955, radio was at its lowest ebb. Radio studios were gathering dust, because everybody was putting money into TV. It appeared that the days of radio might be gone. When I met with the Lutheran Laymen's League's director Paul Friedrich and other LLL officials, I asked what they wanted me to do. They said, "Do whatever you want. We just want to get some mail around here!" True, President Behnken had discouraged Elmer Knoernschild's move toward a dramatic format. Everyone, however, was worried that "The Lutheran Hour" might somehow die and that we would never have another chance at a worldwide radio ministry.

I went to my friend Pamela Ilott at CBS and asked her, "If you had a radio program on which you could do anything you wanted, what would you do?"

She thought for a moment, then she said, "If you put a radio program on the air with good music and good talk, you will have the best program possible." That's what we tried to do.

Let me make clear that we were talking only about the *format* of the program. When I became speaker, the *purpose* of "The Lutheran Hour" remained the same as that of Dr. Walter A. Maier: "Bringing Christ to the Nations." That is, of course, an elliptical statement, because Christ is already there. But the Good News of Christ needs to be told. You cannot tell it in any other way than by telling the story.

Dr. Theodore Graebner, a former professor at Concordia Seminary in St. Louis, used to say, " 'The Lutheran Hour' is a great thing because it not only has the power to *tell* people of salvation, but it has the power to *bring* salvation to people through the Good News of God." That's the way people get to know the Good News of salvation—by the Spirit of God working through the Word of God. That can happen through the Word spoken on the radio too.

Of course, you cannot baptize people over the radio, which means that broadcasting the Gospel does have its limitations. But it is the Word of God being spoken, and the Spirit of God does His work through that Word to bring people to salvation. That is why we never considered "The Lutheran Hour" to be just a bell-ringer to bring people to the church. Wherever and however the Gospel is spoken, "it is the power of God for salvation to everyone who believes" (Romans 1:16).

We know that we are always going to tell people the Gospel. We never trimmed our sails to the wind, and I hope we never shall. We are not worried about the winds of public opinion. We are going to tell the Gospel straight from the shoulder as they did in the apostolic age. It is the apostolic thing to do. C. F. W. Walther, the first president of the LCMS, made that clear in his *Proper Distinction between Law and Gospel* a hundred years ago. Our mission, destiny, and purpose is to get the Gospel out to the world.

MY INTRODUCTORY SERMONS

My first broadcast as permanent Lutheran Hour speaker was from Detroit, Michigan. There was a special reason for this.

Because of a tremendous deficit in "The Lutheran Hour" Fund after its first season of broadcasting, "The Lutheran Hour" went off the air temporarily in 1931. Many pastors and congregations collected funds to erase that deficit. By 1935, they had collected enough money to put "The Lutheran Hour" on the air over two stations: WXYZ in Detroit and WLW in Cincinnati, a "clear channel" station that covered most of the eastern half of the United States. During that year the broadcasts originated live from

163

Epiphany Lutheran Church in Detroit, Rev. Dr. E. T. "Barney" Bernthal, pastor.

When I became Lutheran Hour speaker 20 years later, Bernthal, still pastor at Epiphany, wanted to commemorate those 1935 broadcasts by having my first broadcast as Lutheran Hour speaker originate from Epiphany Church. We all agreed; the idea was a good one.

The topic of my first broadcast was " 'The Lutheran Hour': Evangelical and Evangelistic." That sermon emphasized that we who have the Gospel must also tell the Gospel. Here's some of what I said:

> Dr. Maier had but one message to proclaim. All the speakers who have followed him proclaimed but one message. It is my personal conviction that in this message lies the greatest and the most enduring contribution of "The Lutheran Hour" to broadcasting.

> The whole purpose of our broadcast can be very easily summed up in the words of the apostle Peter recorded in the book of Acts, chapter 15, verse 11 [KJV]: "We believe that through the grace of [our] Lord Jesus Christ we shall be saved, even as they."

That was the evangelical content of the broadcast. Then came the evangelistic purpose.

> There would be no Lutheran Hour if we did not wish to share with you our evangelical faith in the Gospel of Jesus Christ. I want you to know that our only purpose in these broadcasts is to share—and to share—and again to share—Jesus Christ with you.

We recorded the program at Epiphany Church at 12:30, and it went on the air in Detroit at 1:30. We went over to Barney Bernthal's house to listen to the program with his wife (whom he always called "Schatzie") and her parents, Mr. and Mrs. Broeker from Southern Illinois.

We stood in the doorway and watched the Broekers, who were sitting in their bedroom listening to the broadcast. We could hear Mrs. Broeker singing along with the hymns. Mr. Broeker, who was hard of hearing, sat with his ear close to the radio on the dresser, listening to every word. We were almost moved to tears as we watched those two people, who were so devoted to the Lord and so wrapped up in the broadcast that they did not even realize we were there for the whole half hour!

That kind of attention to "The Lutheran Hour" has been characteristic of many people. That was not my doing. It was the legacy of Dr. Walter A. Maier, who began the broadcast and who reached people with his powerful preaching for 17 seasons of broadcasting. It represents the power of the Gospel of Jesus Christ proclaimed anywhere, including over the airways.

My second Lutheran Hour sermon strongly emphasized the content of the Good News of Jesus Christ. The topic was "We Preach Christ Crucified." An excerpt from that message pretty well summarizes the Gospel message that has been the message on "The Lutheran Hour" all through the years.

> Do you have a sense of personal inadequacy? Is there the gnawing feeling at your soul that you aren't everything that you should be? Are you constantly irritated by your business associates, your friends, members of your family? Are you bothered by temptations of one kind or another that keep coming back no matter how hard you try to dispel them?

> I can't promise you that acceptance of "Christ crucified for you" will solve all your personal problems—or will solve any of them immediately. But this I say with complete confidence: making the cross of Christ your own, accepting the crucified Christ as your personal Savior, will change your whole outlook on life. It will bring you into a relationship of friendship with God, the kind that God wants to have with you. It will give God His chance to make you more and more the person that He intended you to be. That's pretty wonderful, considering what God has got to work with in the case of most of us. It's pretty

wonderful all round, that God sent His Son and that He died for us to bring us back to God.

RECORDING THE BROADCASTS

As I mentioned earlier in this chapter, by 1955 all the broadcasts were recorded on audiotape. I did, however, revert to being on the air live one time during my first year. We did it as a favor to my friend and classmate who had been vice-president of the student body during our last year at the seminary: Rev. Dr. Roland Wiederanders. He was at St. Paul Lutheran Church in San Antonio at the time. That was the last live broadcast.

In many ways, it is better to record the broadcast. For one thing, the quality is probably a little better. Besides that, when we did it live, we often would wind up a minute too short or a minute too long. Recording the program on tape, we could avoid that problem.

Still, a mystique surrounds broadcasting live, and somebody usually asks if we ever broadcast live. I tell them, "Sure, it's always a live broadcast as long as the man who made it was alive when it was taped."

From 1955 to 1963, the taping of "The Lutheran Hour" was done in New York. That was because I was still Synod's director of public relations at the same time and continued to live in New York. The place where we worked was Reeves Sound Studio. Some of the people I remember working with at Reeves were Chuck Campbell and Dick Vorisek, both from the studio. Sally Allen, the secretary for the president of the distributor for "The Lutheran Hour" (Art Krohn, of the Gotham-Vladimir Ad Agency and a member of Grace Lutheran, Teaneck, New Jersey) would be there for every recording session. Also, John Tietjen would come in from Leonia (right next to Teaneck), where he was pastor, to be there to check for mistakes and to read the questions for the "Questions and Answers" part of the program. John had been a vicar-intern at St. Matthew during his seminary days.

After the recording was complete, the tapes would be sent to St. Louis to be edited and put together at Premier Studios there. (They were the only studio in St. Louis that had the equipment needed to do the job.) Rev. Elmer Knoernschild would sit in on all those sessions. He insisted on the highest quality for our programs. We owe a great debt of gratitude to Elmer Knoernschild, not only for his many years as announcer on "The Lutheran Hour," but also for the high standard of quality he established for the program.

Over the years, I have met station people who would tell me, "We put your program on the air, because the quality was so good!" I even received that compliment one time from the governor of the state of Arizona, who at one time had been a disk jockey. Studio engineers too would say, "We usually didn't listen to religious programs when we were in the control room, but when your program came on, we did." That was partly due to the content, but it was also a tribute to the technical quality of the program.

Reeves Studio was the top of the line. They recorded about 80 percent of the commercials on radio and television in those days. They invented the first equipment used for editing videotape in this country. Our project was not a big account for them, but they were proud to be involved with "The Lutheran Hour," and they did their level best to put the best product on the air. They were concerned even for the content. I recall one time when the people in the control room stopped me while I was recording a sermon. Not sure which statement of mine concerned them, I asked, "Why did you stop me?"

They said, "Because you said, 'One of these days we shall have a man on the moon.' By the time this is broadcast, we may have a man on the moon."

"No, it'll take longer than that," I said.

I do not know whether they agreed with me or not, but we let it go. I was right!

I had a truly wonderful relationship with Reeves Studio. I recall one summer years later, after our recording was being done in St. Louis, that we needed to go back to Reeves to record a couple of Lutheran Hour sermons. When I arrived, the place was completely dark. As I walked into the studio, the lights flipped on and a large streamer across the ceiling said, "Welcome home!" All the corporate executives came out and greeted me. It almost broke me up to have a big studio treat me in that way.

REACHING LISTENERS' NEEDS

As the state of the art in radio broadcasting became more progressive, the lead time between recording my sermon and the broadcast became progressively longer. At first it was 4 weeks, then 6, then 8, then 10, and finally 12. I was still busy as public relations director for Synod, and always had to be ready to write Lutheran Hour sermons. As a result, I developed a research committee to help me decide topics and titles for the sermons. We generally would meet four times a year.

I would always ask the committee members, "What questions are people asking these days? What kind of problems are you running into?" That way we could stay close to the grass roots. We would talk about the problems and concerns of real people, then bring the Gospel to bear on the realities of life all around us. I always told my research committee that we would never have a program that did not begin and end at the foot of the cross. "This program is about Christ," I said, "about His life, death, and resurrection, and about the forgiveness that is ours through His life and death for us."

During most of my time as Lutheran Hour speaker, Rev. Herbert Kern, who was a pastor in East Meadow on Long Island, was the coordinator of that group. Because he is a person who keeps things and files them, he was a good person for the position of coordinator. Later on Dave Schuller, who was a professor at the St. Louis seminary, served as coordinator of a St. Louis research committee. I had him as a student at Concordia-Bronxville. He became a Lutheran while he was there.

There were all kinds of people on those committees—men and women, pastors and teachers, and laypeople. It was usually a committee of five people, but probably 30 or 35 different people served on the New York committee over the years. Some of them later became rather well-known. Among them were two men who later became seminary presidents: Milton Rudnick, who became acting president of Concordia-St. Paul, Minnesota, and president of Concordia Seminary in Edmonton, Alberta; and John Tietjen, who became president of Concordia Seminary in St. Louis.

We were continually wrestling with the question, "How do you speak the Gospel to those who have never heard it before, to people whom you can't see when you are talking to them?" We figured that communicating the Gospel is putting it out there and seeing what comes back to you.

Sometimes we achieved our goals better than at other times. The only way for us to evaluate was to pay attention to the letters we received in response to what was said. We "listened" to the letters that people wrote, and on the broadcast we answered some of the problems they raised. The questions we chose were those that people were hesitant to bring up with someone in the neighborhood where they lived. I wish, though, that I could have been in the same room with these people to see in their eyes the effect the Gospel was having on their problems. That is why I have never understood pastors who close their eyes when they preach. I think that getting a response from people's eyes is an important thing!

Based on listeners' letters, the audience I visualized included some churched, some unchurched; some sort of half-listening, others listening with great concentration; some who could not get out to church for various reasons and who considered "The Lutheran Hour" to be their church, some for whom "The Lutheran Hour" was a second worship experience that week.

Many people seem to think that it's only older people or shut-ins who listen to "The Lutheran Hour." That's an important audience, and we have to take them into consideration. When I visit nursing homes, as I often do, many of those folks will say, "I listen to 'The Lutheran Hour' every week." But there are also younger people to whom radio talks. Some of the most interesting letters I received came from college students and teenagers. Young people are the ones who carry radios around with them— at the beach, on the street, almost everywhere they go. There are also 200–250 million car radios to which people are listening. People of all ages will listen if we can catch their attention and they think, "Here's someone who's talking intelligently, and he's saying something that needs to be heard."

What you say has to have a compelling sound to it, and then chances are people will listen. We never talked down to our audience. We did not talk baby talk. We respected the intelligence of people, both young and old. We also realized that we had children in our audience, and we tried to speak to them as well. I am always surprised at how many children listen to "The Lutheran Hour." I would often get letters from school children. I got a letter on my 80th birthday from a whole class of children. That was really delightful!

One of the research committee's tasks was to help me visualize my audience. The other task was research on the topics we had decided to discuss on the air. Herb Kern would assign the topics to the various members of the committee. Those who were pastors would write sermons that many of them preached in their own congregations before sending them to me. I encouraged them to do that. I never actually used their sermons, but I would use those and the other research materials I received from the committee to get me started on the topics. Sometimes just a line or a quotation or an illustration would get me going, and sometimes I would not use any of their material at all. (One young man on the committee, though, told me that the material he had sent to me was a lot better than what I put on the air!)

After I received that research material, I would think through the topic and then would dictate my sermon. The only other thing I could have done was to write it out longhand, because I never learned to type. But I felt that dictating it would sound a little more like the way one would speak.

Paul Friedrich, the director for the LLL, and the others responsible for "The Lutheran Hour" had said they wanted to get some mail. That request was certainly fulfilled. I got so much mail that during the time I was in New York, we kept three secretaries busy just answering the mail!

How some of that mail got to me was almost a miracle. Some of the more creative spellings of my name included "Dr. Always Hopman" and "Dr. Alwell Huff." One letter from a listener who couldn't decide whether it should be sent to St. Louis or to our Canadian office in Kitchener, Ontario, was addressed: DR. HARPER. SENT. LOUIS. MURSS. TO. THE. LUTHER. ORS. OFFICE. KITCHEN. ENTUREN.

One classic letter that came to me was a letter addressed to "Dr. Hoffmann Co." Inside was a one dollar bill; a small, folded cardboard box with the label "Dr. Hoffmann's Red Drops"; and a short note that read, "Enclosed $1 for your Red Drops. We always like to have them on hand." I do not know to this day whether that letter was sent to me tongue-in-cheek or not!

I answered all the mail that was addressed to me personally. It was interesting that often people would ask questions of me that they would not ask their own pastor. I did not claim that I could answer all their questions, but I would try to give them a

171

general course they could follow. Often I would ask whether I could request their own pastor or a pastor in their neighborhood to speak to them about their problems. No one ever said no. At other times I would ask if I could find a pastor to speak with them. Many times they would answer, almost by return mail, "Yes. Go ahead and do that." Sometimes I would even ask for a phone number and have a pastor call them. The listeners had faith that I would not violate the confidence they had put in me and that whoever came to their home would not violate that confidence either. Most pastors called on these people willingly. There were only a few times when a pastor did not do so.

Sometimes letters I received would result in an exchange of letters over a period of time. For example, there was a Christian Reformed pastor in British Columbia with whom I carried on quite a correspondence for about six months. He wrote to me, "How can you say on your program, 'Christ died for all'?"

I wrote back to him quoting Scripture passages that said pointedly that Christ died for all. He wrote back, "But how can you say that Christ died for all? He died for some, the ones who are saved."

I replied to him with great respect, "I know you're repeating what you learned at your seminary, and I honor you for that, but that still doesn't make it true. The fact is that Christ died for all. I do not try to explain why some are saved and some are not. Being saved is the work of the Holy Spirit through the Gospel of Christ."

I did not hear from him for awhile. Six months later he wrote again. He said, "I just have to try it once more. I don't want to bother you, but how can you say that Jesus Christ died for all?"

I thought, Well, we have had enough theological discussion now. I thought and thought about what to say to him. Then I wrote to him, "I tell you this with all respect for your ministry. When you go in to visit a person who is sick unto death and you say to that person, 'Christ died for you,' you become a Lutheran." I never heard from him after that.

172

That reminds me of the Swedish bishop Bo Giertz, who became a Lutheran after having been raised outside the church. I asked him why he became a Lutheran.

"Because there is no Gospel but the Lutheran Gospel," he said.

That may seem arrogant, but it is very true. The Bible's Gospel is the Gospel that Lutherans believe and preach: Christ died for all. This is the Gospel we preached on "The Lutheran Hour." That simple Gospel message attracted many listeners. It is also the reason why Lutheran Braille Workers has reproduced Lutheran Hour sermons in braille and sight-saving print for many years.

MR. AND MRS. J. C. PENNEY

Among the listeners to "The Lutheran Hour" were some very well-known people. Two of these were Mr. and Mrs. J. C. Penney. One time after they had attended a luncheon at which I spoke in New York, Mr. Penney wrote me a letter in which he said, "Mrs. Penney and I are both glad that we attended the luncheon at which you spoke and had the privilege of having just a few words with you. We enjoyed your talk. We heard you yesterday afternoon on the radio. You are a great inspiration to us."

After we got to know each other better, Mr. Penney would take me to Rotary Club meetings. He was always pressing me to join, but Rotary Club members have to make up any meetings they miss. I told Mr. Penney that I was gone from home so much that I could see myself making up meetings all year long.

Later, in about 1970, Mr. and Mrs. Penney invited me to their Manhattan apartment for lunch one day. (He was wearing a fine gray suit. He never bought a suit anywhere but at a J. C. Penney store. He said that was the finest suit you could buy.) Our lunch together was on the day of his brother's funeral. Before we could have dessert, his wife had to leave to go to the airport, since the funeral was in Cincinnati. Mr. Penney could not go, because he had fallen on the ice the week before. He was about 95 years old at the time.

I stayed two hours after our lunch talking with him about his life, which was closely interwoven with that of his brother, who had just died. We talked about his brother, and we talked about the meaning of death for anyone who believes in Christ.

When I was ready to leave, the maid brought my topcoat from the closet. After she helped me on with my coat, she extended her hand and shook hands with me. She was a Lutheran Hour listener too.

Shortly thereafter, I was invited to a reception in honor of Mr. Penney's 95th birthday at their home in Greens Farms, Connecticut. Unfortunately, I was unable to attend because I had a previous commitment to speak at a laymen's retreat at Camp Arcadia. In my letter of regret, I explained this to Mr. Penney and added, "I know how important you regard this work of helping laymen to fulfill their mission for Christ in this world."

When Mr. Penney died the following year, I wrote a letter of sympathy to Mrs. Penney, which she gratefully acknowledged. In her letter, she wrote to me, "I will be deeply comforted as I face the days ahead by your beautiful inspirational message, believing in Him is joy, trusting in Him is courage, and hoping in Him is life."

Mr. and Mrs. J. C. Penney were a warm and loving Christian couple. They were among the many people touched by the Gospel through "The Lutheran Hour" over the years.

At the beginning of this chapter, I said that I would characterize 1955, the year I was called to be Lutheran Hour speaker, as a time of great expectations. As I look back on the years since then, I would have to say that I was not disappointed. I saw the opportunity that the media, radio especially, continued to offer and that the Lord could use these things to do great things—and He did. What a thrill to have been a part of His great works!

12

LUTHERAN HOUR RALLIES AND SPECIALS

L UTHERAN HOUR RALLIES AND, TO SOME DEGREE, THE SPECIAL broadcasts were the primary reason the members of Synod's Public Relations Board were apprehensive about my becoming permanent Lutheran Hour speaker. The fact is, these events require a lot of time and energy for preparation as well as presentation. Some other organization might have tried to cut corners, but that was not our way. For us, the Gospel was at stake, and that meant putting together the best and freshest programs we could develop.

LUTHERAN HOUR RALLIES

Lutheran Hour rallies were usually held on a Sunday afternoon in a large auditorium, a gymnasium, or sometimes outside in a stadium. Special music was provided by a mass choir made up of choirs from Lutheran churches in the area. Many times there would also be a children's choir. Local Lutheran clergy would participate, and generally I would be the speaker. The rally often began with a "Parade of Nations," in which local people carried in procession flags representing all the nations of the world where Lutheran Hour programs were heard.

I enjoyed these events, but I must say that the rally schedule was a very busy one. One year there were 26 Lutheran Hour rallies, one every two weeks. I did not speak at all of them, but I spoke at as many of them as I could fit into my schedule. I remember that once I spoke at three rallies in one month.

My first rally as Lutheran Hour speaker was on the afternoon of my first broadcast from Epiphany Church in Detroit. It was held at Veterans Memorial Stadium on the Detroit riverfront. I do not remember a lot about that rally, but I am sure it was well attended, because Lutheran Hour rallies always drew large crowds in Detroit.

One of the next rallies for which I spoke was in the Hollywood Bowl. Marcia was with me, and we had flown to Los Angeles from St. Louis on Saturday afternoon with a stop in Kansas City. When we went to pick up our baggage at the Los Angeles airport, Marcia's suitcase had not arrived.

Some of the Amling family members who had retired to Los Angeles (these were the people who started a large flower business in Chicago) picked us up at the airport. When we told them what had happened, Mrs. Frank Schoenheider took Marcia to a local department store to buy a dress so that she would have something to wear at the rally. As it turned out, Marcia's suitcase arrived at our hotel at about midnight that night. She did not wear the dress she had bought, and before we went back to St. Louis, she took it back to the store. People connections are the kinds of things a person remembers that make certain events stand out among the others.

I also remember rallies held in Washington, D.C. One was at the National Cathedral. It was packed to the doors, with people standing around the huge pillars. Another rally was held at the Sheraton Hotel. The main reason I remember that rally is the people. In attendance was Senator Vance Hartke from Indiana. Before the rally, Senator Hartke, whom I had known when he was mayor of Evansville, came backstage and said, "Chief Justice Warren, his wife, and daughter are sitting out there in the fifth row."

Chief Justice Earl Warren and his wife, Virginia, were regular listeners to "The Lutheran Hour," and Virginia sent us regular contributions. Their daughter, whose name also was Virginia, married John Daley, who was the moderator on the television game show "What's My Line?"

When Chief Justice Warren died, I was invited to speak at his funeral. I was on my way to Europe at the time. When I called Marcia from New York, she told me that a telegram had arrived with that invitation. I had to tell her to send my regrets, saying that I would get in touch with his wife later on—which, of course, I did.

When Senator Hartke's son was married, I was asked to come to Washington, D.C., to perform the marriage. I had to get special permission from the state to officiate at a wedding out in Fairfax County, Virginia. One of Senator Hartke's aides went out there with me and saw to it that all the proper papers were signed at the historic courthouse of that county.

Senator Hartke's wife had been Roman Catholic. When he was mayor of Evansville, she regularly went to the Lutheran church with him. One Sunday the congregation was having confirmation, and the Hartkes were sitting in the front pew where they always sat. Just before the service began, his wife excused herself and said she had to see someone about something. Hartke wondered what that was all about, because she was not a member of the church and did not belong to the Ladies Aid or anything. When the class marched in, his wife walked in with them. She had secretly taken confirmation instructions and was being confirmed.

"When I saw her coming in with the class, I broke down and cried," Hartke said.

I felt very much at home with government officials of both parties in Washington, and they felt at home with me too, because they knew where we stood. We stood for Jesus Christ, and we said, "We'll do everything we can to identify our church with Jesus Christ."

Another rally I especially remember was one in the War Memorial Coliseum in Fort Wayne, Indiana. That rally was in conjunction with an "Each One Reach One" evangelism campaign conducted under the auspices of Synod's evangelism department, of which my good friend and classmate Rev. Oswald Waech was executive secretary.

Sometime before this rally, the Roman Catholic archbishop of Fort Wayne had said that he did not believe that Lutherans could fill the Coliseum. That was all those Fort Wayne Lutherans needed! When it came time for the rally, so many people came that traffic was backed up for five miles. I could not even get to the Coliseum. Someone drove me down the left side of the road. We sped past the traffic with the policemen shaking their heads as we went by!

The place was so crowded that many people could not get in. Ernie Gallmeyer, who now was on Synod's Board of Directors, told me afterwards that his daughter and five children had been there and had not been able to get in. "Was I glad to see that!" he said.

Rallies were also held in small towns. You really did not know what to expect. I would go out to some place in Podunk and would wonder how many people would be there. Usually it was a real surprise when I saw how many people showed up.

I remember one time when Dean Hofstad, a retired Air Force chaplain, flew me in his private plane from Sioux Falls, South Dakota, to Morris, Minnesota, where we were having a rally in the field house of the University of Minnesota at Morris.

I said to my pilot, as we flew over this North Minnesota town, "You mean we're having a rally there?" I did not think we would have much of an attendance.

When it came time for the rally, there were 700 people in the adult choir and several hundred children in the children's choir. The place was so jammed that people were standing in the aisles. My pilot, also a Lutheran (though not from our Synod), was very impressed. So was I.

The last time I spoke at a rally in Fort Wayne, the committee had a dinner the night before the rally. By this time, Walter A. Maier's widow, Hulda Maier, was living at the Lutheran home in Fort Wayne. Her son, Walter, Jr., is a professor at the seminary there. He was in St. Louis attending a meeting at the time of the rally.

I asked the committee whether anyone had made arrangements for Hulda Maier to come to the rally. No one had thought of that. Right there on the spot, I pointed to one fellow and said, "It's your responsibility to get a van that you can put a wheelchair in and get her there."

Mrs. Maier came to the rally and sat up in front in her wheelchair, smiling and waving to everybody. I introduced her to the audience. She could not stand up, but they gave her a standing ovation. It was like one last big thank you for all the things she and her husband had done.

Lutheran Hour rallies did not begin when I became "The Lutheran Hour" speaker. Begun by Dr. Walter A. Maier, they were very popular in the 1930s and 1940s, when he was the featured speaker. The summer after I graduated from high school, when we were still living in Chicago, I went with my parents to a synodically sponsored Lutheran rally in 1930 at Soldiers Field. There were 25,000 people at that rally, probably in commemoration of the 400th Anniversary of the Augsburg Confession. Dr. Maier was the speaker.

When Maier started having rallies, whatever money was collected at the rally was first used to promote the rally and to pay for whatever other expenses had been incurred locally. "The

Lutheran Hour" received the remainder. When I became speaker, the LLL decided to change the system. Money to pay for promotion and local expenses had to be collected from the local area before the rally was held, and all money collected at the rally would go to support "The Lutheran Hour." When money that had been collected prior to the rally was left over after paying expenses, that was also given to support "The Lutheran Hour."

The only time my travel expenses were paid by the LLL other than to LLL conventions was when I spoke at Lutheran Hour rallies. They paid my expenses, but if the local people wanted Marcia to come along, they would have to pay her expenses. That was the understanding we worked with from the very beginning.

The average offering at a Lutheran Hour rally would be between $4,000 and $15,000. The largest offering we ever had, I believe, was at one of the last rallies at which I spoke, held in Cobo Hall in Detroit. The collection there, after expenses, was $29,000.

Lutheran Hour rallies were, I believe, second in importance only to the broadcast itself. The rallies had three purposes: first, to proclaim the Gospel; second, to provide support for "The Lutheran Hour"; third, to increase our listenership. Yes, the income was important—and some years meant the difference between "The Lutheran Hour" ending the year in the red or the black. But after proclaiming the Redeemer, I felt it was more important to increase our listenership. I would often meet people who would tell me that the first time they had heard me speak was not on the radio but at a Lutheran Hour rally. After that, they had become regular listeners to "The Lutheran Hour."

It helped "The Lutheran Hour" for people to see that the man behind the microphone was not just a disembodied voice, but was a real live human being. I was a little heavier in those days, and I'd say to the audience, "I hope you're not disappointed!" They would laugh at that. People always laugh at a fat man!

The larger-city rallies usually were well attended. Yet sometimes I would look out and see two or three hundred empty seats. After the rally I would think, "You know, with just a little more effort, they probably could have filled this place." Then I would remember that this had all been done by volunteers. Realizing that, I did not mind those empty seats so much. This was a remarkable example of the recruitment of volunteers to do things for "The Lutheran Hour." They did it willingly, because they were interested in getting the Gospel out to people. I always thanked those folks publicly.

Committees of local people planned the rallies, but someone on the LLL staff in St. Louis usually assisted. Over the years those staff people did a remarkable job. We owe a debt of gratitude to all of them: Rudy Bertermann, Charles Burmeister, Tommy Thompson, Bill Kniffel, Michael Trinklein, and all the rest. Bill Kniffel may have been one of the best organizers we ever had, even though his talents for organization were not always fully appreciated.

A Special Lutheran Hour Friend: Brownell McGrew

One of the people I met as the result of a Lutheran Hour rally was my friend Brownell McGrew. I went to breakfast at the hotel where I was staying in Albuquerque before going to the early service on the morning of a rally there. I had bought a Sunday paper and was reading it at my table. A woman approached me and said, "I'm Ann McGrew. Would you mind coming over to our table and having breakfast with us?"

I picked up my paper and went over to their table. She said, "This is my husband, Brownell."

"Oh," I said. "What do you do?"

He looked at me with a kind of a twinkle in his eye and said, "I paint."

I saw that twinkle, and I asked, "What do you paint?"

He said, "Mostly Indians."

That is how I got to know them. I invited him and his wife to the dinner with the rally committee that night. It was not until later that I found out that he was one of America's top painters of Indian life and of Southwestern scenes.

The McGrews had driven five hours from their place in New Mexico to attend the rally. He had a chapel at his place where he used Lutheran Hour tapes to have services with the Indians. He was well-known there for his good relations with the Indians.

The McGrews were lifelong Lutherans. Both had been very active in the Walther League. He had even been the president of the California District of the Walther League. They belonged to the Lutheran church in Albuquerque, but they came only about once every five Sundays. Because they lived so far away, few people really knew them. Brownell was a very private person. Many more people came to know his paintings than those who came to know him personally. Both of them were great people, and it was wonderful to know them personally.

Brownell came to St. Louis once, and I took him out to the airport to catch his plane to go home. I said to him, "You know, if it hadn't been for Ann's inviting me to have breakfast with you that morning, I wouldn't even know you."

"Well," he said, with that twinkle in his eye, "that's the last time she introduces me to someone!"

In their later years, Brownie and Ann lived out in the wilds of Arizona close to the Mexican border. Marcia and I tried to go out and spend a few days with them every once in a while. He raised quarter horses and fed them every morning and evening. When I was there, I too had to go out to help feed the horses!

In May of 1994, I received a call from Ann McGrew that her husband, who had been seriously ill for several years, was dying of cancer. On Memorial Day weekend, I was able to fly out to see him. We had a regular service around his bedside in which he participated fully. His wife and three daughters were there, along with other members of the family. A short time later, Brownie departed this life in the living faith of Jesus Christ.

LUTHERAN HOUR SPECIALS

In 1960, someone at LLL headquarters in St. Louis—probably Elmer Knoernschild—decided that we ought to broadcast a special Lutheran Hour program for Christmas. They came up with the idea of doing a program with Marian Anderson, who was at the climax of her great singing career at the time.

No one really knew how to get in touch with Marian Anderson; however, someone had told me that her best friend was a certain Mrs. Brown, the wife of an architect. One day I telephoned her, told her my name, and said, "You don't know me, but I'd like to get in touch with Marian Anderson."

"I do too know you," she said. "We had dinner at Bernie Guenther's house recently!"

Bernie Guenther and his wife, Elsie, were some of the leading members of St. Matthew Lutheran Church in Manhattan. He was the architect who later built the housing at Ebbetts Field and the apartments above the George Washington Bridge from Manhattan to New Jersey.

Then I remembered that there had been an architect by the name of Brown at that dinner at the Guenthers. The lady I was talking with on the phone was his wife.

"Sure," she said. "We'll get in touch with Marianna" (that's what Marian Anderson's mother called her).

Through Mrs. Brown I was able to reach Marian Anderson by telephone. She said she would be very glad to do the program. But she told me that I would have to get in touch with her agent, Sol Hurok, the great impresario, a very expensive man. When I got in touch with him, he said, "She's giving her services; I'll give mine."

We made arrangements to do the taping at Reeves Studio, my regular recording facility. When the appointed time came for the session to start, I started to worry; Miss Anderson had not arrived. I was there, 15 people were in the control room, and quite a few others were milling around, waiting to see Marian Anderson. Anxious, I went down to the street, as if standing there would help more than waiting in the studio. As it turned out, she was only about 15 or 20 minutes late. She got out of the cab, I welcomed her, and we went up to record. She was such a pleasant and wonderfully ordinary person that her late arrival bothered no one. Everyone there was very pleased to meet her.

The Christmas special combined her singing with a personal interview with her, which we did that day at the studio. Most of the songs were taken from her recordings. I do not remember much from the interview, but I remember that she told me about herself. She said she had sung in the choir at her church, then had taken voice lessons. Her opening recital was at Carnegie Hall, and it was a disaster.

She went back home and told her mother, "I'm not going to do a thing with my singing career any more. I'm going to drop the whole thing."

Her mother said to her, "Marianna, you're not going to make a decision like that until we pray about it."

During that year, Marian Anderson continued voice lessons. Whenever she would practice her singing, her mother would go into her room and close the door.

"I knew what she was doing," Marian Anderson said. "She was praying about it."

A year later she had another recital at Carnegie Hall, and it was a triumph. Such a voice! She could sing from the highest register of the soprano to the deepest tones of the contralto and could shift gears as she went down. What she did with a song like Johann Sebastian Bach's "Komm Süsser Tod" ("Come Sweet Death") nobody else could ever do. When she sang "He's Got the Whole World in His Hands" on our Christmas special, it brought tears to your eyes.

When it was advertised that Marian Anderson was going to be the guest on our special Christmas program, all of Radio India took the program. Although Marian Anderson was highly regarded in India, that was a great surprise. Radio India was a government network, and they had not had any Christian programming on the air until that time!

The Czechoslovakian Government Network in the Communist world also took the program. I remember a member of our staff asking me whether I thought we ought to ask the State Department before allowing the Czechoslovakians to broadcast our program.

"What do you mean, ask the State Department?" I said. "We didn't produce the program in cooperation with the State Department, and we're not going to distribute it in cooperation with the State Department. The State Department has nothing to say about it. We have freedom of religion in this country, and that means that we can do anything that we think is the right thing to do. I think the right thing to do is to give the program to the Czechoslovakian Government Network so that they can broadcast it." That is what we did.

We did many, many Lutheran Hour Christmas specials after that one. But I do not think any of them were ever quite as good as that first one with Marian Anderson. In fact, it was so successful that we repeated it the next year.

After the program had aired, I wanted to give Marian Anderson something. I got the idea of giving her a Polaroid camera, which was just coming out at the time. The cameras were great big things, especially the more expensive models. They cost something like $60, which was a lot of money at that time.

I got in touch with the people at "The Lutheran Hour" office in St. Louis. They said, "Oh, yes. Do that. Put a little plaque on it that says it's from 'The Lutheran Hour.' "

I bought the camera, and called up Mrs. Brown. I said, "I don't know whether I should put on the plaque 'Marian Anderson' or 'Mrs.' and then the name of her husband. By the way, what is her husband's name?"

"Well, I do declare," Mrs. Brown said, "I don't remember. We call him 'King.' " Later I found out his name was Fisher. I decided to put "Marian Anderson" on the plaque.

Marian Anderson lived in Connecticut, but she had an apartment in Manhattan, where she lived when she was in New York. She had a big grand piano in there, which she used when she rehearsed. I went to her apartment to present her with the camera. My parents happened to be visiting us at the time, and I took my father along. It was something he never forgot, that he was able to talk and shake hands with Marian Anderson.

Several years later, Marian Anderson made one final tour of the country. She sang in St. Louis at Kiel Auditorium. I think I bought about 40 tickets to that concert (and I didn't charge them to the LLL either!). I felt that was something I could do to repay her for what she had done for us.

After the concert, people filed by to say good-bye to her. Great lady that she was, she stood there and shook hands graciously and courteously with everybody. Then Marcia and I came by. She had never met Marcia. I introduced them, and that's when she did something special. She reached out and embraced me. I will never forget that warm embrace from the great Marian Anderson!

The next Lutheran Hour special we did was in 1962. We called that program "In Excelsis Deo." Congressman Walter Moeller arranged for us to have as our guest on that program astronaut John Glenn. He had just recently returned from his historic space-flight, the first to orbit the earth.

I asked him in the interview, "Did you pray before you went?"

"Oh," he said, "I don't believe that God comes out of the woodwork. I did my praying. But I didn't pray especially for this flight before I went up there." He had his mind fixed on what he had to do. That was a crucial time. We were way behind the Russians, and we needed to get up there.

John Glenn told me that if it had not been for Walter Burke, who was president of Aerospace for McDonnell (and a member of Concordia Lutheran Church in the St. Louis area), we would not have gotten up into space. Glenn said that "Mac" McDonnell (founder of what later became McDonnell-Douglas) was a great promoter. He promoted our aerospace program. But if it had not been for Walter Burke, who was a great aerospace engineer, John Glenn said, we would not have made it.

After we moved to St. Louis, Walter Burke and I became great friends. He would often have dinners at his home with the executives of McDonnell so that they would become acquainted with one another. He would invite me to speak at some of those dinners. It was a wonderful chance to share the Gospel with McDonnell executives.

I also performed the wedding of Walter Burke's daughter, Patty. She married Charles Schlimpert, who became principal of our Lutheran High School in Orange County, California, and is now president of Concordia College in Portland, Oregon.

Patty was 18, and Walter was against the marriage; Patty was too young, he thought. I saw her on the Sunday before the wedding, and she said, "Don't forget the rehearsal on Thursday." Then she asked me, "Are you going to have the part in the ceremony where it says, 'Who giveth this woman to be married to this man?' "

When I said yes, Patty replied, "I don't think Daddy's going to answer that question."

"Just leave that to me," I told her.

When that part came in the ceremony, and I asked, "Who giveth this woman to be married to this man?" Walter Burke stood up bravely and said, "Her mother and I do."

When the first child, a boy, was born to Patty and Charles, Walter was completely reconciled to their marriage. Grandchildren will do that!

The whole power structure of St. Louis was at that wedding. They had a reception at Sunset Hills Country Club for about 500 people. In those days, Pat and Walter would never serve anything stronger than champagne, and very little of that. I was standing there with my clericals on, and the great Mr. Mac McDonnell and his wife came by. "Where do we get a Scotch?" he asked me. I guess he didn't know the Burkes very well after all.

Sad to say, Walter Burke was killed in an airplane crash. He owned his own jet plane, and was flying from Los Angeles to Portland. His wife and daughter were supposed to go with him, but they took a commercial flight because there were two people who wanted to buy his plane and they flew with him. A commercial pilot was flying Walter's plane. It went down somewhere, and all those on the plane died in the crash.

I've wandered a bit from the "The Lutheran Hour" specials and John Glenn, but so often one memory triggers another! I still have the two boomerangs sent in response to the program with John Glenn by a listener in Australia, one for me and one for John Glenn. Some fine day I am going to deliver personally that boomerang to the United States Senator from Ohio!

A CONCLUDING THOUGHT

I have never tired of preaching the Gospel, for it is the power of God both for a believer's eternal life as well as for the abundant life in Christ on earth. I have seen the proof in my own life as well in the lives of many of the people who have been touched by God through "The Lutheran Hour." I will admit, though, that preaching to a microphone in a studio is more difficult and less enjoyable than preaching and speaking to people in congregations and at conventions and rallies. People who know me as well as those who have seen me at these gatherings can attest plainly that it is important to be a "people person." You see in their eyes the work that the Lord is doing in their lives. God's work through Christ in the lives of people has been the purpose for everything we did at the Lutheran Laymen's League as well as over "The Lutheran Hour."

13

To St. Louis, 1963

W HEN I FIRST ACCEPTED THE OFFER TO BE PERMANENT LUTHERAN
Hour speaker in 1955, the sponsoring Lutheran Laymen's League did not have its own recording studio. As
a matter of fact, ever since the League's founding in 1917, the
organization rented space for its headquarters at Concordia Publishing House at 3558 South Jefferson Avenue. Those two factors
were part of the reason that the League was willing to allow me to
continue to live in New York and to serve as Synod's public relations director.

The location of the first LLL offices in Concordia Publishing
House was natural, because that immediate area had been the center of the Missouri Synod since the time of its first president, C. F.
W. Walther. One of his churches, Holy Cross, was only a block
away, and between the two stood Concordia Seminary, which
Walther had started and of which he was president. Lutheran Hospital was also on one of the corners. The treasurer of Synod and its
business office were in CPH. Even the cable address was CON-
PUBHO. And as other full-time offices of the Synod were begun,
they too were housed at CPH. It made no difference whether or
not the Synod presidents were full- or part-time, or whether they
lived in St. Louis or elsewhere; CPH remained the business address
of the Synod for most of the Synod's first century.

Then came the success of American Christianity following WWII, and the space at Concordia Publishing House seemed limited. In 1951, the LCMS dedicated the new Lutheran Building at 210 North Broadway in St. Louis, and 85 full-time workers moved in. In 1959, the LLL moved into the new building it had built at 2185 Hampton Avenue, where it is still located today. I was scheduled to come from New York to speak at the building dedication, but I had such an awful viral cold at the time that I was unable to come.

The LLL had built a recording studio in the new building. Because of this and for other reasons, the officers constantly were urging me to move from New York to St. Louis and to give my full attention to being Lutheran Hour speaker. I did so in 1963, resigning my position as Public Relations Director for The Lutheran Church—Missouri Synod and my call as preaching pastor at St. Matthew, New York, and we moved to St. Louis. I could do so, confident that the Public Relations Department was in the well-trained hands of Norm Temme.

Actually, 1963, the year I would turn 50, was a good year to make the transition to full-time Lutheran Hour speaker. The Lutheran Church—Missouri Synod was changing, possibly maturing. President Behnken, the president I had served for 15 years, urged the delegates at the 1962 Synod convention to choose someone else as president so that he could retire. The structure also was changing. The Public Relations Department would become the Division of Communications and Public Relations, and the director would become more of an administrator rather than a hands-on public relations person. Another great change at the convention—and a definite plus—was that Synod finally gave official recognition and status within the denomination to both the Lutheran Laymen's League and the Lutheran Women's Missionary League.

After 15 years, it was time to turn over control. Norm Temme had been with me for five years; now he would have a chance to revamp the office according to his style. Of course, he would have to be nominated officially and then elected—which he was—but the outcome was predictable.

A discouraging change taking place within Lutheranism at large was the withdrawal of the Norwegian Evangelical Lutheran Synod and the Wisconsin Evangelical Lutheran Synod from the Synodical Conference. Throughout my first 25-plus years in the ministry, I enjoyed the fellowship that the Conference provided, including the coverage of Conference conventions for press and media by our Public Relations Department. With the breakup of the Conference, our previous joint proclamation of the Gospel was silenced.

Elsewhere on the religious scene—and certainly more news-worthy than the breakup of the Synodical Conference—was the death of Pope John XXIII, the man who assembled the Second Vatican Council. He termed non-Catholic Christians "separated brethren" and in his will wrote that he expected to be in heaven "not on my merits but through the mercy of my Lord." This was the same year that the United States Supreme Court banned Bible reading and the Lord's Prayer from being part of a public school opening. Clearly, the religious landscape was changing.

Perhaps the most significant (yet at that point least understood) challenge to the whole Christian church in North America was the civil rights movement that exploded over the six months from April to September of 1963. That was the year of the Birmingham demonstrations, the picture of Alabama governor George Wallace bodily blocking the door to the state university against a black enrollee, the graduation of James Meredith from the University of Mississippi, the murder of Medgar Evers, the march on Washington, D.C., Dr. Martin Luther King, Jr.'s "I have a dream" speech, and the death of four small Sunday school girls when a bomb was thrown into their Baptist church in Birmingham. (For what it's worth, 1963 also saw the introduction of ZIP codes.)

Yes, the world and the church was changing in 1963. I was convinced that the time had come to devote my time and energy full-time to the direct and clear proclamation of Christ the Lord.

For a number of personal reasons too, it seemed like the right time to make the move. By this time our oldest son, Peter, was at Concordia Senior College in Fort Wayne, Paul had just been graduated from the Bronx High School of Science (which Peter too had attended), John was ready to begin high school, and Kate was going into third grade.

We moved to St. Louis in September of 1963. This time we bought our own house in a suburb west of St. Louis, where Marcia, John, and I still live today.

THE NEW STUDIO

The first time I went to record at the studio in the LLL building, I was in for quite a surprise. The studio was a small room overlooking the chapel. There was a large pane of glass through which you could look down on the chapel below. Behind the studio was the control room, even smaller than the studio, with another large pane of glass from which you could look from the control room into the studio. The two rooms together were not as big as the living and dining rooms in an average size house. What a change from Reeves Studio in New York! Still, the LLL building studio was functional, and it was there that I recorded my Lutheran Hour sermons from 1963 until the present studio was built in 1986 as an addition to the current building.

The architect who built the building apparently did not know a whole lot about building a studio. In order to help soundproof the studio, the LLL later had to have additional flooring built above the original floor. That meant that the top step into the studio was higher than any other step in the building. Almost every time I would go up there to record my sermon, I would trip over that step.

Even with the extra flooring, the studio was far from sound-proof. Any time an airplane would fly over or a truck would go by on Hampton Avenue, we would have to stop recording until the noise stopped. Many times when we thought the noise had stopped and we would start to record again, another airplane would fly over or another truck would rumble by, and we would have to stop again.

Studio and Office Personnel

In spite of all of that, thanks to Elmer Knoernschild (LLL Director of Programming) and the other technical people who helped produce "The Lutheran Hour," we were able to produce programs of the highest quality all through the years. The two technical people who were there when I came and who continued to produce "The Lutheran Hour" for many years were Corinne Duever (tape editor) and Earl Birkicht (sound engineer). How they came to their positions is a rather interesting story.

Earl had worked at Premier Studios in St. Louis and had edited "The Lutheran Hour" programs there. He was not a trained sound engineer, but he was intelligent and knew a great deal about sound recording. Apparently the best sound people Elmer Knoernschild knew in St. Louis were the people at Premier. He offered Earl the sound engineer job at the LLL studio. Earl accepted that position and did a fine job for 18 years. He had a degree in music, which meant that he was able to be of considerable help in recording and even choosing the music for "The Lutheran Hour."

Corinne Duever's husband had been a classmate of Elmer Knoernschild at Concordia Seminary, St. Louis. Corinne, a piano teacher, had played a 15-minute piano music program daily over radio station KFUO when Knoernschild had been an announcer there. Elmer knew something about her musical understanding.

When Corinne's husband, a Lutheran pastor, died suddenly of a heart attack in 1961, leaving her as the sole support for three children, including two in college, Knoernschild offered her the job of tape editor for the LLL. As she tells it, her job expanded from there. Not only did she edit the tapes, but she would sit in the control room when I would record my sermons and listen carefully to be sure that everything sounded just right. She also timed the programs, sometimes cutting them in length when they were too long.

Corinne had a knack for hearing when things were wrong. She would rarely interrupt me during a recording session, but sometimes afterwards she would ask whether I had really meant to say what I had said or tell me where I might have misspoken. If there was a mistake we would go back and record that section again.

There was one time, though, when she did not question what I had said and she really should have. I was speaking about the parable of the fig tree, and she thought she heard me say "frig tree." She asked Earl if he had heard it, and he said no, I had said "fig," so she let it go. When she was editing the tape, there it was. I had said "frig tree." By that time I was out of town somewhere and there was no way to do it over. She worked editing that tape until she managed to get the "r" sound out of "frig." She was a remarkably talented woman!

Corinne also chose the music for the programs after Carl Schalk, the former music director for the LLL, left to become a professor at Concordia, River Forest, Illinois. She also did the technical production work for two other programs produced by the LLL: "The Family Worship Hour" and "Day by Day with Jesus." She worked with us for 24 years—from 1961 until her retirement in 1985.

Others followed Earl and Corinne who were also very gifted people. Corinne was succeeded by Mary Brighton, wife of seminary professor Louis Brighton. After Earl left, a young man named

Don Blumenkamp became our sound engineer. Don was killed in a tragic accident while working on an electric line for Union Electric Company after he left us. Then came Bruce Brown, who later became an engineer for CBS-TV. Marilyn Buckmaster is now recording engineer. Mark Eischer, a former music teacher and band director at Lutheran High School South in St. Louis, serves as senior producer of "The Lutheran Hour" at the present time. This task formerly was performed by Pastor Michael Trinklein. All of these people and many others—including, at one time or another, Michael Charles, Bert McGee, Ken Roberts, and Dick Grady—deserve the credit for making "The Lutheran Hour" the fine program that it was and is today.

Then there were my "girls"—those secretaries who served me so well over the years. Someone told me once I should not call them that. But to me it was not in any way a term to put them down. They were my "girls" because I liked them and appreciated all they did for me.

My first secretary after moving to St. Louis was Gaylene LaBore. She had been serving as the secretary for Edgar Fritz, the LLL's Club Services director, and liked working with him. Understandably, she was a little hesitant at first when she was asked to work with me. But I guess we must have done all right together, because she worked for me until she left to raise her children. Then after they were grown, she came back to work for me, first part-time, then full-time, which continued after my retirement as Lutheran Hour speaker. She still serves as my executive assistant. Altogether Gaylene has been with me now over 20 years.

Others who worked with me in my office were Eunice McCormick, who died of cancer while she was my secretary; Susan Hasting, who became office manager; and Lori Parker. Both Susan and Lori worked with me until I retired as Lutheran Hour speaker.

MARCIA

Those were the people who worked most closely with me in the office. All of them were of great help to me. And then there's Marcia. What would I have done without Marcia?

As a human, I owe many debts to many people, but I owe the greatest debt to my wife. If it had not been for her, I cannot imagine what life would have been like over these years. There she was all these years, always ready to take the backseat, never complaining, always doing what needed to be done. She is the one who always packs my suitcase when I travel, making sure I have what I need. Marcia told me that John once said that if she would not do my packing for me, maybe I would stay home more!

Once Marcia was taking Dr. O. P. Kretzmann's wife, Betty, to the airport, and Betty was laughing with Marcia about her always packing for me.

"I wonder if when I get to heaven, I'm going to have to keep on packing," Marcia said to Betty.

"No," Betty said, "I'm going to get there first, and I'll make all the arrangements!" She has always been good at arranging things, something we have found out over the years since we are related to the Brohms, Betty's family.

Marcia was the one who always addressed the Christmas cards, because her husband was not around to do it. She even assembled the Christmas bicycles and toys, taking care of whatever repair work needed to be done around the house. She's the one who did the most to raise the children in our family too, because I usually was busy and traveling a great deal of the time while they were growing up.

I remember the first time I went away for a long period of time—like three months! I think it was when we made the Martin Luther film. The whole family came out to JFK Airport to meet me when I came home. After that, Marcia tells me, it was pretty much the children asking, "Is Daddy home?" and her answering, "No, he's not." Then whoever had asked would say, "Okay." After a while, they did not even ask where I was.

Our Move to St. Louis

That's pretty much the way it has been in the Hoffmann household over the years. And that's the way it was in 1963. Just before we moved to St. Louis, I was off speaking at Air Force retreats in Japan, Hawaii, and the Philippines. That meant that Marcia did all the packing, except for what the movers packed when they came.

The movers were the seven Santini brothers. We had two arm chairs with open-mouthed lions on the arms. When the movers picked those up, they found a piece of a frankfurter in one of the lion's mouths. Apparently one of the children had been feeding the lions!

I was not around when the unpacking was done either. Marcia did all of that too. A few days after we arrived in St. Louis, I had to go to Snyder, Nebraska. I left for my birthplace while the movers were taking our ancient, seven-foot Steinway grand piano out of the moving van.

By the way, the most significant thing about those retreats I spoke at was probably the severe weather we experienced during that time. We were in the Philippines when Typhoon Carmen hit there. In Hawaii, there was a volcanic eruption in one of the craters on the slopes of Mauna Loa, about 12 miles from the place where we were meeting. While both of these caused us some discomfort and concern, they did not result in any serious problems. In fact, we spent hours after my evening lecture watching the eruption on the edge of Mauna Loa's crater!

I have spent a lot of time with the military over the years. I will tell you more about that later. Right now, let's stick with 1963.

Marcia's Health

Sometime later that year, I was out in California. The day I was to return, Marcia remembered that she had forgotten to lock the garage. When she went out to lock it, her nose began to bleed. It was still bleeding when I came home with a bag of California oranges at eight o'clock that evening.

We had not been in St. Louis long enough to have a doctor, so I took her to the emergency room at St. Joseph's Hospital in Kirkwood. An ear, nose, and throat specialist just happened to be on duty doing some surgery. He said she should have her blood pressure checked, because it was very high.

Later, while on a trip together, Marcia had a massive heart attack. A few years later, she had another one while we were in church at Concordia, Kirkwood. I took her home from church, and we tried to call our doctor, Dr. Mortensen, but he was not available. But old Dr. Hanser was at the clinic out of which Dr. Mortensen worked. He told me, "You'd better get her into the hospital right away!"

When I told Marcia that, she said, "Can't I wait until tomorrow morning?"

"No," Dr. Hanser said, "she needs to come in now!"

Before she would let me take her to the hospital, however, she did a load of washing! When I got her to the hospital, they put her in bed and wouldn't let her out of bed at all for 10 days!

That second attack happened the first time Marcia was supposed to go with me to Australia. Of course, she could not go that year, but the next year she went.

Marcia feels one of the reasons she has not had more problems with her heart is that she does not worry about having another attack. She has told many people who have had heart problems not to worry about having another attack. She feels that is an important part of recovery.

Marcia also does not worry about dying. She has told me that if she should die when we are on a trip somewhere, I should just "bury her where she falls."

"Don't bother taking me home," she said. "That's a job! I've known friends who've done that, and it's a difficult thing to do!"

Marcia's like that. Her big concern would be the problems she might cause for other people!

"Mrs. Hoffmann" in Australia

The Australia Lutheran Hour had offered to pay her way to come to Australia. But that was the year they started The Indonesia Lutheran Hour, and they needed all their money for that. The result was that we ended up paying her way anyhow.

Actually I went ahead of her, and she joined me in Australia. She was to meet me in Adelaide, and she had to change planes in Sydney. When she went to the ticket counter to ask about her flight, the man asked her name. She told him, "Mrs. Hoffmann," and he started to laugh.

"What's so funny about my name?" she asked him.

"Oh, it's all over the newspapers here," he told her. "They're looking for a spy by the name of Mrs. Hoffmann!"

Marcia is a remarkable woman. Always a gracious hostess at home, she feels at ease at Lutheran Hour functions and LLL conventions conducting conversations with laypeople as if she has known them all her life. After 55 years of marriage, I have learned to hunt for her at the conclusion of a meeting, because she will be talking to someone and not yet ready to leave.

Packer, mover, Swedish cook, seamstress, bookkeeper and record preserver, tax preparer, and general "Jill of all trades," Marcia impressed even the grandmothers of our children with her ability to "make things look good" with just a sprig of parsley judiciously placed.

She has been my constant companion wherever we could be together, both at home and abroad. She is still a great homemaker and also an avid traveler whenever the opportunity presents itself. And having heard all my old stories many times over, she still laughs with me!

When speaking of Marcia, what else can I say but "remarkable!"

THE ASSASSINATION
OF PRESIDENT JOHN F. KENNEDY

Another event that makes 1963 a memorable year is one that affected almost everyone who was alive at the time. On Friday, November 22, 1963, John F. Kennedy was assassinated. Earlier in the week I had been in New York to attend a meeting of the translation committee of the American Bible Society. Then I had three preaching engagements at the U.S. Military Academy in West Point on Sunday, November 24.

When Kennedy was assassinated, I asked the officials at West Point whether they would prefer to have someone take my place, but they said, "No, you go ahead and speak."

For some reason, Elmer Knoernschild also happened to be in New York City at the time. NBC asked me for comments on this tragedy. I went to their studio to record. They used my comments on both NBC radio and NBC-TV.

I also found out that the Mutual Radio Network was going to cancel all their regular radio programming during the coming weekend and were looking for help to provide special programming. I asked Elmer what we might be able to do. He called St. Louis and told Earl and Corinne to record all the appropriate music that we had in our library. They recorded that music very quickly, and Earl hand carried it on the train to New York. Elmer met him at the train and went straight to the studio. Mutual used music from our Lutheran Hour library for that whole weekend. Elmer stayed there to write introductions to the music, and was able to put the Gospel into the introductions to those selections we provided to mourn the death of President Kennedy. We also changed our Lutheran Hour program for that Sunday to respond to the tragedy that had occurred.

AND MY FATHER

Speaking of death, 1963 also was the year my father died. He had retired in 1957, and he and my mother were living in Saint Petersburg, Florida. That March he died after surgery for a bleeding ulcer.

As you can see, 1963 was an eventful year in many ways, but there were some even more eventful years to come.

14

THE SECOND VATICAN COUNCIL 1964–65

D R. BEHNKEN ALWAYS SAID THAT WE LUTHERANS SHOULD BE READY to discuss doctrine with anyone at anytime. I agreed with him, and I was honored that Dr. Harms asked me in 1964 to be the Missouri Synod representative to the Second Vatican Council. Before I tell you about my involvement, I need to share why our presence there was both important and exciting.

In spite of the differences between the Roman Catholic and the Lutheran churches, there was a time back in the early 1960s when spring breezes seemed to blow through the relationship between our churches. Clearly, that was due to Pope John XXIII and his call for the Second Vatican Council. Some of us prayed that maybe, just maybe, at least a partially unified witness to salvation in Jesus Christ could be made within a world that seemed to be yielding to atheistic communism and secular humanism.

In no way do I want to minimize the doctrinal disagreements between Roman Catholics and Lutherans or other Protestants. Almost everyone knows at least some of those differences. And I have already mentioned at least one difference in practice between the two bodies in the U.S. regarding state aid to parochial education—a difference that came to national attention twice while I was director of Synod's public relations office. Nor did anyone expect that Pope John's Council could or would change basic doctrine in the Roman Catholic Church. Yet ...

Pope John announced in 1959 that a council would be held "to bring the church up-to-date" and to open doors for eventual reunification of all Christendom. To that end, he solicited input from every corner of his church on what the specific topics should be—and from Protestants as well. The Pope also emphasized *collegiality,* the concept that bishops should have almost as much authoritative input into church decisions as the very powerful Roman Curia. (The Curia would be akin to a Protestant denomination's full-time, paid, professional headquarters staff.) And at the sessions, Protestants would be asked for their input into a topic before any tentative or final resolutions were decided.

The cardinal chosen to organize the preparatory work (Augustin Bea) was also named head of a new office: the Secretariat for Promoting Christian Unity. How refreshing for us to learn that Bea was stressing that the Council return to *Scripture* for the church's renewal rather than to tradition or to specific doctrines antithetical to the rest of Christianity.

Sessions for the Council were planned for the fall of each year, beginning in 1962. The initial assumption was that they would last at least five years, with tentative reports coming out during the first years and final decisions in the later years. However, one area was decided on that first session: reform in worship. Christians around the world were encouraged when the Roman Catholics decided to allow services to be held in the members' own language instead of Latin alone, to allow greater participation by lay married deacons in leading the worship, and more participation by the congregation through responses and hymns. These changes may not seem major to Protestants, but they certainly were significant at the time for Roman Catholics. Thirty-five years later, some Catholics are still fighting those modernizations.

When Pope John XXIII died in June of 1963, the world held its breath. Would his replacement be someone who favored and would continue the Council with its openness, or would his successor be chosen because he would put a stop to all this? The man chosen, who took the name Paul VI, turned out to stand somewhere in the middle.

Following the first two sessions of the Council, President Harms asked me to be the LCMS-appointed observer to the Council in response to Cardinal Bea's offer to Protestants to attend as "special guests" of the Secretariat for Promoting Christian Unity. Once again, the Lord brought together a lot of strands in my life to prepare me for attendance in Rome. Three items stand out in my mind as most significant:

- My proficiency in Latin, both because of my love of languages in general as well as having taught Latin at the University of Minnesota and Concordia-Bronxville. (Anyone who went to the Vatican Council had to be able to understand and speak Latin, for that was and is the universal language of the Roman Catholic Church and the language in which the Council was held.)
- The fact that I was already well-known as a spokesman for the LCMS, given my previous position with the Public Relations Department as well as my experience in representing Lutheranism to the media and to the United States government.
- The worldwide reputation as a spokesman for the LCMS as the result of nine years as "The Lutheran Hour" speaker.

There were those in various places in the LCMS who were not happy with our being represented there. In fact, "The Lutheran Hour" lost a $50,000 contribution because I accepted that appointment. Ironically, that turned out to be financially the best year "The Lutheran Hour" had ever had up to that time!

While I was attending the Vatican Council in Rome, I lived in a *pensione* with a lot of other Protestant and Orthodox observers. This was a floor in an apartment building that was operated as a hotel within that apartment building. I think it cost us $9.40 a day.

That included breakfast and dinner. You seldom ate dinner in Rome before 8 P.M.

WEDNESDAY EVENING MEETINGS

On Wednesday evenings between 4 and 8 P.M., meetings were held with the Protestant and Orthodox observers. Cardinal Jan Willebrands of the Netherlands presided at these meetings. He was chairman of the Vatican's Commission for the Promotion of Christian Unity. (Cardinal Bea, you recall, held the top position in the Secretariat.)

One of the meetings was on the Roman Catholic doctrine of matrimony. Father Davis, a Jesuit from England, spoke for about two hours on the topic. He talked about all the changes that were being made at the Vatican in regulations and canon (church) law. He talked about who can get married and who cannot, the problem of annulment in the Roman Catholic Church, along with the many regulations and exceptions of canon law in that church.

In the session were great theologians like Oscar Cullmann, Edmond Schlink, Warren Quanbeck, and many others. During the question period that followed the talk by Father Davis, no one responded with a question. Finally, I held up my hand and asked, "What about the orders of creation?" (My question related to the creation of man and woman by God Himself and the recognition of matrimony as meant for all.)

Father Davis got up and took 20 minutes to answer that question. Cardinal Willebrands looked at me, and I just shrugged my shoulders. Then Willebrands got up and in about three or four minutes explained the Roman Catholic doctrine on the orders of creation, which were recognized also by Martin Luther after he had been excommunicated by the Roman Catholic Church.

"That I can understand," I said. "But what does that have to do with canon law?" This time it was he who shrugged his shoulders.

The other Wednesday evening session I especially remember came after the Council sent the *schema*, the proposed statement, of *De Missionali Activitate* back to be rewritten. The chairman of the commission that produced that document on the mission activity of the church was Cardinal Agaganian, the Vatican librarian, a good friend of Pope Paul VI. They had worked out this document on the mission activity of the church, and it suffered biting criticism on the floor of the Council, even though Pope Paul VI had appeared personally to support it!

A week or so later, Cardinal Willebrands asked for our thoughts and suggestions about how it should be rewritten. I said, "I notice that you always begin with 'the church' this and 'the church' that. Why don't you begin with the Gospel? If I read it correctly, the Gospel creates the church, and the Gospel sustains the church in its mission."

When the new document finally came out the following year, it began with the Gospel.

REMEMBRANCES FROM THE COUNCIL PLENARY SESSIONS

I have some interesting remembrances from the Vatican Council. The Cardinals sat right across from us in the sessions, which were held in St. Peter's Cathedral. They would sit according to rank with the cardinal deacons toward the top and the cardinal bishops sitting on the lower tier. Cardinal Ottaviani was one of the cardinal bishops who sat down below. Every day started with a mass, and every day Ottaviani, who was blind, would stroll in about 20 minutes late and shake hands with everybody around him—right in the middle of the mass!

One day I was sitting in the sessions, right across the nave of St. Peter's Cathedral under the statue of St. Longinus, at the crossing, where you look up at the dome of St. Peter's. These were the best seats in the house! Presiding that day was Cardinal Doepfner of Munich, Bavaria. He was one of the four moderators who chaired the sessions of the Vatican Council. I noticed that he was looking right at our section, trying to catch somebody's eye. I looked around to see whom he was looking for. Then I realized that he was trying to catch my eye!

I had met him previously at one of our meetings and had told him about the Bavarian community in Frankenmuth, Michigan. He was fascinated by that.

"Come on over," I had told him, "and we shall give you a good time among the Lutherans!" Unfortunately, he was never able to take advantage of that invitation. He died young, not too long after the Council was over.

I heard an interesting story about Cardinal Doepfner told by the Lutheran bishop of Bavaria, the Rev. Dietzfelbinger. Bishop Dietzfelbinger said that in Bavaria Cardinal Doepfner never referred to the Lutheran Church as "church." He called it "the Evangelical community," implying a very close relationship between the Catholics and the Lutherans, but that the Lutherans were not quite equal to being "church." In fact, each year they had a civic celebration at the city hall in Munich at which both Bishop Dietzfelbinger and Cardinal Doepfner would speak. After the Vatican Council, Cardinal Doepfner delivered a speech there in which he talked about "this annual occasion where the Roman Catholic Church, and also the Evangelical ... uh ... (taking a deep breath with a following gulp) ... Church get together." (The Council had decided to recognize some Protestant denominations as legitimate churches for the first time in history.)

I especially remember the last day of the 1964 session. Father John Courtney Murray, the leading American Jesuit, and his team had written the great *schema* on religious liberty, which said, "We freely forgive those who have sinned against us, and we beg the pardon of those against whom we have sinned."

They also said, "It is wrong to ask a man to go against his conscience," saying in effect that no church ought use the government to peddle its wares or to persuade those who disagree. The Gospel has its own method of persuasion, and the church must not use government to force its doctrine or opinions on others. The *schema* denied the principle that had been advocated in the Roman Catholic world all those years: "Truth has all the rights and error has none," allowing the Church to use government in support of its beliefs.

"The church must be willing to suffer for its faith," the document said. That *schema* was such a radical departure from the past that all the bishops who were of a different mind ganged up on that document and fought it to the death. The result was that Pope Paul VI had to postpone the discussion of religious liberty from the end of the third session to the beginning of the fourth session.

I was there when Pope Paul VI was carried in on the shoulders of his aides for the final service of the third session. It was appalling. He came in, and not a single person applauded. When he came past us, his face was white. It was a terribly tense moment.

The pope probably did a good thing by postponing that discussion. He was trying to prevent schism in the church. He wanted to give the fathers of the Council time to think that one over. The *schema* on religious liberty was left on the calendar to be voted on in the fourth session, the fall of 1965. The final vote was 1,600 to 400 in favor of religious liberty.

That was, I believe, a very significant vote. As far as I can see, that is the only real change for the better that has been made in the dogmatic foundation of the Roman Catholic Church since the Reformation. All the other issues, including some new additions by previous councils, remain to be faced. The question that Luther raised still remains: "How does a man get right with God?" Luther's answer to that was (in essence), "He does not *get* right with God. He has been *put* right with God through the life, death, and resurrection of Jesus Christ. That's done!"

Sometime after I returned from the Vatican Council, someone asked me whether anything had changed.

"Yes," I said, "a Lutheran went to the Vatican and came back alive!"

THE SUMMER OF 1965

Two events I recall from that summer between the third and fourth sessions of the Vatican Council were not directly related to the Council, but were connected in a way to my presence there.

Meeting Richard Cardinal Cushing

When I was in Boston for the 1965 LLL convention, I was invited to go to see Richard Cardinal Cushing. I think that was probably arranged by the Haffenreffers, who were very close to Cardinal Cushing. Theodore Haffenreffer had gone through Concordia-Fort Wayne, Indiana, but he did not enter the ministry. He went into brewing instead. His brew of Red Lion Ale became one of the most popular commodities in the whole Boston area.

I went over to see Cardinal Cushing, taking LLL executive director Paul Friedrich and a couple of other laymen with me. Cardinal Cushing explained why he had stayed at the Second Vatican Council only one or two weeks of each of four sessions.

"You Protestants have the advantage over us," he said. "You understand the Latin!"

He talked with me about how he had a special heart for the people of South America, having sent nuns and priests down there from the Boston diocese. He said to me, "They go down there. They live their lives there. They die there. And they leave no impression on the culture at all."

"Well," I said to him, "why don't you do what we do? We send a pastor there, and he marries a Brazilian girl. They raise Brazilian children, and the children become pastors and teachers."

"By the way," I asked him, "when are you going to let your priests get married?"

"Never!" he said.

"How about 50 years from now?" I asked.

"Well, maybe 50 years from now," he said.

On another topic, he said, "There was a time when I supported the law here in Massachusetts that forbade the use of birth control devices. But I finally realized that to enforce that law, you'd have to have a policeman under every bed! By the way," he added, "I was supported in my position by a Lutheran down there in Missouri. His name was Walter Maier."

I invited Cardinal Cushing to speak to the LLL convention, and he accepted. After I had done that, I wondered what the consequences of that would be, because we had not prepared our people for a speech by a Roman Catholic cardinal.

"How long to you intend to speak?" I asked him.

"Oh, about 15 minutes," he said.

He spoke for 25 minutes—and captivated the hearts and minds of his audience. Our people did not realize at the time that Cardinal Cushing largely supported separation of church and state, as did his parishioner, John F. Kennedy. I received only one letter of protest about having invited a Roman Catholic cardinal to speak to the LLL convention.

Lutheran-Roman Catholic Dialogues

The other event indirectly related to the Council is the August 1965 meeting in Strasbourg, France, between a commission appointed by the Lutheran World Federation and a delegation from the Vatican. The purpose of the meeting was to discuss establishing Lutheran-Roman Catholic dialogues on the international level and to decide what the subjects should be.

All of the Lutheran representatives had been appointed by the Lutheran World Federation except one. Dr. Harms had appointed me to be there as an observer for The Lutheran Church—Missouri Synod. The Vatican delegation was headed by Cardinal Willebrands and included such people as Archbishop Volk of Mainz; Yves Congar, the great Roman Catholic lay theologian; Professor Witte, who taught in the Gregorian University; and others. The Lutheran delegation was headed by the Bishop of Bavaria and was made up of equally prominent theologians.

When they were talking about what the subject of those dialogues should be, I suggested the topic, "What is the Gospel?" All the others pooh-poohed that suggestion—except Bishop Martinson, the Roman Catholic Bishop of Denmark. He had written his doctoral thesis on Martin Luther. He said the Gospel was the issue raised by Martin Luther and we really ought to discuss that. That is what our group decided.

VISITING THE SICK IN ROME

Among all the events at this time in Rome, there is one of note, which really has nothing to do with the Council. I was informed by one of our Lutheran pastors in Ohio that there was a young man from Elyria, Ohio, by the name of Ronald Bergman in Salvatore Mundi Hospital in Rome. He had been riding his motorcycle and was hit by a car. (Speeding cars are customary in Rome.) He had been in the hospital for three months. While I was there, I visited him almost every day. I have often thought that maybe he was one of the reasons the Lord sent me to Rome.

I have always tried to visit the sick and shut-ins whenever I have had the opportunity. When I am in town, I visit members of our LLL staff when they go into the hospital. When I speak at

Lutheran Hour rallies, I always try to visit some of those who cannot get there because they are shut-ins. I do not think there is anything special about that. I believe the Lord expects you to be a transmission belt to convey His Gospel to others. When the opportunity comes, you should not let it go by. Making those visits, you benefit others, you benefit yourself, and you serve Him. I believe that serving Him is really what life in the ministry is all about.

I remember a visit I once made to a young man in Barnes Hospital in St. Louis, the nephew of one of our strong LLL members in Detroit, Michigan, Joe Foerster. This young man, a farmer about 35 years old, was dying of leukemia.

His wife went with me into his room at the hospital to wake him up. When he saw me, he asked me, "Am I going to go to hell?"

His wife tried to shush him. I said, "No, don't do that. This is one of the greatest honors I have ever received that he would ask me such a personal question."

"Now listen to me," I said to him, " 'The blood of Jesus Christ, God's Son, cleanses me from all sin' [1 John 1:7]. That's true. And I know it's true for you too. Do you want to say that with me?" He did, loud and clear!

After that you could just feel the atmosphere in his room change. We were laughing and talking. His mother, who had stayed outside the room, came in to see what was going on. We were in high spirits. It was really amazing. His wife was laughing too. It was wonderful!

He said, "I recognized you from your picture."

"Where did you see my picture?" I asked him.

He said, "In *The Lutheran Witness.*"

I said, "I'm surprised you'd recognize me from a picture printed in *The Lutheran Witness.*"

We laughed and had a great time.

His uncle told me that he was probably going to go home after treatment there at Barnes. As I went out the door, I said to him, "I hear you're going home."

"Yes," he said, "but not the way you think."

Five days later, he died.

RECAPPING MY THOUGHTS ABOUT VATICAN II

I trust that these few memories of mine can help you catch a bit of the excitement and hope some of us felt about what was happening in the Roman Catholic Church at the time. Luther's main criticism of the church of his day was "they do not understand the Gospel." The medieval church often replaced the Gospel with obedience to the church and obscured a believer's assurance of eternal salvation.

The Second Vatican Council signaled a refocus on the Gospel in the Roman Catholic Church. Granted, what happened in Rome was not near enough to bring about a reunification of all Christians into one church, but how wonderful to see the Gospel lifted up! And to have at least a miniscule part in that happening! I doubt my professors in high school and college could have imagined that any one of their students ever would have the chance to speak the Gospel in so many different ways and during such remarkable times in world history as the one in which we live today.

15

BILLY GRAHAM, THE CONGRESSES ON EVANGELISM, AND OTHER ASSOCIATIONS

L ATE IN 1968, I RECEIVED A PHONE CALL FROM THE HEADQUARTERS of the Billy Graham Association. It was serving as the temporary organizing body for a U.S. Congress on Evangelism to be held in September of the following year. Would I would be willing to serve as chairman of the congress, they asked.

I should explain that the U.S. Congress on Evangelism grew out of the first World Congress on Evangelism, which had been held in Berlin, Germany, during Reformation week, from October 25 through November 4, 1966. The World Congress was proposed by *Christianity Today,* on whose board of directors sat Billy Graham. Graham served as honorary chairman for that congress.

THE FIRST WORLD CONGRESS ON EVANGELISM

I was pleased to be asked by the congress to be present and to be the speaker in its closing session. I jump at any chance to proclaim the Redeemer and to encourage others to do likewise. As I read the New Testament, Jesus did not command just Lutherans to proclaim His Word, He told *all* Christians to do so.

For some reason, when the congress in Berlin started, it still needed a speaker for the Reformation Day service scheduled for Sunday morning. When I got there, Billy Graham came to me and asked me to remodel my talk into a sermon. I agreed to do that. I condensed everything so that it would not go on too long as some sermons do, even the printed sermons of Martin Luther!

Actually, my father always insisted that the sermons of Luther as printed in the various editions of Luther's Works had probably been edited and embellished by him before being published to give them the content he wanted. My father said that to deliver those sermons would have taken an hour or an hour and a half, and he did not think that Luther preached that long.

I think it is very possible that Luther edited the sermons and added to them what he wanted to say, because Luther probably preached as long as we do today: half an hour. Actually we probably do not preach even that long today. It is usually 20 minutes, and it is probably just as well, because what you cannot say in 20 minutes probably does not need to be said.

My topic for that Reformation Sunday service in Berlin was "The Acts of the Holy Spirit." That is probably a more accurate title for the book of Acts in the New Testament than "The Acts of the Apostles." Not all the acts described there are acts of the apostles. Some were acts of other people. All of them highlight the acts of the Holy Spirit.

After the service had ended, a whole delegation of Pentecostals came up to me. They said, "That's the first time we ever heard that Lutherans believed in the Holy Spirit!" Their reaction made me realize that we Lutherans need to convince people of our faith in the Holy Spirit. We have to let people know how deeply we believe that everything good that occurs in the world on behalf of Christ is the work of the Holy Spirit. As Canon Arrowsmith, an Anglican who was once the director of the Australian Bible Society, used to say, "The whole history of the church is the Spirit of God making children of God through the Word of God."

That's Lutheran. It is what we believe. We need to act on this faith too and not claim that *we* are converting people. All kinds of methods are used in the book of Acts to build up the church. Excluding the Holy Spirit from the equation leads to nothing but failure. It is the Holy Spirit who builds Christ's church.

That is certainly true of "The Lutheran Hour" as well as with many other efforts to reach people with the Gospel of Jesus Christ. We cannot claim to convert anybody, but we know who does bring them around. The Spirit does that through the power of the Gospel. That is what the Augsburg Confession says. It is what St. Paul says: "The Gospel is the power of God to salvation to everyone who believes, whether Jew or Gentile" (Romans 1:16).

THE U.S. CONGRESS ON EVANGELISM

Getting back to the U.S. Congress on Evangelism: Graham's association had decided to hold it in Minneapolis, because the moving spirit behind it was Connie Thompson, the evangelism director for the American Lutheran Church, which had its headquarters in Minneapolis. He was ably and spiritedly supported by the Billy Graham Association, which was also in Minneapolis. Billy Graham was asked to be the chairman. But for reasons known only to him, he declined and asked me to be the chairman.

I agreed to do that, but only on the condition that Billy Graham would consent to serve as honorary chairman, just as he did for the World Congress. One of the main reasons for asking him to accept that position was the need to keep the delegates from the wide doctrinal viewpoints of American denominations focused on basic evangelism rather than on sectarian concerns. As Fr. John Sheerin, editor of *Catholic World*, wrote about the World Congress on Evangelism held two years earlier, "Only the Holy Spirit working through Billy Graham as the human instrument could have welded together so quickly so many men of different faiths."

Sheerin credited him with holding together "forces that would have exploded in all directions save for his presence" (so reported *The Lutheran Witness,* vol. 85, p. 314). If his presence was that effective in the World Congress, I was sure it would bring about the same result for the U.S. Congress.

When I called Graham's office to ask him to be honorary chairman, his associates said, "You'll have to get in touch with him yourself and ask him, because we're not going to be able to persuade him to do that."

At the time, Billy Graham was visiting his daughter and her family in Switzerland. I called him there, and he said, "Anything you want me to do, I'll do." On that basis, I agreed to be the chairman.

Later on, during the time when we were organizing the congress, I had lunch with Billy Graham's wife, Ruth, and one of her friends at the Grahams' North Carolina home, after speaking at the Presbyterian college in Montreat, North Carolina. Their home is built of old lumber and sits high up on a mountain. You have to go through three gates, all guarded by dogs, before you get there. Inside the house, over the fireplace, is inscribed *Eine Feste Burg Ist Unser Gott* ("A Mighty Fortress Is Our God"). It was interesting to me to note that the inscription read *Eine.* In the hymn, we use *ein'* to fit the meter, but the word is really *eine* because *Burg* is feminine.

A lot of organizational meetings were held before the Congress, and Billy Graham attended many of those meetings. Paul Freyling, pastor of the First Covenant Church in downtown Minneapolis, was chairman of the executive committee. Many of those on the executive committee were from Minneapolis, but others came from some distance away. There were all kinds of people there: Harold Linsell, the editor of *Christianity Today* at the time; Dr. Knight, the evangelism director of The Church of the Nazarene; Dr. Bill Bright, head of Campus Crusade; and many others.

In order to avoid any problems that might arise from misunderstanding, we set to work defining very precisely what the purposes of this conference were to be. We had at least three meetings of three or four days each to define all the purposes of the congress in order that we might directly confront the problems with evangelism in this country.

Those meetings were very crucial. Many of the evangelicals, who were a formidable part of that executive committee, said, "We have never spent this much time before defining our purposes for a meeting of this sort. It's been a wonderful experience for us, and it has taught us a lot."

The very last problem that had to be overcome in formulating purposes was in one of the purpose statements where we talked about the Church with a capital "C"—meaning all Christians. I put that in there deliberately, and Paul Freyling agreed with me. Harold Linsell, whom I respect greatly, disagreed with us. He suggested that we should change it to "the churches."

"No," Paul Freyling said, "it should be 'the Church,' because evangelism is not just about churches. We are talking about the Church of Jesus Christ throughout the world."

That statement was finally approved as it was proposed. Throughout the sessions our focus was on "the Church."

Besides the plenary sessions, there were 46 workshops held simultaneously each day during the course of the congress. They covered everything from "doing your thing" and leisure time evangelism to dialogical retreats and ministering through the use of the secular theater. Billy Graham, who attended most of the organizational meetings, suggested the right people as leaders for many of those workshops. He knew more about the people who would be appropriate leaders than anyone in his office. That is saying a lot, because the people of the Billy Graham Association were very knowledgeable people!

On the afternoon before the opening session a reception was held at Central Lutheran Church. I was to be the speaker at the session in the evening. Billy Graham and I stood there shaking hands with about 1,000 delegates. Sometime during that afternoon, Graham turned to me and said, "You know if I were speaking tonight, I couldn't be here this afternoon."

That was a very personal disclosure on his part. He was telling me that whenever he had to speak in the evening for one of his crusades or whatever it was, he would have to rest during the day. That is just the way he has worked through a most strenuous schedule.

In my speech that evening, I used a popular slogan of the day as the theme. The slogan was "Get with it!" Then I asked the question, "Get with what?" and emphasized, "Get with Christ, and go with Him!"

In my talk, I apologized to the whole assembly for what we Christians have often done in the name of evangelism. I said that we have acted and maybe even spoken as though we were asking people to be like us, when we need to invite people to be in and with the Lord: to see the Lord, to listen to the Lord, and to follow the Lord. "That is what this meeting is going to be about," I said.

The speaker the next morning was Leighton Ford, Billy Graham's brother-in-law, who was an evangelist with the Billy Graham team. He spoke about "The Church and Evangelism in a Day of Revolution."

"When we see this world convulsed," he said, "it is not a time to despair. It is a time to watch our sovereign God at work. He can take the wild rage of the ghettos, He can take the apathy of the suburbs, He can take the unrest on the campus, He can take the nightmare of Vietnam, and He can bring all these threads together to weave out the fabric of His plans."

Another speaker that evening was Tom Skinner, one of the noted black evangelists in those days. There were people sitting in the front rows from sections of the country where not much progress had been made in race relations, waiting to see what he would say. In his speech Skinner said, "You can take this away from us, and you can take that away from us, but there's one thing you cannot take away from us, and that's the riches of God in Jesus Christ."

When he said that, people who had been sitting on their hands waiting to see what he would say stood up and cheered. It was like a wind blowing through there. The whole meeting felt it! It was the Holy Spirit. His presence was obvious there all the rest of that week.

By the way, we did not spend any time at those meetings talking about race relations. We figured the Gospel would take care of that, and it surely will!

Another featured speaker was Dr. Paul Reese, then editor of *World Vision* magazine, contributing editor to *Christianity Today* and *Eternity* magazines, and well-known author. He spoke to the congress about "The Inward Journey." He reminded the assembly that the whole reason for evangelism begins at the foot of the cross and that it gets its power from the empty tomb.

On Thursday evening, I told Billy Graham he should preside. I sat in the balcony with the pastor of Park Street Church in Boston, Dr. Harold Ockenga, who was a great leader in Protestantism in those days. During that session, a group of American Indians came in and sat down on the floor right in front of the stage demanding to be heard. Dr. Graham promised to talk with them after the session was over.

After the session, the Indians went right up onto the stage. Graham conversed with them for a little while, then he left. The Indians were still standing there on the stage. I went down to talk with them. I stood between two of their leaders, with about 30 others surrounding us, and we talked. I think about 1,000 people from the audience remained to see what they had to say. Mostly they were complaining that black people had received all the advantages, and they had received none. I let them talk. They talked for about an hour, then they left.

The next day I got a call from an official of the United States Department of the Interior in charge of Indian reservations. He told me that he wanted to explain a few things to me about the government position concerning the Indians. I told him that I was very busy, but that if he wanted to come to my hotel room and have lunch with me, I would be glad to talk with him.

He agreed to do that. Over lunch, he told me that the problem with the Indians was that they were all individuals and that only in times of war would there be any individual leadership. "For example, there's an electronics factory in the Southwest completely staffed by Indians," he said. "That factory has the lowest rate of failure of any in the country: about one percent. But our biggest problem is trying to get an Indian foreman for that factory, because they're not used to telling other Indians what to do." If that is true, it may account for some of the strange things that have occurred to these Native Americans over the years.

One of the most publicized incidents of the congress took place during a speech by Christian author Keith Miller. A long-haired student and his wife, both clad in hippie garb and seated on the floor of the hall, were escorted out by ushers. Miller stopped abruptly in the middle of his speech and announced, "They just threw out the man who looks more like Jesus Christ than anybody in the auditorium!"

Soon after that, the ushers brought the shaggy couple back in to the warm applause of the audience. They were given front row seats and sat quietly through the whole session. It was obvious that if the delegates had their say, no one was going to miss out in this meeting on the sharing of God's Spirit!

There was also a large group of young people at the congress. The highlight for many of them was a "happening" that was held on Friday night at the Minneapolis Armory. It was hosted by Pat Boone, and the music was rock, pop, and soul. Thousands of young people showed up to hear that music and to hear about Jesus Christ.

The congress concluded on Saturday evening with a giant rally. Dr. Billy Graham was the main speaker. His Crusade Choir was there to provide the music. A number of other speakers from the congress were also on the program, including me. We expected a large number of people, so we had reserved the Metropolitan Arena, just south of Minneapolis.

This large auditorium seated 17,000 people. The power of the Holy Spirit was with us. The program was scheduled to begin at eight o'clock. By 7:30 the place was packed with 20,000 people. The ushers were forced to close the doors. Traffic was tied up for five miles around the arena, all the way across the bridge over the Mississippi from St. Paul. Someone estimated that nearly 60,000 people were turned away. Hundreds of people gathered on the lawn outside the arena, in the hope that they might participate in what was going on inside.

Even Billy Graham and I, who were scheduled to speak, had trouble getting there. Finally I got a police car to take me in. Even then I had to walk half a mile from the road across a parking lot to get to the arena. None of those who could not get in seemed to be upset. People were smiling and saying, "This is the greatest thing we've ever seen in our lifetime!"

When we arrived, they began. We started 20 minutes before the session was scheduled to begin, because not one more person could get into the building. That was a truly great evening. It was a celebration of the grace and glory that we have in Jesus Christ. To see that kind of response to the proclamation of the Gospel of Jesus Christ gave us a thrill that may be hard to come by again.

Jim Reinhard and Greenville College

I made many friends at that congress, especially in the evangelical community. One of those friends was Jim Reinhard, chapel director and head of the theology department at Greenville College, a Free Methodist College in Greenville, Illinois.

During the U.S. Congress, Reinhard had gone out onto nearby Hennepin Avenue to put into practice some of the things that were being advocated at the congress. There he found an alcoholic man and brought him to the session that evening.

After the session, Reinhard brought the man up to the platform and asked me to pray with him. I put my hands on the man's shoulders and prayed with him. Reinhard told me later that he had put the man in touch with a local pastor, and that he felt my prayer with the man was the beginning of his drying out process.

Sometime shortly after that, Reinhard invited me to come and speak to the students at Greenville College. He was a regular listener to "The Lutheran Hour." In his letter he wrote about one of my question and answer sections that he had heard. A listener had asked whether I could recommend some books that could teach him more about Jesus Christ. I had responded, "Yes. How about Matthew, Mark, Luke, and John?"

By the way, I did accept Reinhard's invitation. As a result, until recently I spoke at Greenville College about every other year. Often I was the speaker for their convocation chapel at the large Free Methodist Church across the street from the campus.

At one time, I met with their faculty at a faculty retreat. At another time, I was the Staley Foundation lecturer at Greenville College. (The Staley lectures were founded by Mr. Staley, a successful businessman who wanted to have the witness of Christ presented to students on college campuses.) For those lectures, I would spend two days on their campus speaking predominantly to students. Through the years I was invited to give the Staley lectures on many other campuses. I always enjoyed those times with the college students.

Billy Graham Schools of Evangelism

Another association of mine as a result of the U.S. Congress on Evangelism is my regular participation over the years as speaker at Billy Graham Schools of Evangelism. Larry Backlund is responsible for setting up all the Billy Graham Schools of Evangelism around the country. He succeeded Mr. John Dillon in that position. This program for professional church workers is funded by a foundation established by Lowell W. Berry, the founder of Best Fertilizers Company, California Ammonia Company, American Plant Food, Occidental Chemicals (with Armond Hammer, although they quickly separated), and American Plant Food Company. As a child, Mr. Berry became a tither, and in 1957 at the Billy Graham crusade in New York caught in a new way "the clarity, simplicity, and power of the Gospel." It was the next year, when Mr. Berry was co-chair of the local committee for the Graham crusade in San Francisco, that he proposed the school of evangelism for pastors and Christian workers. His prayer was that they would receive a new vision of their ministry and be encouraged to concentrate on the Gospel.

Participants in the Schools of Evangelism come from all over the country. Between 800 and 1,000 pastors and their wives usually attend any one of the schools. The auditoriums or convention halls in which they are held are filled to capacity. They usually have to cut off registration, because they cannot accommodate all those who want to come. I have spoken at two or three of those almost every year in different places: Portland, Oregon; Denver, Colorado; Anaheim, California; Lake Louise, British Columbia; Hendersonville, North Carolina; Dallas, Texas; Wheaton, Illinois, and other places. At every one, what a thrill to see the power of the Gospel at work!

THE SECOND INTERNATIONAL CONFERENCE ON EVANGELISM

There was a second International Congress on Evangelism held in Lausanne, Switzerland, July 6–24, 1974. I served as chairman for North America for that congress. The conference began on Wednesday. Billy Graham gave the opening speech. Malcolm Muggeridge spoke that night. I was sitting beside Festo Kivengere, the Anglican Bishop of Uganda, who was chairman for Africa.

Bishop Kivengere served as chairman of the congress on Thursday, and I was chairman on Friday. I opened the meeting that day with a famous old story about the Norwegian in Minnesota who was coming back from fishing and was met by a Swedish friend who said, "Ole, What you been doin'?"

Ole said, "What you t'ink I been doin'? I got this here fish pole and this basket of fish. What d'ya t'ink?"

The Swede said, "If I could guess how many fish you got in that basket, would you give me one of them?"

And Ole said, "If you can guess how many fish I got in dis here basket, I'll give you bot' a' them."

So the Swede guessed, "Five."

Ole said, "Not bad for a Swede. You only missed it by two."

The place erupted in laughter. There had been no real humor since the opening day when Malcolm Muggeridge had said, "The world could use some good eschatology. What Samuel Johnson once remarked about hanging, you could say about eschatology: 'It wonderfully clarifies the mind!' "

Actually, the funniest thing happened the day after I chaired that meeting on Friday. Two German theologians came up to me and said, "Our German translator missed the whole point of that story. Will you tell it to us again?"

I thoroughly enjoyed those congresses on evangelism, and I have had a wonderful relationship with the evangelical community over the years. I have always been well received by them because of my emphasis on the Scriptures and on getting the Scriptures out to people. I always tell them that my theology is Lutheran, that is, the theology of Martin Luther, which is the only theology there is as far as I'm concerned. They respect me for that!

OTHER ASSOCIATIONS

Dr. Billy Melvin, who served as executive director of the National Association of Evangelicals until his retirement in 1994, reminds me that he first met me at the National Sunday School Association meetings some 35 years ago, where I was quite often the featured speaker at national and regional meetings.

I have also served for many years on the board of Christianity Today, Inc. I was asked to serve by Billy Graham, who serves as chairman of the board, although he rarely attends board meetings. The vice-chairman, B. Clayton Bell, Billy Graham's brother-in-law and pastor of Highland Park Presbyterian Church in Dallas, usually chairs the meetings. Harold Myra is president and chief executive officer of Christianity Today, Inc.; Paul Robbins is vice-president and chief operating officer. Harold Myra says that my contribution to the board is that as one who stands outside the evangelical community, when the board gets into areas of disagreement, I can often provide a helpful viewpoint.

Donald Grey Barnhouse

Another member of the evangelical community who became a good friend was a Presbyterian pastor in Philadelphia, Donald

Grey Barnhouse, perhaps the best known American Bible teacher during the '30s to the '50s. (Obviously, I got to know him before the evangelism congresses, for he died in 1960.) He always looked on himself as a teacher rather than a preacher or evangelist. He had a radio program on which he taught the book of Romans, which he never got through in his lifetime. He was such a biblical scholar that he once had three programs on one verse. He published those programs. They are a wonderful commentary and a fascinating teaching tool for anyone who wants to understand Paul's letter to the Romans and the Gospel it proclaims.

I do not remember how it happened, but Donald Grey Barnhouse invited me to come to the annual meeting of his magazine, *Revelation,* which has now become *Eternity* magazine. We met each year at the Nassau Inn, close to Princeton University, where Dr. Barnhouse was a student during the days of Professor "Das" Machen. (Machen's nickname came from the German paradigm *das Mädchen.* The construction is quite unusual, because *das,* meaning "the," is neuter, and *Mädchen* means "young girl.") The Rev. Dr. J(ohn) Gresham Machen was a leading American conservative and a New Testament scholar.

At the meeting of *Revelation* magazine there was an argument going on between Donald Grey Barnhouse, *Jr.,* and Walter Martin about the relative value of the intellectual and the emotional in faith. The argument had apparently started sometime before, because it broke out in full heat in the middle of the meeting. Finally, the elder Barnhouse, who was sitting at one end of the table, broke in and said that he had often wondered how a percolator worked. He investigated, he said, and found out that unless you have grounds on top, you are not going to have coffee. He also found out that unless you have heat underneath, you are also not going to have coffee.

The laughter that followed somewhat eased the tension. In the moment of silence after that laughter, Dr. Kuiper, a Baptist who was sitting at the other end of the table, said, "I'd like to remind you that you also need water." The whole place broke out in tumultuous laughter again, and the argument was forgotten.

My Signature Passage

It was because of Donald Grey Barnhouse that I started to put a Scripture reference with my signature when I gave someone an autograph. He said, "When you sign your signature, put a Scripture passage with it."

I thought that was a good idea, and I picked Galatians 2:20. It does tell the whole Gospel: "I am crucified with Christ; nevertheless, I live; yet not I, but Christ lives in me; and the life that I now live, I live by faith in the Son of God who loved me and gave Himself for me."

Shortly before he died, Barnhouse went to Costa Rica to learn Spanish. He came back and said, "I can't do it."

Members of his congregation realized that something was wrong, because there was never anything he could not do when it came to languages. He used to quote hymns in French and then translate them as he went along. He had a marvelous gift for translation and illustration.

Shortly after he came back from that trip to Costa Rica, he died. His congregation was devastated at losing him.

My other relationships with members of the evangelical community and many other Christians has been through my participation with them in the American Bible Society. My involvement with the American Bible Society and the United Bible Societies over the years has been an extremely meaningful part of my life. The Bible Societies are fiercely dedicated to getting the Word of God out to all people—and so am I!

16

THE BIBLE SOCIETIES

THE AMERICAN BIBLE SOCIETY

M Y INVOLVEMENT WITH THE BIBLE SOCIETIES BEGAN BECAUSE OF
Rev. Ade Meyer. The reader should recall that he was the
pastor of St. Mark Lutheran Church in Yonkers, New
York, who spearheaded the process after WWI to form an LCMS
public relations department and was involved in the American
Lutheran Publicity Bureau. He was also the man who got me
involved in public relations work for him and later as director for
Synod's Public Relations Department. He still was chairman of
the board when I received the call to be Lutheran Hour speaker. In
addition to that, he was the official Missouri Synod representative to the American Bible Society (ABS). When I lived in New
York, Ade would take me with him to their annual meeting.

A person did not have to be a member of the ABS in order to
attend its meetings. People of various denominations were invited
to come and hear what the Society was doing. Ade Meyer and I
would often sit in the back somewhere and listen to what was
going on. The meetings were held at the modest headquarters of
the ABS on 57th and Park, which was at the time a three-story
building. As I recall, space was very cramped.

At one of those meetings, the ABS found out somehow that I
had taught linguistics at the University of Minnesota. The result

was that they asked me to serve on the translations committee, of which Dr. Bruce Metzger was chairman at that time. Metzger was professor of New Testament at Princeton Seminary and one of the world's leading Greek linguists for the New Testament. As such he was chairman of the RSV Bible Committee, a member of the Editorial Committee of the Critical Greek New Testament, and chairman of the American Committee of the International Greek New Testament Project—among other positions. Someone has said of him that if an autograph (original manuscript) of the New Testament is ever found, it will have Metzger's initials on it.

Once again, I was amazed at the way God takes the various strands of our lives and pulls them together in a way that allows us to serve Him in ways we never would have imagined. Doctors Bartling (at Concordia-Milwaukee) and Moenkemoeller (Concordia-St. Paul) never could have imagined that their prep-school student would have the opportunity to serve so many people through this organization. I doubt that Ade Meyer had all this in mind when he first met me at Concordia-Bronxville and asked me to assist his little public relations group at Synod's conventions. And I never assumed when I accepted the position as public relations director for Synod that my experiences there would equip me for meeting leaders around the world. But God pulled together all the strands. How grateful I am that He used me in this way!

At the first meeting I attended as a member of the ABS translations committee, they were discussing whether they should translate the apocryphal books and include them in the translation on which they were working, which happened to be the Good News Bible, Today's English Version (TEV). One older committee member from Hartford Seminary asked, "If we include them, will we have to change our name to the 'American Bible and Apocrypha Society'?"

Eventually Metzger turned to me and asked, "What do you think?"

"Well," I said, "Luther included the Apocrypha in his translation. He said, 'They're not scriptural, but they're good books.' " (Luther always settles a question.) We decided to include the Apocrypha, and we have included them ever since that time for people who wish to read the Apocrypha. We have an agreement with the Roman Catholics that we will include these books, but in a separate printed section rather than scattered throughout the Old Testament as the Roman Catholic Church does. We have adhered to that agreement through the years.

I have served on the translations committee of the ABS ever since I was appointed to the committee in 1964, except for the six months when I served as vice-president of the United Bible Societies for North America. I also served on the ABS program committee. I currently serve as the translations committee chairman, and now Bruce Metzger is a member of my committee. (By the way, in 1994, in appreciation for 30 years of service to the ABS, the Board gave me a framed page dated 1648 from the King James Bible.)

I was on the Old Testament review panel for the TEV. As chairman of the translations subcommittee, I was privileged to present the TEV to the ABS for adoption and distribution. I currently serve in a similar capacity relating to the new version that appeared in the summer of 1995, the Contemporary English Version (CEV). It is translated into language that even school children can understand. Yet it takes into account all the principles of biblical translation, many of them enunciated by Martin Luther in his essay "On Translation."

Most of the scholars who are working on the CEV are in Springfield, Missouri. The chairman of the translation team is Dr. Barclay Newman of Springfield, who is also a poet. Largely because of him, this version offers probably the most poetic translation of the psalms of any English translation in recent years.

I probably should explain briefly how the translations committee works. The translations committee had until recently been a subcommittee of the program committee, which deals with all ABS programs for North America. We are charged with being the point of review for new translations, as well as for the translations of supportive materials that are not part of the biblical text. Eight or nine biblical scholars are on the committee.

When a new translation is being prepared, material in draft form is sent out about every two months to members of the committee and others for review. Not all of the reviewers are biblical scholars. There may be a poet, a college president, or others who have particular expertise to offer in the process of forging a translation.

The material sent to the reviewers will usually consist of translations of two or three books of the Bible at a time. The reviewers read this material, approve it, or suggest changes. The translation team then goes over their suggestions, reacts, and presents findings to the translations committee. In quarterly meetings, the translations committee reviews all of this again, votes on proposed changes, and when everything is agreed on, presents the manuscript to the program committee.

Over the years we have found that you cannot "sell" a new translation to the public. It has to be accepted on its own merit. Even the King James Version was not well accepted when it first came out. King James, who authorized that translation, was not a particularly moral man. The translation named after him had to win its own way.

Speaking of the King James Version reminds me of the woman who wrote to me and asked why I used different versions of the Bible when I preach.

"If the King James Version was good enough for Martin Luther," she wrote, "it should be good enough for you."

I had to explain to her that I usually use my Greek New Testament and translate directly from it when I preach. Then I wrote that there were some problems with her assumption that Luther used the King James Version, since the KJV came out in 1611, and Luther died in 1546. Besides, I said, he would have had trouble reading the language, because I do not believe he spoke English at all.

Bible translation is a continuing process. Even the best translations need to be revised. Often the meanings of words change over the years. Luther revised his own translation 90 times during his lifetime!

The ABS has never limited itself to distributing only one version of the Bible. I always advise people throughout the world that they should not campaign against any version. Some versions are, of course, better than others, because they are more faithful to the original languages. The Living Bible, for example, is probably not as good as some of the others, because it was not translated from the original languages. But it is a noble work done by a layman who did not know Greek or Hebrew. We do not campaign against it, because people have come to know Jesus Christ through the Living Bible too.

Among other items, I was able to influence the committee in the translation of the Hebrew word *almah* in Isaiah 7:14 as "virgin" in the new CEV. The chairman had to push for that translation, and it finally was approved as a good translation. Dr. Eugene Nida, the driving force behind the CEV, agreed with me that it was the correct translation. We pointed out that Luther emphasized that you should translate according to the understanding of the time. Although we could not point back to other writings from the time of Isaiah, we could show that in 200 B.C. God's people understood *almah* as "virgin"—for that's the way the Septuagint (the ancient Greek translation of the Old Testament) translates the

Hebrew into Greek. The Septuagint gives us the Jewish understanding in the centuries before Christ was born!

I have enjoyed working with the ABS on Bible translation, including the opportunities given me to be personally involved in getting the Word of God out to people all over the world. That has always been a priority of the American Bible Society.

UNITED BIBLE SOCIETIES

The United Bible Societies organization is nothing other than an association of the many national Bible societies (including the American Bible Society), designed to coordinate activities between them or common to them all. The UBS recognizes the integrity and independence of all national Bible societies. The UBS does what the member societies tell it to do. I have always supported that, because the national societies know what is best for their own countries.

I was honored to be appointed as one of the American Bible delegates to the UBS Church Leaders Conference in Driebergen, Holland, in June of 1964, and to the first World Assembly of the United Bible Societies in Addis Ababa, Ethiopia, in September of 1972. In 1977, I was elected president of the United Bible Societies. That was a real surprise to me. Here is how that happened.

I had been the UBS vice-president for North America for about six months, when suddenly the Most Rev. F. Donald Coggan, the Archbishop of Canterbury, who had been serving as UBS president for 18 years, retired because of his demanding duties as head of the Anglican communion. They needed to find a replacement to fill his unexpired term. An election by mail was scheduled.

I have no idea who nominated me, but someone called me and asked whether I would accept the nomination for UBS president. I asked them who the other candidate was. They told me it was the Rev. Festo Kivengere, Anglican Bishop of Uganda. (The reader will recall that at the World Congress on Evangelism in Lausanne, he had been chairman for Africa and I was chairman for North America. I knew Kivengere very well and considered him a good friend.)

"Okay," I said, "I'll let my name stand, just so he can be elected."

I assumed that there was no question but that a nominee from a third world country would win the election. When the votes were counted, to my surprise and to the surprise of everyone else including many in America who did not think an American could be elected, I had been chosen. Even some of the African societies had voted for me.

I became president of the United Bible Societies in March of 1977. I was reelected to an eight-year term at a meeting of the UBS Council in Chiang Mai, Thailand, in 1980, and served as UBS president until December of 1988. When I retired as Lutheran Hour speaker at that time, I decided to retire as UBS president also. I still serve as honorary USB president.

The United Bible Societies is a marvelous organization. It consists of 115 national Bible societies that engage in Bible translation, publication, and distribution in about 150 countries. A lot of smaller societies would like to belong to the UBS, but the UBS charter says that you have to be a national society and meet certain qualifications to belong.

For example, the society in the Philippines was expelled one time because of financial malfeasance. After they cleaned house, they were reinstated at the meeting of the UBS Council in Chiang Mai, where I was reelected UBS president. When we sent them word that they had been readmitted, they sent back a cable that said, "Hallelujah!"

Since then, I have visited the Philippines at their Bible society's annual meeting. It was a large meeting held at the Hilton Hotel in Manila. Some of the people who had been responsible for the problem were there. Also present were a professor from the university and a woman executive, who were primarily responsible for getting things cleaned up. Now the general secretary of the Philippine Bible Society is a retired IBM executive, and everything is running just fine.

The Philippine Bible Society now has its own building, which the American Bible Society gave to them. The ABS has done many wonderful things like that throughout the world. We also bought a building in Argentina and gave it to the Bible society there.

One of the most exciting engagements in which I took part while serving as president of the United Bible Societies was presenting the Malayalam New Testament in common language to the people at the Maramon Convention of the Bible Society of India in Kerala, India, in February of 1980. I also delivered a number of messages at that convention. I remember leading a Bible class and looking out over the crowd of 70,000, which looked like a sea of sun umbrellas, under which the people were seated on the ground. Other participants included the bishop of the Church of South India and Metropolitan Alexander of the Mar Thoma Church.

A pleasant addition to that trip was an afternoon visit at the residence of the governor of Kerala in Trivandrum. After the rest of our party had left, she told me that she had been a young disciple of Mahatma Gandhi, but was now reading this Malayalam New Readers version of the Bible in order to become more proficient in that language, since she was a Tamil. What a great thing God was doing!

AMITY PRESS: BIBLES IN CHINA

The ABS was the prime mover in building a plant in Nanjing, China, for printing Bibles. The China Christian Council came to the American Bible Society with a request for $50,000 to buy a printing press to print Bibles. After much discussion about this, UBS representatives said, "You really need more than that!"

Their request for a printing press turned into the $7.5 million printing plant in Nanjing called Amity Press. The Japan Bible Society contributed $750,000, which was ⅒ of the cost. ABS gave $2.5 million, and most of the other societies contributed proportionately.

There were two speakers at the dedication of Amity Press in 1987. One was General Secretary Dr. Ulrich Fick, who spoke for the organization of the United Bible Societies and its general secretaries throughout the world. Then I spoke as president of the United Bible Societies. I said, in effect, "What a surprise!"

Leading Communist party functionaries were present for the dedication, including the vice-premier of the province of Nanjing. There must have been 500 people there, mostly people who had received special invitations to attend. They were tremendously proud of that printing plant!

In front of the building is a great plaza. Flags were flying all over that plaza on the day of dedication. Most of them were red, for in China red flags mean joy—and this was certainly a joyful occasion! It was a most festive sight!

By the way, it was cold inside where the dedicatory ceremonies were held. In China they do not have much heat in the wintertime. We were all bundled up to keep warm. I kept my speech short, because I did not want to make a long speech when it was so cold that you could see your breath when you spoke!

A choir of students from the seminary in Nanjing participated in the dedication. I think every one of them must have been a musician. I said to the seminary vice-president, Pastor Chen, at St. Paul's Church the next morning, "I would like to have that choir on 'The Lutheran Hour.' "

"I don't see why that could not be arranged," he said. That was how our 1988 Lutheran Hour Christmas special, "Christmas in

China," my last Lutheran Hour broadcast, came into being. More about that later.

In the evening of the day of the dedication there was a dinner. At the dinner, I was sitting next to Bishop Ting, chairman of the China Christian Council, at a large round table with 50 people around it at a very nice restaurant in a Nanjing hotel. While we were sitting there, the head of the construction crew, who was wearing his Mao Tse-tung hat, came up to me and offered a toast. He was proud that his crew of 500 workmen had put those buildings up in only five months time.

Amity Press was a large complex when it was originally built, and they have now expanded it. They have put in a dining room for the people who work there, and a dormitory for people who need to stay there while they are working.

The real hero behind the whole enterprise of Amity Press is Han Wenzao, a layman who is vice-president of the China Christian Council. He knows how to work with church people and how to handle government authorities too. Let me give you one example of that.

Until recently, every time Amity Press wanted to print more Bibles they had to get permission from the government to import Bible paper from Hong Kong, and the government would decide how much paper they could import. Finally Han Wenzao persuaded them to allow him to make the decision. Now they can get paper to produce as many Bibles as are needed, and they are also beginning to produce their own Bible paper.

Han Wenzao is truly a remarkable fellow, as are many of the Chinese Christians.

The day after I spoke at the dedication of Amity Press, I spoke at St. Paul's Church in Nanjing. The church and the parish hall were both filled 25 minutes before the service began. There must have been at least 1,500 people in the church and parish hall.

The congregation was all crowded together. They were all wearing padded coats and jackets, because the temperature was only 31 degrees in the church. When they sang the hymns, you could see their breath all over the place.

The vice-president of the seminary was the pastor that morning. He had the same readings we have in church here. I preached the sermon, and he interpreted it for me.

When he was making the announcements at the beginning of the service, I noticed that at one point everybody was looking at me. Since I do not understand Chinese, I had no idea what he was saying. When he came back to where I was sitting, he explained that he had told them that it was my 73d birthday.

"Well, we'll take care of that when I get up in the pulpit," I said.

When we got up in the pulpit, I as the preacher and he as my translator, I thanked the people for the privilege of being there. I thanked them for supporting Amity Press. I told the congregation about the dedication of the printing plant the day before, and how it would serve them and all the citizens of China.

Then I said, "I also appreciate the birthday greeting, but there is only one thing wrong. It is not my 73d birthday. It is my 74th birthday."

At that, they all laughed. The pastor told me afterward that that was the first time he had ever seen his congregation laugh in a church service. Of course, for many years they were so persecuted, that they really did not have much to laugh at.

In my sermon, I said, "You have suffered every indignity of which humanity is capable."

I could say that, and everybody thought it was wonderful that someone from abroad could recognize what they had gone through. Then I told them the Gospel of Jesus Christ in almost apostolic surroundings.

China has problems. They are big problems. China is a big country with a most checkered history. Forty years ago there were 750,000 Christians in China. Today there are more than 10 times that number. Christ is being proclaimed. Bibles are available. The Word increased even in the most unfavorable circumstances.

Amity Press is only one of the many projects of the United Bible Societies. There are 675 translation projects going on throughout the world. Probably in the distant future we shall be translating into fewer languages, because a very few languages (such as English and Spanish) are becoming the *lingua franca* (common means of communication) throughout the world.

ROMAN CATHOLIC PARTICIPATION IN THE UBS

It is interesting that of the 675 translation projects, over half have Roman Catholic scholars on their translation teams. That has not always been true. I once said to one of the cardinals here in America, "We don't get much support from your 'home office.' " He said, "I know exactly what you mean!"

Pope John Paul I changed all that. During his 30 days in office, he had already made plans to meet with us. He had in mind to align the Roman Catholic Church with the movement for people to read and study Scriptures in languages they could understand.

During that month, we were having a meeting at the Far East Regional Bible Center in Hong Kong, when I heard on an English-language radio broadcast that the pope had died. Uli Fick, the UBS general secretary, picked me up for dinner, and when I told him that the pope had died, his face turned white. We had made such progress with Pope John Paul I, and now we did not know what to expect. But the current pope, John Paul II, has received our people and made some statements supportive of Bible society work.

The Vatican has an official representative to the UBS. Archbishop Ablondi serves in that position now. Father Abbott of the Jesuit order served before him.

Speaking of Father Abbott reminds me of an interesting incident. When Marcia and I were coming back from a meeting at Addis Ababa in 1972, we decided to stop over in Rome. I arranged to meet with Father Abbott, and he told me to phone him when we got in, hoping that we might spend some time together.

We were flying into Rome on Ethiopia Airlines, which was run at that time by TWA. While we were in the air, the pilot told us there was a strike at the airport. I was not too surprised to hear that, because somebody is always on strike in Rome.

When we got to the Rome airport, we were all standing in the aisle waiting to get off the plane. I made a kind of joke, saying, "Maybe we'll have to climb down a ladder."

Do you know what we had to do? We had to climb down a ladder! There were no people to handle the plane, which was parked about a block or two away from the terminal. They put a ladder up to the side of the plane, and we all climbed down about a story or two!

There was also no one to handle the baggage. The pilot boosted one of the stewardesses into the baggage compartment of the plane. She handed our bags down, and we carried our own bags into the airport.

I had tried to make reservations at the *pensione* where I had stayed during the Vatican Council, but it was full. We stayed at the Hilton Hotel, which was a little farther out, but we could take a bus downtown, which at that time cost only seven cents. That was a lot cheaper than taking a cab!

It was about 4:00 P.M. when we got to the hotel. I tried to call Father Abbott, but I could not reach him. I called and called, but he did not answer. Finally about eight o'clock, which is about the time people in Rome eat dinner, I said, "I'm going to make one more call before we go out the door to dinner."

The phone rang only once or twice, when Father Abbott answered.

"I'm sorry you couldn't reach me before," he said. "I've been in a meeting all day. But now, come right down here. Take the Number 7 bus to the Via Veneto. Get off there, walk four blocks to the right, and you'll come to a brick wall. Follow that brick wall to a gate. I'll be waiting for you there."

We followed his directions, and there we were—at Jesuit headquarters for the world! He welcomed Marcia and me in and showed us around.

The building is an old Roman mansion where the Lucullan feasts had been held in classical days. It had been owned by the German embassy for years. They had never been able to change anything, because it was a historic building. The Jesuits bought the building from them, but they were not allowed to change anything either. Finally they built a library five stories down into the ground!

In the ballroom upstairs were paintings worth at least $2 million. Those paintings caused the press to criticize the Jesuits for their affluent life-style, but they had actually come with the building.

When we got to that ballroom, Father Abbott said, "You sit down and look at the paintings. I'll meet you in 15 minutes."

I was not dressed in clerical garb, but Father Abbott was. He took off his clerical garb and rejoined us.

"We've got a date at Alfredo's," he said.

Alfredo's is a restaurant at the Spanish Steps, famous the world over. When we went in, there must have been a line of 75 people waiting to get a table. We walked past all of them, right into the middle of the establishment. They put us at a table, and this man with a little mustache came to our table. It was Alfredo himself! He whipped up a batch of fettuccine Alfredo right there at the table and served it to us. He handed a plate to me and a plate to Father Abbott. Then he handed the platter with all the rest on it to Marcia. We had one of the best meals I have ever eaten in my life. That alone would have made a visit to Rome memorable!

The next day, I was able to take Marcia around and show her the Roman Forum, the Coliseum, and all those other well-known places we had talked about when I was teaching Latin.

Another memorable trip I made on behalf of the United Bible Societies was a visit to East Germany in 1983, before the Brandenburg Gate was opened. I was there as a guest of the East German Bible Society for the celebration of Luther's 500th birthday. Even though at that time most foreign drivers had to stay on the autobahn, we could go everywhere, because Ekkehard Runge, General Secretary of the East German Bible Society, drove me in an East German car.

We went to Naumburg, where we drove through the streets that had been rutted by Russian tanks. We even drove right by the Russian tank encampment located there. I got to see the wonderful cathedral of Naumburg with its beautiful statues. Those statues are smiling. They have become Lutheran!

Even though the East Germans had downplayed Luther and made Thomas Münzer, the leader of the peasant revolt, the bellwether of the Reformation, hundreds of thousands of people turned out for the celebration of Luther's 500th birthday.

For the first time since World War II, the churches had gotten permission to put up posters. What they did was put up only a few words from Luther's explanation of the First Commandment: *Gott über alle Dinge* ("God over all things"), which in the Communist world was a direct challenge to the very basis of the whole regime!

That was also the year of Karl Marx. We drove all over East Germany, and I saw only two signs saying, "This is the Year of

Karl Marx." In contrast, every telephone pole and every bus stop had the *Gott über alle Dinge* posters.

That's when the East German Communist regime began to realize that the jig was up. Finally, and I think thoughtlessly, they allowed a certain number of people to go through the checkpoints without being checked. Almost immediately, they had tens of thousands of people flowing through there. The government did not plan it that way, but that is the way it happened. It must have been exciting to be present there during that time!

THE AUSTRALIA BIBLE SOCIETY AND THE OLIVER BEGUIN MEMORIAL LECTURES

In 1984, I was chosen by the Bible Society in Australia as the Oliver Beguin Memorial Lecturer. The man after whom those lectures was named was a remarkable man. He was a Belgian who reached out in a missionary way with the Bible to German troops, French troops, and British troops during World War II. He did that in all kinds of ways. For example, he went through the prisoner of war camps and gave out Bibles. He was the one to bring the Bible to Uli Fick, who had been a soldier in the German Alpine troops. As a result of that, Fick became a Christian, and after the war became a Lutheran pastor. He later became manager of RVOG in Addis Ababa, Ethiopia, the powerful radio station that "The Lutheran Hour" helped to build. (The call letters stand for "Radio Voice of the Gospel.") That station transmitted Christian radio programs—including our Lutheran Hour programs—all over the third world for 15 or 16 years, until it was nationalized by the government when the Communists took over Ethiopia. When I was elected president of the United Bible Societies, Uli Fick had just been elected General Secretary of the UBS.

I met Oliver Beguin at the first General Council meeting of the United Bible Societies at Driebergen, Holland, in 1964, which

I attended as one of three representatives of the American Bible Society. Beguin conducted that meeting at which Donald Coggan, who was then Archbishop of York, served as chairman.

As the Oliver Beguin lecturer, I spoke all over Australia. My topic was "The Authority and Relevance of the Bible in the Modern World." The subject was Bible translation.

The first lecture was presented at the Academy of Sciences in Canberra. The auditorium was packed. During the question period following the lecture, one of the women who was organizing the reception asked me, "Which do you regard as the best translation of the Scriptures?"

I believe she was asking about English translations, but my reply was, "I think it was Martin Luther's translation."

"But I can't read that," she said.

"I know you can't," was my reply, "but that's an absolutely marvelous translation."

Another man got up and said, "You used the Twenty-third Psalm as an example of how Luther revised his own translation. How did he translate 'though I walk through the valley of the shadow of death' [Psalm 23:4]?"

Fortunately Luther's translation of those verses came to mind right away. His German translation would be translated into English as "in the dark valley." Incidentally, the translators of the King James Version interpreted that passage not as "the valley of death," but as "the valley of *the shadow* of death." The shadow is with us all the time!

Those were three of many memorable international trips for the United Bible Societies. I also made several memorable trips as Lutheran Hour speaker, and on those trips too I met some very interesting people.

17

WITNESSING WITH KINGS AND OTHER WORLD RULERS

On My account you will be brought before governors and kings as witnesses to them and to the Gentiles. ... [D]o not worry about what to say or how to say it. At that time you will be given what to say, for it will not be you speaking, but the Spirit of your Father speaking through you (Matthew 10:18–20 NIV).

In this Bible passage, Jesus actually was talking about people who will be arrested and therefore will have a chance to witness. I was never *arrested,* but I have witnessed before kings and other rulers. I never suspected as a student that such opportunities would be presented to me, but when the Savior opened the way, I was not about to turn Him down.

NORWAY AND KING OLAV

One of the first times I had a chance to speak personally with a national leader of a country other than the U.S. was at the end of a preaching trip in Norway in 1959. Here's how it happened.

Two years earlier, in 1957, at a meeting of the leaders of the Lutheran World Federation just before the LWF Assembly in Minneapolis, Bishop Fridtjov Birkeli of Norway (also head of the LWF Mission Department) proposed a Lutheran radio station that would broadcast the Gospel to Africa and Asia, at least a third of the world. The site chosen: Addis Ababa, Ethiopia. This is the station that ultimately would become RVOG, the "Radio Voice of the

Gospel." Birkeli's interest came in part from his prior experiences as a missionary somewhere in Africa.

Well, we in "The Lutheran Hour" could hardly turn our backs on such a project. After all, at that LWF Assembly Bishop Birkeli had praised "The Lutheran Hour" for its mission work and used the Hour as an example of what a new station could do for spreading the Gospel. I was at that meeting as part of a large delegation of LCMS observers appointed by President Behnken. (By the way, this all took place while I was still serving as both public relations director for Synod and as "The Lutheran Hour" speaker.)

Building such a station would take time and money (it would take until July 1963, before Emperor Selassie would officially open the station), and since Birkeli thought up the idea, he thought that his own Church of Norway should start the fund drive. As part of that, he asked me to conduct a preaching tour of Norway to raise funds for the station. I was more than happy to do so. I preached in almost every bishopric in Norway, from Oslo all the way up to Tromsøo in the Arctic Circle, which the Germans took over during World War II.

In the home of Lutheran Bishop Norderwald in Tromsøo hung a picture of former King Haakon and the then Crown Prince Olav meeting with the cabinet for the last time before they left for England. That meeting had been held in the Bishop's dining room after the German invasion of Norway during World War II.

Norderwald was a great man. He had been a seaman's pastor. He would often be out on a ship for three months ministering to the men on board. He said that those seaman, as rough as they had to be to face the perils of the North Sea, were often great Christians.

Now Norderwald was bishop in Tromsøo, deep in the North Country along the Arctic Coast. His diocese included the Lapps, even those in the Soviet Union. He went over into the Soviet Union, and nobody ever bothered him. It was so far north that there were no customs stations or checkpoints up there.

Norderwald told me about a time when he was invited to the palace for the annual dinner that the king gives for the 12 or so bishops of Norway each year. When he got there, he remembered that he had forgotten the medal that the king had given him. He asked the aide whether it would be possible to go back down to the hotel to get that medal, because he was sure the king would notice that he was not wearing it.

The aide said, "Sure, you should still have time."

Now, you have to picture that the palace sits high on a hill. The road down winds around a set of steps that go straight down from the palace to the plaza at the bottom.

Norderwald jumped into his Volkswagen and drove right down the steps—187 steps to the bottom! The only thing that was damaged was the tailpipe when he hit the bottom. The king had been looking out the window and saw this.

"Norderwald," the king said at lunch, "what were you thinking when you went down those steps?"

Norderwald, who always had presence of mind, said, "I thought I'd be the first man in history to drive down these steps."

"Unfortunately, that's not true," the king said. "A lawyer tried it two years ago and was seriously injured."

I preached in Norderwald's church in Tromsøo. It was a frame cathedral built in the year A.D. 900. When I finished preaching, there was a terrible crash, but no one seemed very excited about it. A picture of the Virgin Mary on the opposite wall from the pulpit had come crashing down.

"Oh," Norderwald said nonchalantly, "that's happened before."

When I finished my preaching tour, King Olav invited me to come and see him. I went by cab from my hotel to his palace, and as far as I could tell I was the only one invited. I was met by an Air Force captain who was the aide to the king. He said, "The king has someone in there right now."

The man who had been with the king came out and introduced himself to me. "I'm Folke Johannson," he said—the admiral of the Norwegian Navy and commander of NATO for all of northern Europe at that time. This important man was the one who took me around the palace, showing me all the gifts on display there that had been given to the king.

Finally the captain who was the king's aide came up to us and said to me apologetically, "The king is waiting to see you."

I went in, and we started talking right away. I complimented him on his English, and he said, "I should be able to talk English well. English was my first language. My mother was an English princess." His father, King Haakon, had married the granddaughter of Queen Victoria!

We talked about the Roman Catholic Church. "It's so brittle," he said, "because they failed to confront the issues that faced them in the 16th century."

He told me about his grandchildren who had come back from Brazil to be confirmed in the Lutheran Church of Norway. (His daughter had married a man from Brazil.) The king told me that his grandchildren had taken their confirmation examination and passed it with flying colors. He was very proud of them.

That reminded me of Bishop Eivind Berggrav, who had died shortly before my visit with the king. He had been the Presiding Bishop of the Lutheran Church in Norway, the first president of the United Bible Societies, a president of the World Council of Churches, the leading theologian in Norway in the first half of the 20th century, and the leading pastor to organize church resistance against the Nazi occupation in WWII (which brought him imprisonment from 1942 to 1945).

I include this background so that the reader can understand in contrast his gentle, shepherding heart when it came time to go around the diocese confirming the classes, which had been instructed by the pastors. The following story that Berggrav told is one that I passed on to the king.

At one place the local pastor told the bishop that there was one older boy in the class who had been left behind. He had not passed the examination for the last two years.

"You'll know him," they said, "because he's so much bigger than the others."

The bishop examined the children. When he came to this boy, he looked for a question that would be simple enough that the boy could answer it.

"Do you know anything about God?" the bishop asked him. The boy stood on one foot, and he stood on the other foot. He smiled and said that he didn't know anything about God.

Bishop Berggrav was embarrassed, and he searched for a question that the boy could answer.

"Do you know anything about Jesus Christ?" he asked the boy.

"Oh, yes," the boy said. "I know about Jesus Christ."

"I learned a lesson that day," the bishop said. "And that is that you should never talk about God except in Jesus Christ."

On a different topic, I shared with the king an observation I made while on my preaching tour of Norway: "I've talked to your people—taxi drivers, all kinds of other people—they all have great respect for you. They tell me that they can be in the supermarket checking out their groceries, and the king may be there in line right behind them checking out his groceries. They respect you, and they love you too." When I said that, his eyes filled with tears.

Our interview was after the two visits of our astronauts to the moon. I said to King Olav, "You know, your people were much impressed with our astronauts. The first group up there read, 'In the beginning God created the heaven and the earth' [Genesis 1:1 KJV], and the second group coming back said, 'What is man, that Thou art mindful of him? and the Son of Man, that Thou visitest Him?' " [Psalm 8:4 KJV].

251

"No one told them that they had to do that," I said to him, "and no one told them they could not do it either. That's what we have in our country. Freedom of religion. But one thing our astronauts did not do," I said to him. "They did not take Jesus Christ to the moon."

At that, his face fell.

"Christ was there when they got there," I said with a chuckle. "He is Lord of heaven and earth!"

That's the way we talked for 45 minutes. It was wonderful.

Christmas in Norway

Our Lutheran Hour Christmas special in 1970 was "Christmas in Norway." We wanted to do that because of all the marvelous Norwegian Christmas customs such as the Santa Lucia festival. That's the one in which the oldest girl in the family brings in breakfast for her parents 12 days before Christmas with a regular procession of the children through the household. We also wanted to use the great music of Norwegian and Swedish composers. It is interesting that much of the music sung in Norway is by Swedish composers, although there are great Norwegian composers, like Edvard H. Grieg, who adapted a folktune into the melody for "Behold a Host Arrayed in White."

On our "Christmas in Norway" special, I did an interview with Bishop Birkeli, who was by then the primate of The Lutheran Church of Norway. I thoroughly enjoyed getting back together with him.

When I interviewed him for the Christmas special, he told me about how he had lost one kidney to infection, and then his other kidney had become infected. That was shortly after WWII, in a day when they did not have kidney transplants or other treatments that we have today. If the kidney had failed at that time, he would have died. He said they brought him over to the United States to the Mayo

Clinic in Rochester, Minnesota, and gave him the first little bit of streptomycin that had been developed. They had only an ounce and a half or so, but they tried it out on him—and it worked! As a result, he went back to Norway well. That had happened about 25 years before our interview, and by that time he had become the presiding bishop of The Lutheran Church of Norway.

After that Christmas broadcast, I got a letter from a doctor at the Mayo Clinic in which he told me that he was the intern who administered the streptomycin to Bishop Birkeli when he was in the United States 25 years before. "I pulled out his file," the doctor wrote, "and I made a notation that now 25 years later he was still alive, and I listened to him on 'The Lutheran Hour.' "

I was very impressed with King Olav and with Bishop Birkeli. You have to be impressed with the Lutherans in Norway. They have always been a vital group, more so than in most of the northern countries. The proof is that the bishops and pastors are always arguing with each other about some point of theology. That shows something is alive there in that part of the world.

People have the idea that the faith is dead in the Scandinavian countries, but the faith is never dead in countries like that. The church may be dead, but the faith never is.

HAILE SELASSIE AND ETHIOPIA

The first emperor with whom I "worked" in connection with the "Christmas in ..." specials for "The Lutheran Hour" was Haile Selassie, the emperor of Ethiopia. I had the privilege of interviewing him for the first special, "Christmas in Ethiopia," broadcast in December 1968. At the time, Ethiopia was a Christian country (and had been since the fourth century), and the Selassie family claimed to be descendants from King Solomon and the Queen of Sheba.

I did the interview with Haile Selassie at the Jubilee Palace, which is near the old hotel where I was staying in Addis Ababa. Although the emperor spoke fairly fluent English, protocol demanded that he speak in Amharic and be translated. I could see the palace from the hotel. I could also hear dogs barking at night. That was rather disquieting, because I always wondered what might be causing the dogs to bark, maybe two or three miles away. I was told those dogs were a part of the palace security system.

When it came time to do the interview, I was taken by car to the Jubilee Palace. There we had the interview, just the emperor and I—and a little dog, the emperor's personal companion, walking around between our feet all during the time the interview was going on.

I had been instructed that I was to back out of the emperor's presence when we finished the interview, but, as it turned out, I did not have to do that. The emperor was going to visit a friend in the hospital, and we walked out together. Outside a big limousine was waiting to take him to the hospital. There were also two big mastiffs out there, barking and jumping around.

We were standing in the foyer of the palace, and I said to him, "You have a great protector here!"

He looked at me rather puzzled, and I pointed to the little dog. He laughed and then got into the limousine to go to the hospital. I left too. That night, the emperor's chamberlain brought over to the hotel a beautiful bracelet made of gold and engraved with the emperor's insignia for me to take to Marcia.

Sometime later, I went to the Ethiopian embassy in Washington, D.C., to deliver a copy of the record of "Christmas in Ethiopia" for transmission to the emperor. The Rev. Dr. Lambert Brose went with me and gave me precise instructions about exactly what I was to do when I met with the Ethiopian ambassador. I should greet him, then Lambert would unwrap the package, and so on. In those years Lambert was the associate director of the News Bureau of the

Lutheran Council in the U.S.A., a cooperative agency of the LCMS, the Lutheran Church in America, and the American Lutheran Church. Brose, with his office in Washington, D.C., and a longtime writer-editor for the Synod's Armed Services Commission, was as "up" on protocol as I was back in the '50s when I was public relations director and often visited Washington.

When Brose and I got into the embassy, the ambassador just happened to be in the outer room and said, "Oh, Dr. Hoffmann! I was the interpreter for the program. Let's go into my office!" That pretty much took care of the protocol Brose had tried to get me to follow! The ambassador himself opened the package, and that was that!

About half of the Ethiopian ambassadors at that time were Lutheran. I met many of them when I preached in their church in Addis Ababa. There were about a thousand people in that service. The whole church was filled. One long bench that ran the length of the church against the wall was filled with ambassadors, supreme court justices, and other government officials.

In that service, Ato Emanuel Gabre Selassie (no relation to the emperor) translated my sermon sentence by sentence into Amharic. He was a very good interpreter who also interpreted for the British embassy and for the Lutheran radio station in Ethiopia, RVOG (Radio Voice of the Gospel).

During my sermon, I told one story that had a funny punch line. When I came to the punch line, about 30 percent of the audience laughed. Then Ato Emanuel interpreted it, and the other part of the audience laughed. You know you have a good interpreter when he can translate humor into another language!

Six years later, when the United Bible Societies met in Addis Ababa in 1974, Haile Selassie spoke at one of the sessions. He was well over 80 years old by that time, and he read his speech in English. After his speech, Ato Abraham, another Lutheran who was Selassie's minister of communication, came striding across as representative of the emperor to indicate who would be the first people to greet the emperor. The very first ones he picked were Marcia and me.

When we went over to greet the emperor, I said to Marcia, "Show him your bracelet." When she did, he said, "I see you've been here before!"

FERDINAND AND IMELDA MARCOS IN THE PHILIPPINES

In 1970, in connection with a trip to Vietnam to visit the troops during the Christmas season, the producers of "The Lutheran Hour" arranged for me to stop in the Philippines to do an interview with President and Mrs. Marcos. The producers wanted that interview for a Lutheran Hour Christmas special they were planning for the following year, "Christmas in the Philippines."

We were ushered first into President Marcos' office, where the recording equipment had been set up. After being introduced to us, the president asked an attendant where Mrs. Marcos was. The attendant left, and soon Imelda Marcos, beautifully dressed, made her grand entrance.

President Marcos then said, "Let's go into the music room"— which meant that we had to transfer all the recording equipment to that room. As it turned out, the music room held a big Christmas tree, which made a great background for publicity photos— which may be why he wanted to move in there, even though this was a radio interview. At any rate, both of the Marcos contributed to the interview, speaking perfect English. It was a good interview.

Later on, the Marcos unfortunately got into ways characteristic of some of life in the Philippines, and that was their downfall. But at the time of the interview, they spoke very highly of Christ and of His coming at Christmas.

In 1958, Hoffmann and John W. Boehne, a member of Synod's Board of Directors and the Board for Public Relations, present to President Dwight D. Eisenhower a special leather bound copy of Hoffmann's newly released book *Prayers for Peace*.

Dr. Hoffmann receives best wishes from Senator Warren G. Magnuson prior to Hoffmann's 1960 trip behind the Iron and Bamboo curtains. Magnuson was chairman of the Senate Interstate and Foreign Commerce Committee.

In 1960, Congressman Walter Moeller, Ohio *(seated)*, arranged for Dr. Hoffmann to meet privately in Moeller's office with presidential candidate John F. Kennedy.

In 1971, Dr. Hoffmann chatted with President Nixon at the White House, giving a personal report on his recent visit to Vietnam and Korea. During the visit, Dr. Hoffmann presented to the president a specially inscribed copy of the recently published *Psalms for Modern Man* in Today's English Version.

Dr. Hoffmann and Suzanne Johnson stopped in Chu Lai during their 1969 Christmas tour to Vietnam. Accompanying them was their escort, Chaplain (Col.) Hunt.

In Vietnam, Dr. Hoffmann made it a point to visit with the men. Two of them from the greater St. Louis, Missouri, area were William H. Ratliff (*left*) and Bob Finck (*below*).

Brig. Gen. Gerhardt W. Hyatt, deputy chief of chaplains *(center)*, presents LLL President Thomas McDougall *(left)* a thankoffering check from Lutheran military congregations for allowing Dr. Hoffmann to make the 1971 Christmas tour to Vietnam and Korea.

On September 13, 1980, Dr. Hoffmann received the Secretary of Defense Award for Outstanding Service for his many years of service to the military. Congratulating Dr. Hoffmann is General John W. Vessey, vice-chief of staff, U.S. Army. Hoffmann first met General Vessey on Christmas Day in 1970, while visiting the U.S. troops in Vietnam during the holidays. At that time Vessey was commander of the Army in Thailand.

Dr. Hoffmann and John Meredythe Lucas, the director, discuss the script and staging of the 1984 movie *Yeshua* as they stand on a gigantic map of the Mediterranean area.

In *Yeshua,* Hoffmann shows how the inscription of Jesus' cross might have looked. The words, dictated by Pilate, say in Aramaic, Latin, and Greek, "Jesus of Nazareth, king of the Jews."

Dr. Hoffmann stands beside a model radio tower that honors those who contribute $1,000 or more to the Lutheran Hour Endowment Fund, honoring Dr. Hoffmann.

Dr. Hoffmann, now honorary Lutheran Hour speaker, with *(left)* Dr. Wallace Schulz, associate Lutheran Hour speaker, and *(right)* Dr. Dale Meyer, Lutheran Hour speaker.

The annual OCJH White River Float Trip has been a highlight for Ossie as well as many of his close friends. The 1988 group includes *(left to right)* Rupert Dunklau, Harry Barr, Dick Barr, Will Hyatt, Larry Barr, Bob Peregrine, John Drager, John Hoffmann, Larry Knutson, Ralph Reinke, Ossie Hoffmann, and Walter Rugland. Tom Barr took the picture.

At the *Schlachtfest* in Frankenmuth, Michigan, on the Adolph Riess farm, Ossie spreads the spices over the meat before grinding it into sausage. The fest has been carried on for some 20 years.

Marcia and Oswald Hoffmann, married Sunday, June 23, 1940.

THE KING OF TONGA

I also did an interesting interview with the king of Tonga for our "Christmas in the South Pacific" special in 1973. The king was a regular listener to "The Lutheran Hour," as is almost everyone else out there. The 150-island kingdom, about 2,000 miles northeast of Sydney, Australia, has been Christian since the mid-1800s.

King Taufa' ahau Tupou IV (whose name I never could pronounce) weighed about 375 pounds. His prime minister was his brother. He was not that heavy. In his younger years, the prime minister had been a great rugby football player for England. He had such tremendous legs that Marcia simply could not take her eyes off them!

The prime minister had a reception for us when we came. The food was supplied by the Australians and was served to the guests by Tongans. Since the servers could not pass in front of the prime minister, they went around and came in the back way to serve us.

Marcia and I sat with the prime minister, and everybody who came in from the front scooted in on his behind. They were not forced to do that, but did it as a sign of respect for the prime minister.

When they were preparing the recording equipment for my interview with the king, the people setting up the equipment all scooted around on their rear ends too. Then we did the interview, and it went very well.

After we had finished the interview, the king asked me about a book he had been reading. It was a book written by a German and translated into English. (Someone has remarked that if a theologian in Germany sneezes, theologians throughout the world get pneumonia!) The book, about the death of Christ, claimed that maybe He did not really die. The king wanted to know about that.

"That's not the story in the New Testament," I told him. "You listen to our broadcasts all the time," I said, "and you hear it all the time. When we talk about Him dying, you can be sure He really died. He didn't just look as if He died."

While I did the interview with the king, Marcia and the queen sat out in the dining room of the palace with all the windows open. Tonga is in the hot part of the South Pacific, but they have the prevailing westerly winds. The open windows made the place comfortable.

By the way, the king is the son of Queen Salote Tupou III (who ruled from 1918 to 1965). She was the one who at the coronation of Queen Elizabeth, which was on a very rainy day, did not ride in a closed carriage but stood up in the open and greeted the crowds. Because of that, people all over the British Empire remembered Queen Salote. The best-known girls school on the islands is named "Queen Salote College."

We went to visit the college and to tape the young women's choir for the program. There was one American out there. Her name was Mrs. Schudt. Her son is a three-star Air Force general who used to fly Air Force One in the Nixon days. I saw him later at a Christmas service I spoke for at the Pentagon.

After a long career as a teacher of English in the United States, Mrs. Schudt had joined the Peace Corps at age 76. She was the most honored citizen in the whole realm. At Queen Salote College we sat beside her while the girls all sat on the floor—maybe 250 of them—and sang like angels for us.

That night they had a reception for us. There 700 singers sang three selections from the *Messiah* without any music in front of them—and sang beautifully. They use the solfa system for teaching and memorizing music, in which tones are represented by the syllables of the scale. Often they do not use music at all.

After they sang, they asked me to speak. I did not know I was supposed to speak and had not prepared anything, but I got up and started by saying, "Well, I know what the angels at Bethlehem did after they left. They came here!"

I preached on Sunday to 2,000 people. The royal family was there, and the whole cabinet was sitting in front.

When we were getting ready to leave the country, the prime minister, the king's brother, came over to our hotel to say good-bye to us. That's when something interesting happened that we were not even aware of at the time.

The prime minister had his aide with him, who was carrying the minister's things. "You know, it's so warm down here," I said, "why don't we go up to our room where we have air-conditioning?"

"Sure," the prime minister said. "Let's do that."

Later I found out that was the first time the members of the hotel staff had ever seen a member of the royal family go to a room and visit with anybody in their hotel. They always met with people in a public room downstairs.

SAMOA

After we left Tonga, we went to Samoa and then to Fiji. In Samoa, we met the wife of the prime minister. She invited us to dinner, but I told her we could not come because we had a previous engagement with people at the radio station. She finagled it, however, that we had to go and see her anyway.

We went with her to this small village with four large houses that belonged to the four families from which the prime ministers come. All kinds of huts surrounded each large house. We spent most of the evening there. I thought we were just going out to have a drink of Coca Cola with them, but when we were ushered into the dining room, there was a full dinner. The radio station people with whom we were supposed to have dinner knew what had happened. They just had to wait with eating dinner until we got back.

Well, that's the way it works. You are not always exactly sure what is going to happen. You play it by ear. My ear had to be tuned in those days!

THE RULERS IN TAIWAN

Since the last true emperor of China was deposed in the late 1800s, the Chinese rulers I could visit with would have to be ordinary mortals. One of those visits, however, was only two steps removed from the last emperor.

In December of 1978, I was in Taiwan for two events in celebration of the 25th anniversary of the China Lutheran Hour. A week or so before the first of those, I went down from Taipei (the capital, at the north end of Taiwan) to a place on the seacoast to inaugurate the new translation of the Old Testament that the Presbyterians had done. The next day I read in the paper that the moment our plane had left Taipei, there was an earthquake there.

A day or so later I was having dinner with the 95-year-old daughter of the famous Sun Yet Sen and with two or three other people. I was quite honored to be invited to the dinner. Sun Yet Sen was the father of the nationalist movement in China following the overthrow of the last emperor. He also provided the philosophical basis for modernizing China: the "Three Principles of the People"—nationalism, democracy, and economic security for all. When he died in 1925, Sun was president of the new China and mentor for Chiang Kai-shek, who should have ruled all China, had he not been pushed onto Taiwan by Mao Tse-tung. Anyway, that was my two steps from the emperor: to Sun Yet Sen, then to his daughter.

At this dinner, James Shen, the former Taiwanese ambassador to Washington, D.C., was sitting next to me. I asked Shen, who was not a Christian, "How does it feel to be in an earthquake?"

"Well," he said, "it makes you think about things."

His observation was not unusual, but it would serve me well about a week later at a Christmas program for the older people of Taipei, sponsored by the China Lutheran Hour. The event was attended by 2,000 people, 90 percent of whom were non-Christian. We began the program by saying, "We Christians simply want to greet you on our day of celebration when the Lord Christ was born, and we want you to know that we would like you to have the joy that we have. We greet you on this day as your friends, and we wish you all things good."

I was scheduled to speak at the end of a three-hour program that included dancing, singing, and other forms of entertainment, all very properly done. Sometime during the program, I said to Steve Tsui, my interpreter, "I don't think anybody will be here anymore to hear me speak."

"Not a soul will leave until you speak," he said, "because they came here to hear you."

That was true. Even after three hours, none of those present had left. That just shows how other cultures can differ from ours!

Before I got up to speak, I was wondering how I was going to attract the attention of those people who had been sitting there all those hours. Then I thought about what had happened to me the previous week. I asked Steven, "Would I be out of line if I mentioned that earthquake you had here?"

"No," he said, "that would be the thing to do. That would focus their attention right away."

When I got up to speak, I began, "I'm here to greet you from the Christians of Taiwan. I hear you have earthquakes."

When Steven interpreted that, everyone's face lit up. I told them about my conversation with the former ambassador. Then I reused a favorite quote of mine. I said, "That reminds me of Samuel Johnson's statement about hanging." Steven interpreted that. Then I repeated what Johnson said, "It wonderfully clarifies the mind!"

Steven had to laugh even before he interpreted that. Then he interpreted it, and everybody laughed. With that, the audience was with us, and we got to the message right away. I told them that the Lord came to this earth, a place where we have earthquakes, sickness, and sorrow, the results of all the things we do wrong. I told them it was into this real world that Christ was born as a baby. I was able to give them a nice little Christian talk. And they listened to it raptly.

The other main event celebrating the 25th anniversary of the China Lutheran Hour was a rally three days later, on December 15, at Sun Yet Sen Auditorium in Taipei, which seats about 2,500 people. Marcia was there with me. They seated her in the front row next to Mrs. Lee Teng-hui, wife of the provincial governor of Taiwan. On the day before the rally, Mrs. Lee went out with Marcia and bought for her a red Chinese dress. She brought it to the rally, and Marcia had to go into one of the dressing rooms in the auditorium to put it on. It was slit up to the thighs, which is the way Chinese dresses are. They need to be that way so that they can walk in them. It looked mighty good on Marcia!

That December, George Beverly Shea and his pianist, Ted Weiss, were coming back from a Billy Graham Crusade in Singapore. Henry Go, who was the manager of the China Lutheran Hour at that time, had been the manager of a previous Billy Graham Crusade in Taiwan. He asked them to participate in our Lutheran Hour rally, and they did.

I've met George Beverly Shea many times since then at Billy Graham Schools of Evangelism, and he always recalls with pleasure that stop in Taiwan. His first wife died, and he has been married again. It was during that time just after his first wife died that he participated in that Lutheran Hour rally. It was a comforting experience for him.

And a Third Step from the Emperor of China

During one of my visits to Taiwan I had the chance to talk with Chiang Ching-kuo, the son of General Chiang Kai-shek. The General was one of the military leaders under Sun Yet Sen and became president of all China about the time WWII was beginning. As it turned out, he and his supporters were pushed out of mainland China in 1949 and were relegated to Taiwan, where he ruled until 1975. Shortly after that, his son, Chiang Ching-kuo, was elected president.

The son, Chiang Ching-kuo, was not a Christian, although his stepmother was a Christian. Because of her, his father became a Christian too. Chiang Ching-kuo said to me, "The Bible must be one of the most important books in the whole world, because in every house in every village I go to, there is a Bible."

Another leader of the Republic of China (Taiwan) I came to know is Lee Teng-hui. (His wife was the lady who sat next to Marcia at "The Lutheran Hour" rally.) As I mentioned, in 1978 he was the governor of Taiwan Province. He is an agricultural expert who got his Ph.D. at Cornell University and was a professor before being called into politics. He is a Christian, one of the 10 percent of the population of Taiwan that embraces the Christian faith. In 1984 he became vice-president of the Republic, and Chiang Ching-kuo became president. What an honor that, while in Taiwan for the 30th anniversary of the China Lutheran Hour in May of 1984, Marcia and I, at the invitation and expense of the new government, attended their inaugurations! By the way, Mr. Lee was elected president in 1988 upon the death of Chiang Ching-kuo. We have visited with him on several occasions since that time.

TRAVELS IN THE CARIBBEAN

The only royalty I met in the Caribbean were the kings and priests in the kingdom of God. That is not disappointing, though. Christ Himself said, "Where two or three come together in My name, there am I with them" (Matthew 18:20 NIV).

I was privileged to travel to the Caribbean several times. The first trip was in 1969, when I spoke to a meeting of AAL general agents. Elmer Knoernschild, LLL Director of Programming, wanted to do one of our Lutheran Hour Christmas specials from Jamaica. I stayed there for a few days after that meeting to see whether I could arrange that. I took a taxi from Ocho Rios, where the AAL meeting had been held, across the island to Kingston in order to visit with the Governor General of Jamaica, Sir Clifford Campbell, at the King's House, official residence of the Governor General. I went to see him to find out whether he would do an interview for the program.

When I asked him about doing the interview, he said, "Sure. We could just do the interview now, right here."

If I had brought recording equipment and someone to run it that day, we could have done that, but we did not. We had to go back later to Jamaica to record for the 1972 broadcasting of "Christmas in the Caribbean." On that trip, I spoke to a pastors meeting, and found out that "The Lutheran Hour" was the second most popular program of any kind on the air in Jamaica.

When I got in the cab to go from Ocho Rios to Kingston and told the cab driver where I wanted to go, he asked me whether I would mind if he stopped at the taxi stand first. I told him that would be all right.

When we stopped at the taxi stand, he brought all the taxi drivers over to meet me and shake hands with me. That was the only reason he stopped there. He had recognized my voice, and he wanted the other drivers to meet me. They had "The Lutheran Hour" on in their taxis every Sunday morning!

While I was in Kingston, one of the most popular disc jockeys there asked me to be on his program. He picked me up early in the morning before breakfast, and we went over to the station to do the program. When we pulled up at the station in his Jaguar sports car, there were about 50 people standing outside.

"Are you always greeted with a bunch of people like that when you arrive at the station?" I asked him.

"They're not here to greet me," he said. "They're here to greet you!"

That's the way it is in Jamaica. They love "The Lutheran Hour." We had some people in our congregation at St. Matthew's in New York from Jamaica. Their name happened to be Campbell, the same as the prime minister of the country, but they were not related. The man was a cameraman for NBC. They went back to Jamaica and, when they got there, they told people there that I was the assistant pastor at their church. People in Jamaica would not believe them, because they were hearing me on the radio every Sunday. Some of them were convinced that I was somewhere right close by.

It's the same way all over the Caribbean. Everyone listens to "The Lutheran Hour." On Sunday morning you can walk down the street in the shopping areas and hear "The Lutheran Hour" in stereo. The shopkeepers on both sides of the street have radios in front of their places of business, and all of them are tuned to "The Lutheran Hour."

When we had a Lutheran Hour rally at the ball park on St. Thomas, one-sixth of the population of the entire island turned out. The place was absolutely jammed with people swinging and swaying to the music and having a good time.

In 1992 I was at a service at our Lutheran church in Nassau in the Bahamas for the celebration of the 500th anniversary of the coming of Columbus. The prime minister and the governor general were there. So were the president of the senate and the members of parliament. The church was jammed with people for that special occasion.

After that service I went and visited prisoners at two jails. They did not have to come to see me, but more than half of them did. There must have been about 100–125 in each place. They sang hymns enthusiastically and were grateful that I had come to talk to them.

After that I had a few hours before my plane was to leave. I went to the shopping area near the wharf where the ships come in. I started to buy things, and the woman at the place where I first stopped gave me a great big bag. She recognized my voice and said, "You're the one. You're the speaker on 'The Lutheran Hour.' "

As I went around doing my shopping, they would not let me buy anything. They just put things in my bag without charging me for them. They gave me all kinds of handcrafts and other things like that. The only thing I had to pay for was some perfume that I bought for Marcia.

The people in the Caribbean appreciate "The Lutheran Hour" because they know that we are bringing them the true Word of God. We represent no one but our Lord Jesus Christ. We proclaim the Gospel of the Lord and Savior, Jesus Christ.

TWO OTHER TRIPS

England

I commented earlier that the church in Norway may suffer from small attendance, but the faith of the people is strong. That is true also in England, where there is often pitiful church attendance. A strong strain of evangelical faith runs through the people of England too. That accounts for the large audience we had during the time when the English language "Bringing Christ to the Nations" program was being broadcast there.

I was there in 1966 on an eight-day tour through England, Ireland, and Scotland with the chorus of Concordia Seminary-Springfield, Illinois, directed by Fred Precht. Bill Kniffel had organized that tour, and he did his usual masterful job. Even then, some people did not know very far ahead of time that we were going to be there.

That was true in Plymouth, England, where the Plymouth Brethren come from. They did not know we were going to be there, except from the announcement at the end of "The Lutheran Hour" broadcast from Luxembourg the week before. When we got there, there were a thousand people in attendance. They filled the hall.

The Gospel does work!

India

Once when I was in India, I had the opportunity to proclaim the Gospel over national television. It was sometime around Easter, and I was interviewed for 15 minutes by an Anglican pastor who had been ostracized by his Hindu Brahmin family because he had become a Christian. He told me that in spite of that, he never regretted his decision to become a Christian.

Our interview was a rather historic occasion. It was the first broadcast on which anyone representing the Christian faith was allowed to speak on national television.

As I reminisce on these events, I recall again my 1988 visit back to the town of my birth (Snyder, Nebraska), which I mentioned in chapter 2. Inside, I *am* just a small-town preacher's kid, and I was as overwhelmed as anyone to be asked to interview and witness to Jesus with these world rulers. On the other hand, the Lord had prepared me through the years as a public relations person so that I was not so awed that I would hem and haw or stammer in their presence. Underneath the pomp and the office, these people were the same as I: sinners in need of the magnificent forgiveness won by Jesus Christ. That's what I was there to say, and that's what I said. After that, what more is there to say?

18

WITNESSING AND THE MILITARY

M
Y INVOLVEMENT WITH THE UNITED STATES MILITARY BEGAN IN February 1958, when Martin Poch, one of our LCMS chaplains, was senior chaplain for all the military in Alaska. He had invited me to come to Alaska to speak at all the military installations in the territory. (That was also the year Alaska became our 49th state.)

After a brief start at the University of Alaska in Fairbanks, I believe we went next to Ladd Air Force Base just outside Fairbanks. As some may recall, 1957 was in the midst of the Cold War. Ladd AFB was the post where we had all our warning signals to detect aircraft flying over Alaska from the Soviet Union. There was a big glass display board there that showed what kind of plane it was, how fast it was flying, at what altitude, and everything else. In those days, that was all done by hand. People wrote backward on one side of a glass wall, and people on the other side could read what they had written. Only a very few people were allowed to go in there. They let me go in and view it in operation during an exercise. (By the way, in about 1960, Ladd AFB in Fairbanks was moved to different land nearby and renamed Eielson AFB; Ladd's property was converted to Fort Wainwright Army Base. That's how it is today.)

On Sunday morning I preached three times in the Anchorage area: at Fort Richardson, at Elmendorf Air Base, and at Anchorage

Lutheran Church. After lunch Pastor Joe Frenz and his wife drove me up to Palmer (about 40 miles north) in the ice and snow. We saw several moose along the way. I preached at Palmer in the afternoon at the little log church. Then in the evening we had a Lutheran Hour rally back at Anchorage's Lawrence Auditorium.

The next day the Air Force took me down to Kodiak Island (about 300 miles south-southwest), where there was a naval base at that time. The trip there was very interesting. The two officers who were flying me out there were Air Force men who were "getting in their hours" with some tough flying. The runway at Kodiak ran directly from the sea right up against the mountains. If you came in for a landing, you *had* to land. You could not go up again, or you would crash into the big mountain at the end of the runway. We landed at Kodiak controlled solely by instruments, and we made it just fine.

At Kodiak, I watched the fishermen bringing in king crab and dumping them out of the boat. I also visited with the Russian Orthodox priest there. He had been a Russian merchant marine captain and had left that occupation to become a priest. As you may know, the Russian Orthodox Church was the first church in Alaska, and some of the Eskimos learned to speak Russian very well. Therefore, I asked the priest, "On Sunday morning, in which language is your service conducted?"

"Before the service I look out to see whether the congregation is mostly young or old," he said. "If it's mostly old, I conduct the service in Russian. If it's mostly young, I conduct the service in English."

After Martin Poch invited me to make that trip to Alaska, word got around, and I began getting all kinds of invitations to speak to military personnel. I spoke at military bases, at chaplains retreats, at all of the military academies, and at the Pentagon.

On a later trip to Alaska, I was taken by helicopter to an alternate command post on the DEW Line, about 100 miles north of

Fairbanks. (The DEW Line covered the outer defenses of the U.S. against attack.) While we were flying up to that post, we went low over the woods to see a herd of moose. When we landed at our destination, we were met by a junior officer who said, "We're very sorry, but this is the alternate command post, and you won't be able to go inside, because an alert has been called, and everything's going on here that usually goes on farther south."

"I can understand that," I said. "I am a member of the Federal Civil Defense Religious Advisory Committee. I have to pass security and everything else like that. I know what you're talking about."

Ten minutes later he came back out and said, "Come on in. The commander says it's all right!"

Just to explain, I had been a member of the Federal Civil Defense Religious Advisory Committee in Washington, D.C. This committee consisted of five representatives of churches—persons suggested by the churches and appointed by the United States government—to handle alerts and other emergencies in case of an attack on our country.

The five representatives on the Federal Civil Defense committee were from the Jewish community, the Roman Catholics, the National Council of Churches, the Southern Baptists, and the Missouri Synod. The main purpose of the committee was to see to it that we would be able to perform our spiritual mission if the U.S. ever should be attacked, and that the church would have the same access across the lines as the police or others dealing with the emergency.

The government at first opposed us. They wanted to limit us only to social welfare to protect people after everything had occurred. We and the Roman Catholics said, "Oh, no. We won't stand for that."

A government official came back at us saying, "I thought it was your business to teach people how to live."

"No," the Roman Catholic representative responded, "it's our business to teach people how to die."

I agreed with him about that. He and I had a very fine friendship going at that time, because we had the same interest in seeing that the church was not pushed into being just a social welfare organization but would be able to maintain its spiritual ministry no matter how bad the disaster might be.

I was able to prove that point sometime later during a mock A-bomb attack at 41st Street and Sixth Avenue in New York. I went down there and walked right through the fire lanes, just as anybody would who was there to keep order. Clergy need the same access as any others who deal with an emergency situation.

On one occasion when I was in Alaska, the people at our young Lutheran Church in Homer wanted me to come down and preach there. (Homer is about 200 miles from Anchorage, on the Kenai Peninsula, a drive not always possible in winter.) They said they would pay whatever it cost to get me down there.

I asked whether the Air Force would be willing to take me down there, and they agreed to do that. On the day when we were supposed to go, there was thick fog, and the Air Force notified me that they were not flying at all.

I called the people at Homer and told them that, and they said they would pay for a private plane to bring me down there. I asked the Air Force people with whom I was staying at the time what they would advise me to do.

"We advise you, if the Air Force is not flying, not to fly," they said.

That was good advice. Just before that time one of our leading representatives in Congress, Hale Boggs, tried flying on a day the Air Force was not flying, and he went down. I do not think they ever found his plane.

On another trip to Alaska, I was invited up to Fort Greeley, about 85 miles southeast of Fairbanks. It is not very big, and there are only two chaplains up there, but it is a very specialized place. They are not happy there unless it is 60 below zero! That is where they train our Alpine troops to operate under all kinds of conditions.

Those who go through the training course at Fort Greeley are required to go out and spend three days in the wilderness in that 60 degrees below zero weather and survive having only a revolver and a box of matches. They have to build an ice pillbox for themselves, just big enough for a man to crawl into for the night.

They told me that the worst part of that experience is right before you crawl in to spend the night in this little igloo you have built. You have to take off all your clothes, otherwise you'll freeze to death. They said that you make a block of ice to cover the doorway into the place. If you take off all your clothes your body heat will keep you warm enough so that you can sleep comfortably. Then you can get up in the morning, and put your clothes back on. You then go out and look for a rabbit to shoot, which you can cook for your breakfast on a fire started with your matches. They said that it takes a lot of faith to follow the instructions to take off your clothes.

SPEAKING AT THE PENTAGON

Because of my initial contacts with visiting the troops, I was asked many times to speak at the Pentagon also—for Good Friday, Easter, Christmas, and other times. The last time I spoke at the Pentagon was for their Christmas service, December 1993. They gave me a little plaque as a memento of the occasion.

One Good Friday I was speaking there to about 1,500 to 2,000 people on the concourse. At the beginning of my sermon, I said, "Today there is no rank. We are all equal at the foot of the cross." General Lyman L. Lemnitzer, a Lutheran who was commander of all the NATO forces in Europe was sitting there in the congregation. Afterwards he came up to me and said, "I'm so glad you said that!"

I also preached at the Pentagon about a month or two after the Vietnam Memorial was put up. The chaplains took me to see it, and I found it very moving to read all those names. But I knew that many of the people at the Pentagon did not like that monument.

When I got up to speak, I said, "I was just down at the Vietnam monument, and I think it's wonderful. For once, we don't have a general sitting on a horse, but we have the names of the troops." There was a three-star Air Force general sitting in the front row. "No harm intended, General," I said, and he laughed.

I can talk that way to the military. I think it is because the Lord gave me a facility for talking to men. I had been dean of men at Bethany College, had coached basketball at Bethany College, and had a lot of experience in dealing with men. They recognized that I could speak to them man to man.

I can do that because they are real people. There is very little sham in the military, even in the highest ranks. Officers are really interested in the troops. It is that way at the Pentagon too. It is filled with very human people—who also are very honorable people. They will not lie to you. Everything is very straightforward. That was especially true about two military men who became close friends of mine: Jack Vessey and Will Hyatt.

GENERAL JOHN "JACK" VESSEY, CHAIRMAN OF THE JOINT CHIEFS OF STAFF

I first met General Vessey on Christmas Day in 1970, while visiting the U.S. troops in Vietnam during the holidays. At that time he was commander of the Army in Thailand. I and the rest of my group had left Vietnam Christmas morning at 6:00 A.M. in an Army plane to go to Bangkok and U Tapao, the air base in Thailand from which the B-52s took off to carry out their missions in Laos and Vietnam. We had a Christmas service at U Tapao at 10 o'clock.

General Vessey, attending with some of his troops, invited me to lunch with his staff afterwards.

During our conversation at lunch, he made what seemed to me to be an impulsive statement: that he was going to retire from the Army. Then, without allowing time for any reaction, he looked over at my plate and said, "Where's your steak sandwich?"

I said, "I guess somebody else must have eaten it while we were talking."

General Vessey left the table and went out to the kitchen.

One of his staff members said, "I'll bet you're going to get your steak sandwich in about 30 seconds!"

General Vessey came back from the kitchen, after giving me a little time to think about what he had told us about his retiring from the Army. I said to him something that I had learned myself in life, "Why don't you let the Lord decide that?"

A little later he said to me, "You know, I think I'm going to do that."

Everybody around the table was looking very relieved, because their whole careers depended to some extent on his career.

I found out later why he was thinking about retiring. He thought he had been "passed over." In the military that means you are not going to go any farther, and people expect you to retire. Others may have felt that Vessey was passed over because he was not a graduate of West Point. He was an enlisted man, a sergeant who had risen up through the ranks and become an officer. At this time he was a one-star general. He had been trained in artillery at Fort Sill, Oklahoma. In spite of that, he had been all over. He knew the Army!

Later, after we became good friends, he told me about a comment he had overheard the day after I had been at U Tapao. One of his men asked another whether he had attended the Christmas service the day before. "No, I didn't," the other man said. "How was that girl singer? Was she pretty good?"

"Oh, she was all right," his companion said, "but what you really missed was that little fat guy. Boy, could he preach!"

Once I was speaking at the War College in Carlisle, Pennsylvania, after General Vessey had been there for a meeting. They had also had the chief of staff of the Army, the head of the CIA, and many others there, but they said, "Don't be taken in by that 'soft shoe' approach of Vessey's; nobody knows the Army the way he does. He can answer questions about the Army that nobody else can answer!"

After General Vessey left Thailand, he was in Laos for about nine months. Then he was given a second star, then a third star and made deputy chief of staff in Washington. Then about a year later he was given a fourth star and made commander of all the troops in Korea. While he was there, he advised President Carter not to draw down the troops, which was the president's intention at the time.

When the time came to appoint the new chief of staff of the Army, Vessey was passed over—but he did not quit! He could have, but he did not. Instead, the new chief of staff of the Army, General Edward Meyers, who had been one of Vessey's subordinates, asked Vessey to be vice-chief of staff of the Army. That meant he actually ran the Army. He had an office in the Pentagon which covered a good deal of the building!

Of course, General Vessey was finally appointed chairman of the joint chiefs of staff. I happened to be speaking at West Point the weekend when he was appointed. I was scheduled to speak there on Sunday morning. Then they asked me to speak for the banquet of the yearling class too, because Mayor Koch of New York, who was supposed to have been the speaker, was running for governor and begged off.

At that banquet on Saturday evening, without mentioning any names, I talked about a military man who just put all his trust in God and did his duty day by day. He let God take care of opening the doors. When I finished that speech, General Davidson, who was the superintendent of the Academy, came over to me. "I know whom you were talking about," he said. "You were talking about Jack Vessey. I was a member of his staff, and I know the whole story." He added that the talk about doing one's duty was just what the cadets needed, after spending crucial years at the Academy mostly competing with one another.

Earlier that afternoon I had telephoned Jack Vessey to congratulate him on his appointment. He said to me, "Do you know what Avis [his wife] said? She said, 'You lied about your age when you entered the National Guard in Minnesota, and now God is punishing you!'"

For their retirement, Jack and Avis built a beautiful home up in Minnesota, something they had been planning to do for many years. Marcia and I have stayed there as their guests.

The main house, of course, has every kind of communication you can imagine. You can talk to Washington by satellite, and the fax machine is going all the time. The Vesseys also built a little hideaway back in the woods for their children and grandchildren. Every log comes from Minnesota and was cut to specifications.

Once when I was visiting him, he had just come back from Washington. It was a time when the military was trying to meet expectations in a highly political situation. "What did you tell them down there?" I asked him.

"Oh," he said, "I told them to keep their nose clean."

When Grenada was invaded, Jack Vessey was called to the White House. "When do we have to make this decision whether or not to invade Grenada?" President Reagan asked him.

"You have to make it in the next hour," Vessey said. "We're ready to go!"

WITNESSING AND THE MILITARY

That's the way it is with Jack Vessey. Our government still relies on him in many ways. He is a quiet man but very knowledgeable. He's also a fine Christian gentleman and a very good friend. He is one of the fellows who have gone with me on the famous White River float trips, which I will tell you about in a later chapter.

U.S. ARMY CHIEF OF CHAPLAINS, MAJOR GENERAL GERHARDT W. "WILL" HYATT

I first met Will in New York when I was public relations director for The Lutheran Church—Missouri Synod. Will was on the faculty of the chaplains school in New York, which was located at Fort Slocum on an island right off of the Bronx. I was often invited to go over there and speak, and I got to know him. We also had him over to our home and had a wonderful evening together. Then I met him later under other circumstances and really got to know him. He was one of the greatest people I ever met in my lifetime.

Will did not play partisan politics, but he was ready to help anybody or to get help from anybody when it affected those he served. Once he found out that Congress was considering consolidating all the chaplains' schools into one school where they would all be trained. Will felt that would be a big mistake, because the military services are so different. Marine chaplains need different training from Air Force chaplains, Air Force chaplains need different training from Army chaplains, and so on.

After talking to some of the people in Washington, Will found out that it was legislative aides to Congress who were cooking up this idea. He met with some of the senators and representatives personally and explained his position. The whole idea was dropped.

Will's career as military chaplain spanned almost 30 years, from 1945 to 1974. The highest positions began in 1970, when he was made Duty Chief of U.S. Chaplains and then, in 1971, U.S.

Army Chief of Chaplains. With the rank of Major General, he was appointed Chairman of the Armed Forces Chaplains Board of the U.S. Department of Defense in 1974.

When Will retired from the Army in 1975, I was asked whether he would make a good president of Concordia College, St. Paul. I said, "You couldn't get a better man." He was called to that position in 1976, and he did a lot for that school, my alma mater. His presidency there lasted until his "retirement" in 1983. At that time, as one of the vice-presidents of the Synod, Will was appointed as a special assistant to the denomination's president. In order to carry out those duties, Will moved to St. Louis, but he maintained his house in St. Paul for his wife, who stayed there. He would usually stay in St. Louis during the week, then go to St. Paul on the weekend. But there were some weekends when he could not go to St. Paul, and often I would be away. Then Marcia and our son John would take him out to dinner.

"Where are we going to dinner?" he would ask them. "Is it someplace from which I can find my way back?"

Will could never find his way around. I would go to Washington after he had been in the Pentagon four years, and he would take the wrong route into the Pentagon. Once we had to go back over the bridge into Washington, D.C., and start all over again.

Our whole family got to know Will very well. When he died suddenly on August 30, 1985, it was a shock to all of us. He had gone to Washington, D.C., to do some oral history for the military. While he was there he had a heart attack.

I am not exactly sure how long he was in intensive care at Walter Reed Hospital. It may have been a week or two. I called him every other day.

Then he was finally taken to a private room. General Vessey was immediately informed. He called his driver to take him to the hospital to see Will. General Vessey's driver went up to Will's room first to look over the scene and make sure that the way was clear for General Vessey to go in. Then he went down to get General Vessey. When they got back to the room, the doctor came to the door and said, "Would you please sit down out there?"

A little later, the doctor came out and said, "He just died."

I found out about his death later, when I tried to phone Will.

I preached his funeral sermon at the Fort Meyers Chapel near Arlington Cemetery. The military honored him just as they would have honored the highest ranking general. A whole company of troops and the whole Army band were there. Rev. Gerry E. Kuhn, his pastor and former member of Synod's Armed Services Commission, arranged the funeral service. General Vessey was sitting in the front row with his wife, Avis, together with the deputy chief of staff of the Army, General Max Thurman, who later became known as the commander in Panama.

Those of us, including an Army chaplain, who were participating in the funeral stood out in front of the military chapel. At just the right moment the hearse arrived, and the band played "A Mighty Fortress" as Will's body was carried into the chapel.

Two of Will's good friends from Canada were there: the president of his district and another pastor. I made a reference in the sermon to the fact that we collected Will from Canada and brought him down here. He was the first U.S. Chief of Army Chaplains ever born in Canada.

When the service was over, a caisson carried his body to the cemetery. My good friend Dr. Ewald Mueller, who was also a good friend of Will, rode with me to the cemetery. As we came up to the grave on a hillside, a horse without a rider was standing at attention, and the band was playing "Beautiful Savior."

Will was buried at the national cemetery in Fort Meyers. Pastor Kuhn had the committal service. They gave each one of us a flower, which we put on his coffin. Then they blew taps. General Vessey and Avis came over to me and we embraced. We had lost a good friend.

After the funeral, we went back to one of the buildings at Fort Meyers for a reception. Will's friends from Canada were there, as were his three brothers, one from eastern Canada, one from central Canada, and one from western Canada.

When I walked in the door to that reception, I got the shock of my life. There was Will! One of his three brothers looked just like him. He also had the same quiet, yet forceful personality as Will.

Will had another brother, who had been the comptroller of the Studebaker Corporation in Canada. He had died earlier in an automobile crash in which his wife had been severely injured. Will called me at that time and asked whether I would call Aid Association for Lutherans insurance company and see that she was taken care of, because she was in the hospital and needed money right away. (AAL was still operating in Canada at that time.) I called up and asked whether they would take care of that.

"Oh, it's taken care of," the fellow I talked to said. "I already took a check over there for her."

People had respect for Will Hyatt. He was a great man and a wonderful friend. Will's widow, Elda, still lives in the house they owned in St. Paul. I see her whenever I am up that way.

CIVIC RIGHTEOUSNESS

As I think about the absolute trust and obedience that soldiers must give to their superiors and to the military itself, I think the civilian population could learn a lot. Soldiers have to have a lot of faith in the organization and its regulations, under which they are to operate. The men and women have to believe that this is the best thing they can do under the circumstances.

People in civilian life could learn that the best thing they can do is listen to God and live according to His laws. Those laws work very well out in space, and they work just as well here. You can live a much happier life if you conform to the regulations God has written even into the hearts of people.

Luther was asked what those regulations were. He said that they are pretty much like the Ten Commandments. He would not have included the Third Commandment, though. That is an invitation to worship God, and you do that in the freedom of the Gospel. You cannot expect people who do not know the Gospel to do that. But you can expect people who do not know the Gospel to honor their parents in order that the family structure may not be destroyed, and that they may live happily ever after. You can also expect them not to kill, not to commit adultery (and to wreck family life that way), not to steal—those are the laws of the universe.

Those universal laws were recognized even by the pagans. Cicero, in his book *De Republica,* said that there is not one law in Athens and another law in Rome; there is only one law that covers the whole world. And he added, *Rector huius legis est unus: Deus* ("The director of this law is one: God"). Not all the pagans were polytheists. Their philosophers realized that there was one mind behind this world, one God who rules the universe. They did not know that God, because they did not have the opportunity to know Him, as do people who know Jesus Christ. To know Jesus by faith is to know God! It is also great to know the laws of the universe. You can appeal to people to observe those laws, because it makes sense to observe them.

That is what Luther meant when he talked about civic righteousness as distinct from the righteousness that saves. You can live with civic righteousness. A Turk can be a good father, Luther said, and he can raise a good family too as a matter of civic righteousness. But civic righteousness does not save.

In fact, civic righteousness sometimes leads people to believe that they can be saved by observing those laws, and that is not true. No one is going to be saved by observing those or any other laws. There is another righteousness revealed apart from the Law, although it is witnessed to by both the Law and the Prophets: the righteousness which is of God by faith in Jesus Christ. That is the righteousness that saves!

Sometimes the people who are saved by the righteousness of God are not nearly as righteous in their ways as those who live by civic righteousness. That is one thing you have to recognize. There are people out there who live better lives than the people who are going to church every Sunday, because the people who are saved by the righteousness of God do not recognize that they need to observe the Law too for their own good. But they are not saved by observing the Law. People are saved solely by grace.

That is what I as a pastor preach to the military too. I talk to them about sin and grace—sin a person recognizes, and grace a person receives. Military people receive that message very well. I tell them that God is so good that He receives you in spite of yourself. We just need to keep telling people that: by grace you live, and without grace you die.

I notice that the most gracious people are those who have received the grace of God in truth. They have received faith in God from the Spirit of God. With that faith go a lot of other things: love, joy, peace, gentleness, forbearance, patience, self-control. Those are all the gifts of the Spirit. If I read it correctly, they are also the mark of a true gentleman or a real lady. We need a lot more of that in the church.

Well, these have been some of my experiences with the military. Through the years I have had many opportunities to serve in this way—more than I can recount here. I spoke a number of times at the United States Military Academy at West Point; at Colorado Springs; at the Field Artillery Center at Fort Sill, Oklahoma; at Armed Forces prayer breakfasts in different locations; at the U.S. War College; and the like. But the most memorable experiences were my four Christmas visits to Vietnam.

19

VIETNAM

I N 1969, I RECEIVED AN INVITATION FROM GENERAL CREIGHTON W. ABRAMS, the commanding general in Vietnam, to make a Christmas visit to the troops there. I was to leave on December 17 and spend eight days in Vietnam. I would be scheduled for up to six appearances each day at bases of the Army, Navy, Air Force, and Marines.

The military, being what it is, made me a simulated two- or three-star general during each of my four trips so that I could receive their VIP treatment. They did that for all Department of Defense (DOD) guests. The honor didn't last. Besides, it didn't make any difference to me whether they wanted to call me a general or not for a few days. I felt equally at ease with the real generals as I did with the GIs.

The military also planned all the details of each trip. That assignment fell to the Air Force chaplain assigned to MAC-V (Military Assistance Command-Vietnam), the joint command responsible for conducting the war in Vietnam. The chaplain was responsible for planning, coordinating, and escorting all DOD visitors. The first year I was there, the chaplain was Lt. Col. Lloyd B. Trautman. The second year it was LCMS Chaplain Mel Witt, who later did an outstanding job of heading up Lutheran World Relief. I don't remember who went with us the third and fourth years.

By 1969, the Vietnam War had become a very unpopular war with many in the United States, and some of the clergymen who had been going to Vietnam were now refusing to go back. But I accepted General Abrams' invitation without hesitation.

On the first three trips I took along a female entertainer/singer. The first two years it was Suzanne Johnson; the third year, Jane Briggemann. The fourth year's invitation came such a short time before the holidays that I had no time to arrange for a singer to accompany me.

Suzanne Johnson, a graduate of Augustana College in Rock Island, Illinois, previously had been Miss Illinois and had won the talent competition at the Miss America contest. By 1969, she was a professional singer and had been on the concert stage for 10 years. (She also was married by then but had no children as yet.) She had a beautiful soprano voice and had made several records. She was a very talented and a very feminine young lady, and she related very well to the men. Some of the entertainers who went to Vietnam brought women who were tough, because they thought that was what the troops would want. But the men appreciated Suzanne Johnson. "Whoever arranged to bring that girl over here was a genius!" one colonel said to me.

After our 1970 tour, Suzanne Johnson became pregnant with the first of her three sons. As a result, she was not able to accompany me the following year. In 1971, Jane Briggemann went with me. She was one of our Lutheran students from Concordia Teachers College in Seward, Nebraska. She had been Miss Nebraska in 1969 and had won the Miss Congeniality award at the Miss America Pageant. She too was a singer, although not a professional like Suzanne Johnson.

The second year (1970) I also took along Bob Garmatz, a member of the LLL staff. His assignment was to get some film of the trip and some sound recordings of me interviewing some of the men. Unfortunately, that did not work out too well. The military had assigned one of their people to go with us to do the filming, but for some reason it all came out very yellow. We did get some still photos and a little usable film footage, but that was about all.

In 1971, Charles King, a singer from Walla Walla, Washington, who had been the director and soloist for the Wings over Jordan choir, also went with us, as did Tommy Thompson, the director of domestic operations for "The Lutheran Hour."

It cost the military $50,000 for each one of us who went around out there. We paid our own way out there and back, but once we were out there, the military took care of us. Francis Cardinal Spellman started that arrangement. At first, the government paid his way even to get there, but Spellman was criticized for spending government money. So he said, "Okay, I'll pay my own way." Actually, the LLL paid my way to get there, and we made arrangements for private funding to get the singer's transportation paid. Of course, once we were there, none of us could have paid our own way to get around from base to base.

Each year I took along 20,000 small crosses to give to the men. The second year I added copies of the psalms from the American Bible Society as a give-away. I had to find funds for these items too.

TO VIETNAM, 1969

Before I made that first trip, I called Dr. Martin Scharlemann, one of our seminary professors who was also a retired general in the military, and asked him, "What am I going to talk about to them?"

"Oh," he said, "you'll find out." And I did.

When we left the United States, we were in the air for 29 hours. We arrived in Saigon at noon, and they took us right over to the Third Surgical Field Hospital. Helicopters were constantly bringing in the wounded. I spent the whole afternoon there visiting with the men.

One fellow who had just been brought in that day was lying on a bed in the hallway, because they did not have enough room for him in the hospital. Because every man brought in wounded was allowed a free call home, I asked him, "Have you called home?"

He told me that he had.

Then I asked him, "What's going to happen to you now?"

"I'll stay here until I recover enough to be taken to Japan by air," he said. "I'll probably spend two or three weeks there, and after that I'll get back to the real world."

That fellow told me what I needed to talk about. He told me to talk about the real world. Anyone who thought of St. Louis or other places as the real world had to be disabused of that notion. The real world is where you are right now. I had to tell that to the men out there, "Where you are is the real world—out here at the fire support base, with the tanks pointed out into the woods in order to protect the base, and with one unit out there reconnoitering in the woods."

That night I had dinner with a very secret organization that was not even allowed to make its presence known. With the helicopters headed for the Third Surgical Field Hospital flying right over us, the men said they wanted me there, because they would not have a chance to see me otherwise. I talked to them and they talked to me. That gave me a good idea what I was going to meet all over Vietnam. We stayed there until ten o'clock.

The next day the military took us out to the fire support bases. We went to seven bases and had 40- to 45-minute meetings with the troops. The men sat there in a semicircle with their shirts off because it was so hot, and I spoke to them. Fortunately, I have a voice that carries well, because in most of these places there was no PA system.

I talked to them about Christmas and the real world. I told them that it was into a real world that Jesus Christ came. He did not come into a make-believe world; it was a very real world. He was born in a barn. He lived that way too in the real world, without a mortgage to His name.

That is the way He was, I told them, and that is the way He is even today. He takes people as they are and receives them as they are. He says, "Come to Me, all you who labor and are heavy laden, and I will give you rest" (Matthew 11:28 NKJV). That is just as true today as it was then. That is what I told them. "Right here and now is the place to be real men and to carry the name of Christ with honor," I said.

After 50 minutes we had to leave, because the troops at the next place were already waiting for us. No roads were available, of course. We would go by helicopter to the next fire support base, maybe 50 miles away through the woods.

By the way, those helicopters that took us around were often accompanied by gunships, because we were flying through dangerous territory. Sometimes they would fly as high as 3,000 feet, but usually they flew about 100–150 feet above the treetops, because that was the best way to avoid being fired on. The gunship fellows told me that it would be a brave man who would fire at a helicopter with a gunship behind it, because you can see the flash of the rifle or whatever the sniper is using, and within two seconds the ship would fire a 20-millimeter cannon and wipe him out.

We always flew from one place to another with the doors of the helicopter open. We would be wearing seat belts, but we would be right out there in the open. I had a camera with me, and I sat right on the end seat and took pictures all over Vietnam. Sometimes firing was going on around us, but we were never attacked. I suppose there was some danger there, but the military was more worried about me than I was worried about myself—I suppose because I did not know any better!

We were in Vietnam that first year from December 19-26. We traveled all over South Vietnam, going mostly by helicopter, but also by car, jeep, and jet plane.

I had Christmas dinner that first year with the commanding officer of all Vietnam forces, General Abrams, all alone in his hut, just the two of us. I knew him from Washington, D.C., and he had, after all, invited me to make this tour.

The general was a very well-informed Protestant Christian. His wife was Roman Catholic. I was surprised when, at dinner that night, he announced to me that he was going to become a Roman Catholic the next day. "I've left my family so much alone, and I'm going to be confirmed tomorrow," he said.

He had taken instructions in the Roman Catholic faith, and the next day he flew to Bangkok, where his wife was waiting for him, and was confirmed. He did it for his family. I was impressed.

The Background of the Crosses

Those 20,000 small crosses I distributed to the men were donated by a Lutheran layman by the name of Bill Rohn, who has a metal stamping company in Michigan. He had a contract with General Motors and discovered that the residue from one of the parts that he was stamping for them was in the shape of a cross. It was made of a bronze-colored material that went into an automobile somewhere.

Bill put a Chi-Rho on the metal and gave me 20,000 of those to take to Vietnam. I talked to the Air Force about getting them over there, and the Air Force willingly had those crosses transported to Fort Dix in New Jersey, where they had planes taking off to Vietnam from the Air Force base nearby. When the truck driver who transported them to Fort Dix saw what it was he was transporting, he insisted on transporting those crosses free of charge. I gave them to the troops at the various places as a little Christmas remembrance. I still meet men, sometimes generals, who are wearing that cross under their uniforms.

Later on, the Lutheran Laymen's League used that cross. It became so popular that they wanted to prohibit anyone else from using it; then they could give it away to anyone who contributed $10 or more a year to "The Lutheran Hour." It was really Bill Rohn's cross, and its first use was in Vietnam.

Arranging for Suzanne's Travels

As I mentioned earlier, the military did not pay our way to Vietnam. And although the LLL picked up the tab for me, we needed to find some special funding for the female singer. The first year, the way for Suzanne Johnson was paid for by R. V. Lehner. I need to tell you about this gracious and dedicated layman.

The previous winter I combined a pheasant hunting trip in Kansas with a meeting set up by Vernon Bryant, an LLL officer from Great Bend. He had put together a gathering at a restaurant in Topeka to encourage people to support "The Lutheran Hour." He had invited about 40 people from all over Kansas.

I remember saying good-bye to the people at the door of the restaurant as they were leaving. One of the men introduced himself to me as R. V. Lehner and introduced me to his wife. He shook hands and said, "Good-bye." Then he said, "You'll hear from us."

When I got the first invitation to go to Vietnam, I still had not heard from Lehner. I called up Vernon Bryant and asked him whether he had a list of the people who had been at the meeting that night. He said he did, and I asked him to go over it with me. When he went through the list, I said, "That's the one. R. V. Lehner. Do you have his telephone number?"

Vernon gave it to me. I called him up, and his secretary answered the phone. That told me that this farmer out in Kansas had other interests besides farming. I found out later that he also had oil wells.

"He's over in Ness City celebrating his mother's birthday," his secretary told me.

"Will you give me the number over there?" I asked. She did, and I called over there. He answered the phone.

"Mr. Lehner," I said, "This is Dr. Hoffmann."

"Oh," he said, "how good to hear from you!"

I told R.V. about the 20,000 crosses that Bill Rohn was making available. Then I said to R.V., "I want to take Suzanne Johnson out to Vietnam with me. How would you like to make that possible?"

"How much would it cost?" he asked me.

I said, "Twelve hundred dollars."

There was a long pause on the line—and a sound as if a man was sobbing.

When he came back on the line, he said, "You've just done me the biggest favor that anybody has ever done in my life. I've got to go back home and have my secretary write a check. It will be there on Monday morning."

On Monday morning his check was on my desk.

A week after I got back from that trip to Vietnam, I was in Jamaica speaking to a meeting of the general agents of the AAL when we got word that R.V. Lehner had died.

The next year it cost $3,000 to take Suzanne Johnson to Vietnam. Anita Lehner, R.V.'s widow, paid for that. The Men's Club of Trinity Lutheran Church in Mansfield, South Dakota, paid for the crosses that year.

THE SECOND VISIT TO VIETNAM

The next year, 1970, General Abrams asked me to make a return Christmas visit to Vietnam. In my acceptance letter to him, I wrote, "This trip is in no sense a sacrifice on my part. My family feels the same way. It is one small thing I can do for you and all the personnel in your command who are really giving up a great deal for our country and for the world."

It was on this second trip that everyone was glad Suzanne Johnson was a professional. We had arrived at Fire Support Base Baldy, a Marine encampment. For some reason, there was a sullen feeling—almost anger—on the part of the troops who were there. Our escort, Chaplain Mel Witt, thought it might have been that the men were ordered to be present rather than attending of their own free will. We didn't know whether that had happened or not, but it was possible.

At any rate, during the course of our presentation, we came to that point when Suzanne would sing Christmas carols and invite the men to sing along. But this time, no one would join in the singing. That never happened anywhere else, and I think if she had not been a professional, she would have broken up.

When I saw this, I got out there with her. I started to direct, and I said, "Come on, fellows. Now is the time." When I said that, three Marines started to sing. Then the rest started singing too. We sang and sang, and it got to be a real blowout. I talked too, and they were right with me. Chaplain Witt said he actually could see the eyes of the men change during the course of our presentation.

That year I had brought along with me 20,000 copies of the TEV version of the psalms, which had just been published. When we finished, I handed out those copies of *The Psalms*. At least 75 of the men lined up and asked me to sign their copy.

Too quickly Witt told me, "You've got to go. They're waiting for you at the next fire support base." After I apologized to the men that I didn't have time to sign all those copies, I got in my jeep and was driven back to the helicopter. On the way the driver said to me, "This is the greatest day that I've seen out here since I got here."

I'm happy to say that even if these soldiers were forced to be present, they were not forced to have a change of heart. That was due to the Lord.

Roger Anderson and "the Old Man"

Suzanne Johnson and I went to all the fire support bases. When we got to Fire Support Base Green, we were met by the base commander, a colonel in a dusty uniform with ammunition strung all over it. There was also a captain there who was a Missouri Synod chaplain. The chaplain introduced me to the commander. Then the chaplain took me over to where the troops were already gathered waiting for us. On the way over there, the chaplain said to me, "There was a young lieutenant here by the name of Roger Anderson who wanted to be here. He gave $10 to help bring Suzanne Johnson over here."

I do not know how he did that. I suppose it was through a contribution to "The Lutheran Hour" or something like that. Anyhow, the chaplain told me he had made that contribution. Then he said, "But Roger won't be here. At the beginning of December he was on patrol about 10 clicks [kilometers] out, and he was killed out there."

I started out my sermon there by saying, "You all know Roger Anderson." Of course, they all did, because when you are at a base like that, all alone out there in the woods, everybody knows everybody else.

I said, "Roger Anderson knows exactly what Christmas means. He does. Right now. 'In Him is life, and that life is the light of people everywhere. And the Light shines in the darkness, and the darkness has never been able to put it out' " [John 1:4-5].

We used various texts like that out there. I mentioned Roger Anderson and the fact that he believed in Jesus, the one who came into the real world, the one where they were. I told them, "This is the real world. The one where you are right now. Now is the time to believe. And now is also the time to learn all the good things that come with having faith in Jesus Christ. Now you can be a real person here, redeemed by the blood of Jesus Christ." I just told them the same old story.

When we got ready to leave, the chaplain said to me, "The old man won't be here to say good-bye to you. When you mentioned Roger Anderson, he broke up. The old man went down to his hut, and he won't be able to come out."

"That's okay," I said. "I understand."

That just shows you the feelings between the commanders and the men who served with them. By the way, to call the commander "the old man" is a real sign of affection in the military. That is not downgrading him; that is upgrading him. It means he is a real guy. If they like their commander, they call him "the old man." If they do not like him, they have other names for him.

Commanding officers generally had a high respect for the men that they commanded. They said that these men did not ask to come out there, but they came out and did a fine job. I think the country should know that too. They had a great problem out there, and they solved it the best way they knew how.

Silence for "Silent Night"

At one Army post we could hear the large guns going off. Fortunately the shots were all going out, not coming in, but that continued while we were getting ready for the service and as we began the service. Then, just as Suzanne Johnson began singing "Silent Night," the guns stopped. When she finished, the guns resumed almost immediately.

Afterward, Suzanne asked our escort officer whether it was possible that they knew that she was singing "Silent Night" and had stopped the guns during that time.

"No, Suzanne," he said. "That was just something that happened. Maybe the Lord intervened and kept the guns silent while you sang 'Silent Night.' "

Suzanne Johnson Collapses

It was on this trip that Suzanne Johnson collapsed. We had had the experience at Fire Support Base Baldy, had a Christmas Eve service at Long Binh Army Headquarters, then went on to MAC-V for Christmas morning. General Frederich C. Weyand, commander-in-chief, was in attendance at the Christmas morning service.

As I recall, Suzanne sang before I spoke. Then General Weyand got up from the pew where he was seated and said, "I think we ought to thank Dr. Hoffmann for being here today." After that, Suzanne sang again. At the end of the song, she collapsed.

Escort Chaplain Mel Witt came rushing forward, and they took her out. I did not see her again until about 3:00 that afternoon. She was just exhausted, and after sleeping for several hours she was fine. We were scheduled to go from there to Korea, but we stopped in Hong Kong for a day for all of us to rest. Then we went on to Korea and Okinawa. We always stopped at places like that on our way back from Vietnam. (Later on, I also went to Korea when General John Vessey was there. That time I took Marcia along.)

I found out later about something interesting that happened during this visit to Vietnam. Escort Chaplain Mel Witt wanted the commanding general, General Weyand, to host me and the chaplains there on our first evening in Saigon. Mel and the command chaplain, who were trying to arrange this, were frustrated because the general's aide was not giving them an appointment to see the general. Finally they decided that since General Weyand was in chapel every Sunday, they would ask the general if they could come up and see him. They did this when he left the chapel service one morning, and he said, "Sure, come on up."

When they got to his office, he asked, "What can I do for you chaplains?"

They told him what they wanted him to do, and he called up a three-star general who was the U.S. Army commander at Long

Binh and canceled an appointment with him so that he could serve as host for us, even though he had never met me. Also, on the Sunday before we left, he invited all the chaplains and their staffs, including the enlisted men, to his quarters and hosted a breakfast.

General Weyand was a very gracious and generous man, and we became good friends. The following year he invited me to come back and visit the troops again—which I did.

During our 1970 Vietnam trip we visited both Army and Marine fire support bases, large Air Force installations, and smaller naval installations. We also spent several nights on an aircraft carrier in the Gulf of Tonkin at the invitation of a three-star admiral, the commander of the Seventh Fleet. I had an opportunity to have dinner with the admiral and his staff and to preach to the men on the ship. We flew off from Vietnam to Yankee Station in the Gulf of Tonkin on a small propeller-driven airplane that landed on the ship. When we left, it was like being shot off the ship into air!

Dr. Henry Bast

There is another interesting story about something that came about because of that second trip to Vietnam. Dr. Henry Bast, who taught theology at the Reformed seminary in Holland, Michigan, was the speaker on their radio program, "Temple Time," for many years. The year they observed the 25th anniversary of the program they asked me to speak.

Dr. Bast and his son, who was also a pastor, picked me up at the airport. In the car, they told me why they had invited me to come. After that Christmas Eve service at Long Binh, I had given out copies of *The Psalms,* and about 100 fellows lined up to have me sign their copies. Another one of Dr. Bast's sons, a helicopter pilot in Vietnam, was one of those whose book I signed, although I did not know who he was at the time.

About 30 days later he was killed in his helicopter. Among his personal effects that the military sent home was that copy of *The Psalms*. In the book was my signature, with the passage I always write down, Galatians 2:20, and a little message from me.

"You are the last one we know who saw him alive," Dr. Bast said, "and we wanted you here for this occasion."

All of that was a result of my second trip to Vietnam. It is always a surprise to me how the Lord leads a person from one apparent chance occasion to another.

THE THIRD TRIP, 1971

As I mentioned at the beginning of the chapter, our third trip to Vietnam included Jane Briggemann as our female singer-entertainer, Charles King as our male soloist, and Tommy Thompson, the director of domestic operations for "The Lutheran Hour." On that trip we spent only three and a half days in Vietnam, but we also spent three days in Okinawa, two and a half days in Thailand, and two and a half days in South Korea.

THE FOURTH TRIP TO VIETNAM, 1972

In 1972, the invitation for me to visit Vietnam at Christmastime came at the very last minute. I was up in Alaska with the military in the early part of December, when I got a wire from General Fred Weyand asking me whether I could come out to Vietnam.

I called Chaplain Will Hyatt, who was Chief of Army Chaplains in Washington, D.C., at the time, and asked him what he thought I should do. He said he thought I should go. That meant going home, rearranging my schedule, repacking, and going to the Far East. But I went.

Secretary of State Henry Kissinger had suggested that all of our troops would be home by Christmas, but it did not work out that way. There were still 13,000 troops left there, and I visited them.

On Saturday evening I went out to Long Binh with the Judge Advocate General of the Army, who was the son of Pastor Henry Gericke in St. Louis. Pastor Gericke had been a chaplain in the Army in WWII. He was one of those who ministered after the war to the prisoners at Nuremberg. He was the last one to see Hermann Goering alive.

For some reason, his son had never told anyone that he was the son of a chaplain. I mentioned that to some of the people there, and they kidded him about that.

Long Binh was the former headquarters of the U.S. Army in Vietnam. By this time there was nothing left there but a stockade in which prisoners were being held, some of whom had committed murder. Gericke asked them whether they were being treated well, whether they were getting good food, and things like that. Then I got a chance to talk with them.

Bob Hope

When we finished, we got in the helicopter and went back to Ton Son Hut Air Base. I preached in the chapel there the next morning. That afternoon Bob Hope and his troupe came in from Bangkok for a show in the late afternoon.

Hope's people never stayed in Vietnam overnight. They had too many people with them to be accommodated easily at the military bases. Besides, they had a whole floor rented at a hotel in Bangkok and a Chrysler-sponsored plane that they had chartered to bring in their people and equipment.

I was supposed to have dinner with General Weyand that afternoon, but when I got to his home for dinner, the attending sergeant said, "He's out at the airport picking up Bob Hope."

A little later, General Weyand came back with Bob Hope and his wife, Delores. His wife asked me whether there was a Roman

Catholic service she could attend somewhere. I told her, "I'll take care of that." I went to one of the Roman Catholic chaplains and found out that they did have a service that evening at five o'clock, and Delores was able to attend.

While she was doing that, Bob Hope and I had dinner with General Weyand. Then the general wanted to take pictures of Bob Hope and me. Bob Hope came about up to my shoulders. I said to him, "Say something funny," and he said, "Crosby."

That was the only time I saw one of Bob Hope's shows. He had been in Vietnam the other times I had been there too, but he was always two days ahead of us or two days behind us—something like that. I watched the whole show. I thought that with his reputation as a great ad-libber, in this situation he would ad-lib a lot. But I was sitting in the front row, and I could see the big screen where his cues were being displayed.

The only time he departed from the script was when he had to introduce a Vietnamese commander. He introduced him as Lieutenant So-and-so, and General Weyand, who was sitting about three seats in back of me, got up and said, "Lieutenant *General.*" Bob Hope on the spur of the moment said, "I just promoted you ahead of Al Haig." He *could* ad-lib! I guess the show required that people would know what was going on, to have their timing right. Timing is very important for a program like that.

I believe Lola Falana was the entertainer with him. She danced and sang. It was a good, clean show.

That was in 1972. It was my last visit to Vietnam. A year or two later all of our troops pulled out.

FACING THE CHALLENGES

In those four years, my meeting with the troops was canceled only one time. We were going up to a corps in the DMZ, where the Marines were in charge. We had flown by helicopter almost to the place where we were supposed to land, when we turned around and started back.

They told me that they had just gotten word that there were seven or eight infiltrators coming in across the DMZ, and we were ordered back because they did not think it was safe to go up there. It might be that the enemy knew we were coming, because they had the best spy system in the world. They seemed to know everything that was going on.

I guess there were spies everywhere. In fact, they told me that a fellow could be cutting your hair at a base one day, and you would find him dead on the barbed wire in the morning, because he had been one of those who had attacked the base during the night.

I talked to General W. C. Westmoreland about that one time afterwards at the Pentagon when he was chief of staff. He was having an important meeting in "the Hole," where they have all classified information. Everybody was gone from the Pentagon, but I was still waiting there with my escort officer, Chaplain Will Hyatt.

There was a three-star general there waiting to see General Westmoreland in his office. Westmoreland came walking up the hall. He recognized me, because we had met and talked in Vietnam.

"Come right on in," he said. He saw the general who had been waiting to see him and said, "Hi, Jim." We walked past him right into General Westmoreland's office, and that fellow was left standing out there.

I asked General Westmoreland, "How did it feel when you got out there to Vietnam?"

"Well, Dr. Hoffmann," he said, "I didn't know friend from foe out there."

That's the way it was with all the troops. It was a very difficult assignment. I think they did very, very well. It was not the military that wanted this war to happen. They did not create the problem. Yet some folks got to be antimilitary, as though the war was the soldiers' fault.

I had one or two letters that came in criticizing me for being with the military at Christmas. I wrote back and said that I did not ask to go out there. I went out there because our people were there. I added, "I'm not going to quit going out there either."

I told them that it was just like visiting someone who is sick in the hospital. "I did not put the patient there, and the hospital is not responsible for his being there either. He is there, and I am going to visit him." I never got a letter back in response to that.

At every service where I spoke in Vietnam, I told those attending that there were all kinds of differences of opinions in the United States about the war in Vietnam, but that there were no differences about the concern of all American people for those who were fighting the war. "First, the country cares about you," I told them. "Second, the church cares about you. And what is most important, God cares and saves."

That was the message everywhere I went: God cares and God saves. That always had been my message. I was especially grateful to the military and especially to my Lord that I had the privilege of participating in this "work" of "PR"—*P*roclaiming the *R*edeemer to real people in the real world.

20

EXTRA-VOCATIONAL SERVICE AND THE AAL

I STRONGLY BELIEVE IN SERVING PEOPLE AND JESUS CHRIST IN EVERY situation open to me. Sometimes a person's schedule gets so full that one has to choose between this and that, but at other times the opportunity is so significant that the moment must be seized. That was the way I felt when I was given the opportunity to make those Christmas trips to Vietnam. That was the way I felt also when asked to serve on the boards of the Bible societies, when invited to attend the Second Vatican Council, and when given the opportunity to sit on the Religious Public Relations Council. Nor could I have refused the chance to be involved with the movies *Martin Luther* and *Question 7* (and *Yeshua,* about which I'll write in the next chapter).

In 1962, when I was asked to sit on the board of directors for Aid Association for Lutherans (AAL) fraternal insurance company, I saw that too as an invitation to serve God's people. True, some people see AAL as nothing more than an insurance company, but it has always been more than that; it has always existed as a *fraternal* company for the benefit of its members. The local association of members is called a branch, and those branches (run by volunteers) do an awful lot for the members, for their congregation(s), and for their communities. So, when I was asked to serve

God's people through the AAL, I accepted. Let me tell you how the invitation came to me.

In 1962, AAL was having a Presidents Club meeting in Mexico for its top salesmen—the first time outside of the U.S. The president of AAL, Walter Rugland, one of the great men of God in our generation, invited me to preach at the service they had at that meeting. At the time, I thought that they assumed the presence of "The Lutheran Hour" speaker on Sunday morning somehow would help make the weekend special for the agents. Since I love preaching the Word of God anyway, and since AAL was picking up the tab for my presence, I accepted the invitation. (By the way, Alex Benz was chairman of the board at the time. He is the person who developed the agency system for AAL.)

Prior to that meeting, AAL board member Jack Fleischli, an executive of the Cupples Corporation, had resigned from the board, and without my knowing anything about it, Walter Rugland proposed that I fill the vacancy. Conveniently, the board was meeting in Mexico City at the same time as the Presidents Club. While I was in my room, I received a phone call from a representative of the AAL board informing me that I had just been elected a member of the board.

They asked me to take a cab to the hotel where the board was meeting, but I walked. I even made it across the street through that crazy Mexico City traffic. The traffic there is controlled by the horns of people in the cars. Everybody honks his horn, then proceeds directly to where he is going. You have to be aware of this as you walk across the street. If you keep moving, the drivers will avoid you.

I'll always remember my first 15 minutes on the board of AAL: I voted to spend $7.5 million so that the company could add an addition to the home office building in Appleton, Wisconsin. The rest of the board had had a big discussion about that, but the talking was over by the time I got there. Since everyone else was voting for the building, I did too.

The next time AAL built a home office building, I was the one who made the motion that we go ahead and build it—this time for $52 million. Before making that motion, they talked long whether they should cut something out in order to save money. After a long, long discussion about that, I asked, "Is there anyone here who thinks that five years from now it will be more reasonable to build the part of the building that you are proposing to cut out than it is today?"

They all said no.

"Then," I said, "I move that we build the whole building."

As it turned out, I was chairman of the board the year that building was dedicated and was one of two speakers for the dedication; the other was Lieutenant Governor Schreiber of the state of Wisconsin, who was a Missouri Synod Lutheran. It was a great day.

That was 15 or 20 years ago, and I think AAL is now adding to the new home office. When that new building was built, we were planning to sell the old building downtown, but we kept it instead. The building was assessed at something like $7.5 million, and we were going to deed it to the city of Appleton for something like $2 million. They wanted it for a municipal building. Then somebody in city government started a campaign claiming that our price was too high. As a result, we decided not to sell it.

It turned out to work well for us. Since the city had decided that it was not worth the $2 million we were asking, then the city could no longer tax it with an assessment of $7.5 million. Our property taxes went way down after that.

It was a good thing we did not sell that building. AAL has expanded so much since then that most of that older building, maybe all of it, is still in use by AAL.

A TRAGIC PLANE TRIP

The AAL board met four times a year. Once when we were flying back to Chicago from a board meeting in Appleton, Elsa Johnson, the wife of one of our board members, Henry Johnson, became ill on the plane. We were on an Air Wisconsin plane, one of those smaller planes that seats about 30 people. Henry came up to me from where he and his wife were sitting in the back, and said, "Say a prayer for Elsa."

I looked back, and there she was: lying on the floor, becoming black, as heart patients often do. The poor girl who was the stewardess on the plane did not know what to do. She was trying to give Elsa artificial resuscitation and trying to use oxygen, but she did not know how to do that. A young lady sitting right in front of us was watching this. Suddenly she jumped up and took off her jacket. Then she asked me whether I thought it would be all right if she would help. I said, "Sure."

I found out later that she was an American Airlines stewardess who was coming back from visiting her mother in Appleton and was going to Chicago to pick up a flight there. She knew what to do. She worked on Elsa until we made an emergency landing in Milwaukee, where an ambulance was waiting. They took Elsa out of the plane, and the ambulance attendants started to work on her right there. They would not let anybody get off the plane except me. I went out, then came back and reported to Henry Johnson what they were doing.

They had Elsa looking as if her skin was perfectly natural, but they could not get a pulse. After about an hour they gave up. The plane stayed there all that time, and when they could not revive her, Henry got off. He went with her body, I suppose, to the hospital, where they had to fill out the death certificate. The plane took off and we went on to Chicago.

I took down the name of the girl who had helped on the plane, and wrote a letter to the president of American Airlines, thanking him for what they were doing to educate their flight attendants on how to handle a crisis like that. I also wrote a letter to her mother, whose address she had given me, and thanked her for raising a daughter like that.

So often we do not think of thanking people for some helpful thing that they have done. I am always grateful for thoughtful acts on the part of people, things they actually did instead of just thought about doing.

Sad to say, it seems to me that the people who usually act on their intentions are those who are out to hurt people. This is the essence of humanity without God and without hope in the world. When nobody is looking, humanity will go the other way. It is the nature of the beast!

To act on love requires a definite orientation and an actual decision that you are going to do it the right way—even though you may not be appreciated at all. That is the way Christ wants it to be. That is the kind of love I believe I saw in that stewardess.

Now back to AAL.

WALTER RUGLAND AND AAL'S FRATERNAL BENEFIT PROGRAM

As a board member, I also sat on the fraternal benevolence committee for many years. We said, "We are chartered as a fraternal benefit society, and it is our mandate to benefit our members." We developed a whole new fraternal program under the direction of President Walter Rugland. He was the one who made a real fraternal benefit society out of AAL. Until then, it had been mostly an insurance-selling society. Of course, the company had to sell insurance; that is why AAL exists. But it also was to be a fraternal benefit society, existing for the benefit of the members.

Walter Rugland remodeled AAL so that it became a *genuine* fraternal benefit society, truly benefiting the members—and even the congregations to which they belonged. The churches have no right to demand anything of AAL, and AAL does not have to give anything to the churches. But because our AAL members are such strong members of their congregations, we also give money to the churches to help our members. We have the Matching Funds program for the congregations to which our members belong, the Gold Star program (which benefits the local branch and the congregations to which they belong), and other programs like that. We also sometimes contributed something to the communities where our members live—funds to help build a park or some other civic improvement supported by our members.

Few of these programs were in existence before Walter Rugland's presidency. As a result of him, AAL became a leader in the whole fraternal system throughout the United States. We made such strides that George Romney, the head of volunteerism in the United States, saw to it that AAL was given a medal by the White House for its efforts in that area.

Walter was a giant of a man, not only in the AAL but also in the church. He became chairman of a group of 32 people, mostly laymen, who met at the LLL building. They decided to set up a category of contributions to "The Lutheran Hour" that would begin at $100 a year. They all pledged $100 apiece. That program was quietly dropped along the way, I am told, because the staff opposed it. They said that they did not want to alienate the people who contributed smaller amounts, who have always been very important to us. I can appreciate the fact that an organization does not want to exclude the small contributor. Walter Rugland and his group did not want to do that either. But they felt that those people who could contribute more should be encouraged, even stimulated to do so. Walter definitely is one of the great men in my pantheon of heroes of the faith.

I was on the AAL board for 21 years. That was one of the longer terms on the AAL board. Fred Kuhlmann, a Lutheran in St. Louis, the longtime president of the Cardinals baseball team owned by the Busch family, and a member of many boards of the LCMS, may have beat my 21-year stint with AAL. Two years younger, he came on a year or so after I did and stayed on another two years after I left. We were both members of the executive committee when I retired in 1983 at the mandatory retirement age of 70.

HENRY SCHEIG AND SOME THOUGHTS ABOUT HUMOR

Henry Scheig was introduced as Walter Rugland's successor as president of AAL at a Presidents Club meeting in San Antonio. I was the speaker at that meeting, and Ernie Schoenfeld was the toastmaster. Ernie had a native wit that enlivened many an AAL Presidents Club meeting. He had sold pots and pans when he arrived in this country from Germany and became one of the top producers for AAL. He never became a general agent, because he did not want to be. He made more money as a district representative.

As toastmaster, Ernie turned to Henry Scheig (a rather large fellow at that time) and said, "Hank, you'll never be able to fill Walter Rugland's shoes."

Nobody knew exactly how to take that.

"But," Ernie said, "you certainly can fill his pants!"

Everybody loves a good joke. By "good," I mean of course that people are laughing with other people and at themselves (not at other people). A good joke does not try to make fun of other people but to share some fun with them. Good humor need not be offensive to any group. That's why over the years, I've told "Hittite jokes." As far as I know, there are no Hittites around any more to find them offensive.

To be human is to have a sense of humor. I do not think we should be afraid of using humor. Scripture uses it. See, for example, Luke. In Acts 19:2-3, Paul comes to Ephesus and asks the people there, "Have you received the gift of the Holy Spirit?" And they say, "We have not so much as heard whether there be anything like the Holy Spirit!" That's human, and it's humorous.

It was that way in the Reformation too. A priest once wrote and asked Luther whether as a Lutheran he could use the mass vestments at the Holy Communion. Luther wrote back to him that as far as he was concerned the priest could use any vestments he wanted to, and if he wanted to dance up and down the aisle the way David did when he brought the ark of the covenant back from the Philistines, that was all right too.

I believe that one of the reasons humor is so successful in public speaking is that it plays on the foibles of our humanity, including our human propensity to do everything we can to hide our frailties. Roman Catholic Bishop Fulton Sheen once said that humor is the difference between who you think you are and who you really are. Or it's the difference between what you want your neighbors to think about you and what your neighbors actually do think about you! Humor helps us laugh at and go around our facades, and to do so together. Good humor builds a sense of fellowship and community.

In my opinion, humor belongs in a sermon. We who are Christian are not afraid to be fully human. We already know that we are far from perfect, but that we are loved by God in Christ anyway. That in itself should make us laugh with joy. Preachers sometimes are scared off by the fact that people are so stolid, maybe even so hostile that it is nigh impossible to warm them up with anything human. But that is what humor does. It warms people up to their own humanity, first of all, and then to the humanity of others around them.

Sometimes some people have a problem with certain forms

of humor because they take it too seriously. That's especially true of satire. Consider, for instance, the letter supposedly from Xanadu, Nebraska, that John Strietelmeyer used to write in *The Cresset*. This was a letter from a Lutheran businessman who was writing to a friend, asking for his opinion or his help. I think the letter writer supposedly was president of the North American Lutheran Implement Dealers Association. The organization split, and he became president of the North American Lutheran Implement Dealers Association—Orthodox Division.

This Lutheran Babbitt had a P.S. on one of his letters. He wrote something like this: "I have to give a speech to the Rotary Club next week. I've been looking around for a certain Scripture passage and I've not been able to find it. Could you give me any help with that? The passage is, 'God helps those who help themselves.' " [Lest any reader should miss the satire, there is no Bible passage that says that.]

Yes, some people have trouble with satire—and there were those who took this satirical letter seriously. *The Cresset* eventually dropped it. Some people just do not appreciate humor. They are very serious people! They are also not too human!

As I said, there were these two Hittites, and one says ...

21

YESHUA

A FTER 20 YEARS, WITH THE MAKING OF THE FILM ON THE AUGSBURG Confession in 1980 and plans for *Yeshua* in 1981, I finally was in the movies again. Let me tell you why that made me so happy.

As I have mentioned before, growing up toward the beginning of radio, television, and the movies, I have been enamored of the technology and captivated by these tremendous channels for proclaiming the Redeemer. That is one of the reasons I eagerly accepted the opportunity to do public relations work for Concordia-Bronxville and why I jumped at the offer to establish a true public relations department for the LCMS. I would also be less than honest if I did not admit how much I enjoyed doing TV programs, first as a volunteer under Ade Meyer's public relations office and then full-time as the director of the new Public Relations Department. And I fully appreciated the extra "frosting" God provided when I had the opportunity in 1952 to work on the film *Martin Luther* and in 1960 on *Question 7*.

I see the Lord's hand, though, when he called me to be radio's "The Lutheran Hour" speaker rather than to focus on television work. Therefore, following my work on the movie *Question 7*, I spent 20 years on radio work alone—until 1980 and '81 when I was asked again to be on film. Maybe the Lord thought my energy for radio work would be recharged if I received another taste of film work. At any rate, 1980 was marked by work for the film on the Augsburg Confession (which I mentioned briefly in chapter 8), and 1981 brought my role in *Yeshua.*

NARRATING *Yeshua*

In 1980, Arnon Zuckermann, the former head of Israeli television and founder of his own production company in Jerusalem, was looking for someone to coproduce with his company a television documentary about the Jewish roots of Jesus. This idea had been sparked by a book he had read about Jesus called *The Israelite.*

Arnon Zuckermann got in touch with the executive producer for Lutheran Television at the time, Ardon Albrecht, who became very excited about doing this project. Ardon got in touch with John Meredythe Lucas, a Roman Catholic director with whom he had worked in the past (not the Lucas of "Lucas Films" fame), and asked Lucas if he would be interested in working on the project. Lucas was extremely interested. As it turned out, Lucas not only directed, but also helped to write the script for the series. Aid Association for Lutherans, the fraternal life insurance company on whose board I sat at the time, provided a grant to fund the project.

Ardon decided that, because of my position as Lutheran Hour speaker and president of the United Bible Societies, he would ask me to be the host and narrator for the series. I agreed to do that, even though it meant canceling a number of engagements for which I had already made commitments.

This was not a small project. It required three and a half months of filming, mostly in Israel. Several weeks before the filming was to begin, Albrecht and Lucas went over to Israel to meet with Arnon Zuckermann, who was to provide the technical people for the shoot, to scout out the sites where the filming was to be done, and to get whatever permission might be needed to shoot in those locations.

After they had made all these arrangements, they sent for me. That was in February of 1981. I flew into Israel and arrived at the Jerusalem Hilton Hotel, which would be our headquarters for the next three months or so. Marcia did not go with me at that time, although she did join me during the last two or three weeks of filming and spent the rest of the time in Israel with me.

The first day, we began shooting at an archaeological site in the city of Jerusalem, an Iron Age tomb where archaeologists had done some digging. As was the custom with Lutheran Television over its 30-year history, before filming began, they opened with prayer.

Ardon asked me to say that opening prayer. It was interesting that the whole crew was Israeli, and that the only Christians there—in fact, the only Gentiles—were Ardon, John Meredythe Lucas, and myself.

In my prayer, I asked the God of Abraham, Isaac, and Jacob, the Father of our Lord Jesus Christ, to guard and keep all those involved in the work ahead. After the prayer, I said to the Israeli crew, "You know, most of us Christians in the United States grew up with the stories of Abraham, Isaac, and Jacob. When Christians are at their best," I told them, "they have always identified closely with Jewish people. But as you know, we have not always been at our best."

When I said that, it was like a cloud between us had been lifted. Until that time, I think that Israeli crew was not too sure how well they could work with us Christians, especially on what was going to be an essentially Christian production. From that first day on, we worked together just fine.

And when I say we worked, I mean we *worked*. Every weekend, I would go over the script for the next week to memorize it and to rewrite what needed to be changed.

On the days when we were doing the filming, Arnon Zucker-mann and his people would use every hour of daylight that was available. Ardon, John Lucas, and I would get up at 4 A.M. We would have breakfast in our rooms, because there were no restaurants open at that hour of the morning. Then we would wait in the hotel lobby for a van to pick us up and get us to the place where we were shooting by 5 A.M. The crew would get ready there quickly and put my makeup on me. And right at 5:30 every morning we would hear, "Zene vun. Take vun. R-r-rollink," and the filming would begin.

We would work until about 9:30 A.M. Then we would break so the crew could have its breakfast and we could have a snack. The caterer, a fellow named Avrahan Rappaport, prepared quite a feast. We would have these big Arab bagels or pita bread with cream cheese, sardines, olives, and all kinds of other things.

Later on, we were filming during the seven days of Passover. During those days there could be nothing with leaven in it. That meant there could be no Arab bagels. It was interesting to see all the creative ways Avrahan Rappaport had to get around that. For example, he put scrambled eggs between two pieces of matzo to make a "Matzo McMuffin," and he would put chocolate frosting between two pieces of matzo to make a matzo chocolate cake. Fascinating man!

After that break, we would usually shoot until early afternoon. Then we found a restaurant somewhere nearby and had a light lunch. Usually this would be an Arab restaurant, because there are few Jewish delicatessens in Israel like those we have in the United States. Their owners come primarily from Eastern Europe.

After lunch, we would start again and work until 5:30 P.M. Film directors love the afternoon sunlight! Then a van would take us back to our hotel. John, Ardon, and I, and later on Marcia and John's wife, Pat, would have dinner together. After that, I would go back to my room and review the narration for the next day, which was usually about 10 pages, single spaced. Often I edited the narration again at that time.

One of the things that had to be changed was the material that had been written about Abraham's sacrifice of Isaac. The script made a big deal about how there had been human sacrifice in Israel, and that when Abraham took his son up onto the mountain, God made it clear that He did not want any more human sacrifice. I changed that, because that was not the meaning of that incident. The Bible makes clear that Abraham, in obedience to God, would have gone through with that sacrifice of his son. However, God provided a substitute. God's action symbolized the whole future history of the people of God: their/our relationship with Him depends on His grace, not on our obedience.

The other thing I would sometimes change would be the Scripture sections. Instead of using the narration they had prepared, I often told the story based on my own translation of the Greek. I did that, for example, when we told the story of Jesus talking with the woman at Jacob's well and also when we told the Easter story.

They had provided very little narration in relation to the Easter story, and I felt we needed more. I suggested that I walk down the road and tell the story of the Emmaus disciples. They agreed to let me do that, and it turned out very well.

I ad-libbed a lot of those things. The rest of the narration I did from memory. When I first got over there, they had prepared cue cards for me. I told Ardon I did not need the cue cards and really could not use them. The whole crew was a little skeptical about that, but it worked just fine.

That was the routine almost every day we were there. We would start at 5:30 A.M. and work until 5:30 P.M. Then I would have those two hours in the evening to prepare for the next day. The only time that routine varied was when the weather changed our plans.

CHANGES IN SCHEDULE FOR RAINY DAYS

A couple of days when we had planned to shoot outside, it rained. Then Ardon and Arnon Zuckermann would have to try to find a spot somewhere where they could shoot indoors on short notice. When they would find a place like that, they would come with a different script from the one I had worked on for that day, and I had to memorize it on the spot.

I remember once after we had been working on this project for several weeks, we had to change locations because of rain. When we got to the new site, Ardon put three pages of narration in front of me and asked me to learn as much of it as I could. I guess I was a little tired after those long days, and that was the proverbial straw that broke the camel's back. I think I said something to Ardon like, "I can't do that." And he said, "I'm really sorry, but we have no other choice. Take as long as you want. If it takes two hours, that's okay. We'll wait for you."

About a half hour later, I said to Ardon, "I guess I'm ready," and we got started. That evening, I had to call Bill Kniffel in St. Louis about something else. When he asked me how things were going, I told him, "They're trying to kill me!"

I never got sick during the whole time I was there, but I did sometimes get tired at the end of those long days. Finally Ardon told me that he could tell when I was getting tired, because I would pull on my ear.

"You know," I told him, "I've been told that I did that ever since I was a baby. When I got tired, I would pull on my ear."

CONVERSATIONS WITH JANET NAEH

The first person I would see every morning when I arrived on location was the script supervisor and makeup/wardrobe person: Janet Naeh. She was a Sephardic Jew, whose ancestors went back 12 generations in Palestine. I would spend the first half hour of each day with her while she applied makeup to give me a suntan. After several weeks of shooting in the sun, I got my own suntan. Then she had to tone down my tan, so that it would match the one in previous scenes.

Janet was a very intelligent woman. She was fluent in both Hebrew and English and could get along pretty well in several other languages. Every morning while she was making me up, we would talk about the narration I had done the day before. On the second or third day, she said to me, "I'd like to have a copy of your Bible."

I called up the headquarters of the Bible Society in Jerusalem, and they sent over five Good News Bibles, which I gave to her and members of the crew. The next morning she told me, "I read your Bible last night, and I discovered that it has our Bible in it too!"

After that, she started asking me questions about Jesus and asking me to explain things that bothered her about Him. One thing that bothered her was that He seemed to be lacking in humility.

"If people had said 'He must be the Messiah,' that would be one thing," she said, "but He didn't show much humility in saying that about Himself."

"But if He was the Messiah," I said to her, "why shouldn't He say so?"

She struggled with that and all kinds of other things about Jesus during the eight weeks of the filming. We had a particularly strong and interesting conversation about John chapter 6. It helped me understand why Jesus responded to the religious leaders the way He did.

We had quite a number of fascinating experiences during the three and a half months we were shooting in Israel. One time when we were filming near the Red Sea, we were shooting from a cliff down over a huge wadi. The only way John Meredythe Lucas could get the shot he wanted was for the camera to be high and for Lucas to hold me over the edge of the cliff by his belt. If he had dropped me, that would have been the end of the filming—and probably of me.

One time after Marcia had joined me, we were shooting a shepherd-sheep scene with a Bedouin boy. Ardon had negotiated with the boy's father to give him a certain amount of money for his son to do the scene. We shot it near their tent. After we finished, the father offered us a cup of tea. It was obvious from the situation that the tea had undoubtedly been prepared under less than sanitary conditions. I felt we could not offend our host, and urged Marcia to drink some of the tea—and to pretend to enjoy it. She came back home with hepatitis. Whether the tea had anything to do with that, we do not know.

PASSOVER

As I mentioned before, part of the time we were there was during the seven days of Passover. I understand now what was happening when the Lord was crucified, because I was there during the Passover. It has been estimated that a million people came there during the Passover during Jesus' day. People came to see the marvelous temple Herod had built. It was a real tourist attraction. At the same time, they came to celebrate the Passover. They came from all over, even from Cyrene on the coast of north Africa.

It was that way while we were there. The streets were crowded with people. Every once in a while, there would be a group of people with someone carrying a cross, winding their way through those gangways that serve as streets in the old city.

We could not eat in the hotel during this time, because the restaurants there were filled with people from New York who had come to celebrate the Passover. They would sit there singing songs, because Passover is a very joyful time. We stood at the door and listened to them. It was a happy occasion for them.

We were shooting our film in the midst of this whole congregation of people. One of the places we shot during that time was on the road going down from Jerusalem to Jericho. There is a sign in Hebrew there forbidding priests from going down that road. They are not supposed to travel that road, because they are not allowed to go through a cemetery. They had to go a roundabout way to go down to Jericho. We put an English translation of that sign on the road for our film, so that people would know what it said.

That sign is typical of the legalism that has arisen, not so much from the Old Testament but from Rabbinical literature. That kind of legalism is woven throughout life in Israel today too. In our hotel, the elevators were programmed on the Sabbath to stop on every other floor. One elevator would stop on the even-numbered floors, the other on the odd-numbered ones. You did not push the button to call for the elevator. It opened automatically when it came to your floor. That way you were not doing any work on the Sabbath.

The other law that affected everyday life was the law against mixing meat and dairy products. Once we were having a script conference in the evening in Ardon's hotel room, and we called for room service. Someone wanted a glass of milk and John Meredythe Lucas wanted a steak sandwich. There was a long discussion in which they explained that they could not bring meat and milk at the same time. Finally Lucas, who was the one on the phone, told them, "Okay, bring the milk to this room and bring a steak sandwich to room 412." He then went to his room to get his steak sandwich and brought it back to Ardon's room where we were meeting.

PROBLEMS IN A MUSLIM CEMETERY

That kind of legalism pervades life in Israel for Muslims also. One morning we were shooting a scene in a Muslim cemetery right outside the east wall of Jerusalem overlooking the Brook Kidron. We had to do that before someone came to chase us away.

I had just 30 seconds to finish the narration about how the Muslims buried their dead there outside the original Golden Gate, which is now closed up. The theory was that when the Messiah came, He would come through the Golden Gate. He would have to raise the dead that were in the way before He could go through there. That meant that those who were buried there would be the first to rise from the dead. Followers of Islam had more faith in the resurrection of Jesus than did His own people!

Just as I had finished this narration, people came running to chase us out of there, and we went running too.

Another time, we were filming in the famous Muslim mosque at the Dome of the Rock. We had official permission to shoot there, but certain people who were there tried to chase us out. They were angry, first of all because we were there and then because we were taking pictures in a holy place.

GOD OPENED A WINDOW

In terms of the political situation in the Middle East, it seemed that God had opened up a window for our project. Just before we began, our crew, who were all in the Israeli military, had been off on some kind of military maneuvers and would not have been available had that not ended in time. Then, just after we finished filming, Israel invaded southern Lebanon, and our crew left again. We could not have continued had we not finished shooting a few days earlier.

Even though those were relatively quiet times, things were tense in Israel, but that is always true. We were often shooting film on the West Bank, because Bethlehem, Jericho, Nazareth, and a number of other places, such as Jacob's well, are located there. It was a little disconcerting to notice when we were in those places that when the cameramen leaned over, you could see a revolver in their belt. You would also never see children getting out of a school bus without two or three people armed with automatic weapons getting out first to make sure that the way was clear.

Let us hope that a time will come when people in that part of the world can put some of those hatreds behind them. That is going to be very difficult. Having seen all of this, I know that the hatred on both sides is so thick you can cut it with a knife. I am thankful to see in 1996 that the leaders are doing something to change the situation. Still, a lot of those people have to be convinced that something needs to change for peace to be lasting. A lot of the people there have been raised to think that hatred is the order of the day. I do not know how you change that, except in one way.

CHANGING THE HATREDS

On a plane later on, I was sitting next to an official of United Technologies in Connecticut. He was in charge of the division dealing with Boeing Aircraft. He told me all kinds of things about Israel and about the help being given them by the United States. Then he told me about his 12-year-old daughter, whom he was teaching the Old Testament.

I asked him whether he taught her about the chosen people of God. Jews do not usually like to talk with Gentiles about that, because it makes them seem to be arrogant.

He said, "What do you mean?"

"Well," I said, "you know the chosen people of God were not picked because they were mighty or numerous. Deuteronomy makes a big point of this. It says in effect, 'I picked you in spite of the fact that you were the least of the nations' [e.g., Deuteronomy 7:7]. It was an election of grace. And the name of the game is love. You know how often that appears in the psalms: 'His stead-fast love lasts forever' " [e.g., Psalm 136].

"Yes," he said, "I remember that very well. That's interesting."

"That's the theme that runs through the New Testament too," I said to him. "It is not so much that we love God, but that He loved us and gave His Son to be the sacrifice for our sins. You know, I think I have the solution to that problem in Israel."

"You do?"

"Yes," I said, "the solution is the Good News from God that we have forgiveness in Jesus Christ. You cannot go back to the fork in the road, but you can receive forgiveness for the past from God, and then go on from there and do the right thing, which is to forgive the past."

There was silence for at least a minute, and then he said, "That's very interesting."

That is what I think our friends in the Middle East have to learn. It is what we have to tell them too. We are not peddling ourselves here. "We preach not ourselves, but Jesus Christ as Lord, and ourselves as His servants for Jesus' sake. For the great God who first elected for the light to shine into our hearts has given us the light of His glory in the face of Jesus Christ" (2 Corinthians 4:5-6).

That is all we have. That is what we have to tell people. Nowadays people need that more than ever. They cannot go back to the fork in the road to start all over again. All of us have to start anew from day to day, forgiving as we have been forgiven. This is a big order. It takes the work of the Holy Spirit, with the Good News of salvation by the grace of God through faith in Jesus Christ.

Without taking any credit for ourselves, without any self-aggrandizement, and with no ecclesiastical competitiveness, we need to tell people there and everywhere that the Gospel is for them. If we do not do it, someone else will. The time has come. Nothing else will do.

This is not "religion." This is God saving people from themselves, from their sins, from their past. The past is just full of all kind of things that can never be explained or covered up. The only thing that can be done is to forgive.

Of course, that is not worldly. The world says, "I'll forgive, but I can't forget." That is not forgiveness, at least in God's language.

When I was at the seminary, I used to go to a men's Bible class at Third Baptist Church that was led by the president of the International Shoe Company. There were about 400 men in attendance. I usually stopped in on Sunday morning on the way to my own church. The Bible class leader said, "You can say, 'I can forgive, but I won't forget,' but when you say that, you're not forgiving him, you're just laying for him."

I have never forgotten that. You do not really come to the fullness of the stature of Christ until you learn how to forgive.

How true that is of a marriage! A marriage begins, not so much on the day of the ceremony, but on the day when the new groom discovers for the first time that his new bride is not perfect. Now she has known that about him all along, but how he handles finding out that she is not perfect will determine what kind of marriage theirs will be. Forgiveness is the name of the game in marriage. People need to forgive one another and then put it behind them. From there you can go on!

What is true in a marriage is, I believe, true of the situation anywhere in the world. The Israelis and the Arabs have to learn how to forgive one another, how to forget the past, and how to then go on from there. That kind of forgiveness is not mere sentimentalism. It originates at the foot of Christ's cross!

A DISASTER!

Now back to *Yeshua,* which is what the name of this documentary eventually became. After we got back to the United States and the footage had been edited, Ardon Albrecht looked at the first cut. It was a disaster. Ardon said that I had done a fine job, but the whole two hours was "talking head" shots of me. That did not make for interesting television.

Ardon told me this over dinner with Marcia and me in California shortly after he had viewed the first cuts.

"Well," I said, "that happens. Sometimes you think something is working, and it just doesn't work."

"But we're going to make it work," Ardon said. And he did.

The film editor with whom Ardon was working had worked on the "In Search of ..." programs and others. Ardon asked him what needed to be done. He told Ardon that the narration needed to be interspersed with some reenactments, and that it needed some "gee-whiz" material. For example, we had interviewed Israel's leading archaeologist Yigael Yadin at the Shrine of the Book about the Dead Sea Scrolls and showed the copy of the Isaiah scroll displayed there. What needed to be added was a reenactment of the little Bedouin boy finding those scrolls.

Ardon did a lot of research and study. Then he wrote those reenactments. He and Lucas went back to Israel to do some more shooting. That meant they needed some close-ups of me. They also needed to record more narration to cover the new things that Ardon had added to the script. I went out to California to do those things.

I also walked across the world in California! They had constructed a huge section covering the whole floor of a large studio showing the whole Mediterranean world. I was the only one allowed to walk on that map. Even then, they had to cover my shoes with material that would leave no footprints. At the opening of the whole series, they had me come in from outer space and walk across the Mediterranean Sea to Israel, then to Greece, Italy, and Spain. That was John Meredythe Lucas's idea. I found out later that it cost $80,000. As Ardon said, Lucas had expensive ideas.

With all the things now added, *Yeshua* became a five-hour miniseries. It was shown exclusively on the CBN Cable Network during the Lenten season of 1984 and 1985. In 1986 it was shown as a syndicated series over 79 stations throughout the United States. It is also now in many church libraries. It is good background material for Sunday school classes, confirmation classes, and also makes for interesting Bible classes. It is still available for purchase through Concordia Publishing House.

Yeshua won an Angel Award from Religion in Media, a nonprofit organization that encourages and honors top quality religious productions. It also won a Gold Award in the category of special documentaries at the International Film and TV Festival of New York.

Yeshua in Russian

There is an interesting footnote to the *Yeshua* story. Marilyn Wolf, a member of Canoga Park Lutheran Church, where Ardon Albrecht had been a member when *Yeshua* was produced, went over to Russia in 1992. While she was there, she got the idea of dubbing *Yeshua* into Russian. She thought it would be appropriate for Russian television, because unlike Americans, for whom television is primarily an entertainment medium, the Russian people still use television to learn things.

Marilyn talked to Ardon Albrecht about her idea, and he asked the LLL about it. Walt Winters, the LLL's assistant director of international ministry, told Ardon that they had just finished a study with some consulting group to see which programs would be most appropriate for Russian TV. He said that the number one choice was *Yeshua.*

"If that's the case, we're going to do it," Marilyn said.

Having found out that it would cost about $30,000 to dub *Yeshua* into Russian, she got together with Sharon Hartwig, and they formed a committee to put together a fund-raising event. They called it "An Evening with Dr. Hoffmann and Yeshua." It was sponsored by the Southern California District of the LLL. Ardon was there, and Marcia and I were there. John Meredythe Lucas and his wife, Pat, had been invited, but could not be there because they had a previous engagement.

The Southern California LLL District presented a beautiful copy of the Rosetta stone to both Ardon and me in appreciation for our work on *Yeshua*. By the end of that evening, with the help of Lutheran Brotherhood and AAL, they had raised the entire $30,000 needed. *Yeshua* has been dubbed into Russian, and in 1995 was shown on Russian television.

Truly, our gracious God has given me opportunities beyond anything I ever could have imagined. Not only did He call me into full-time service doing what I loved to do anyway, He also let me have the fun of occasionally working professionally in film and TV—and having that go to Russia, a country closed to the West almost my entire life. How grateful I am!

22

RELAXATION, RENEWAL, AND A FEW VACATIONS

W HAT DO YOU DO FOR FUN?" SOMEONE ONCE ASKED ME. I KNOW what the question meant; that is why I wanted to say, "My work *is* my fun." Yet I am thankful that I live in an age and a country in which a person has time away from one's full-time vocation—leisure time—in order to pursue additional interests.

I word my thoughts here carefully, because I do not view time away from the job as "free time" or "goof-off time." Nor do I view my time on the job as only putting out energy for others, while time away is my turn to receive. Of every day—and of every evening and every weekend and vacation—I say with David, "This is the day the Lord has made; let us rejoice and be glad in it" (Psalm 118:24 NIV).

As a Christian, I am equipped to enjoy every moment, even though as a sinner I do not. But I could. For some people, time is the passage from the past to the future. For me, time is the present, because the past has been forgiven in Jesus Christ and the future offers new opportunities not yet here. Therefore, while this imperfect world may force upon me a time to weep or a time to mourn, with God's strength I will celebrate the present as a time to laugh and a time to dance (Ecclesiastes 3:4)—and to do so with other people, because laughing and dancing alone is nothing.

After we moved to St. Louis in 1963, one of the sports I picked up was golf. Walter Burke, the president of McDonnell's aerospace division and a member of the same congregation to which Marcia and I belong (whom I mentioned at some length in chapter 12) gave me a membership at Forest Hills Country Club. I played many a delightful round of golf there with him and other friends, associates, and family members. I no longer play golf, but I do enjoy dining at the club house, and have spent many, many enjoyable evenings there with a variety of good friends. I was saddened greatly when Walter died; he was a fantastic layman!

As another favorite pastime, Marcia and I belonged to a duplicate bridge club here in St. Louis. The members were a great mixture of lay and clergy leaders of the LCMS in the city: Rev. Dr. Oliver Harms, the LCMS president, and his wife, Bert; Mr. Fred Kuhlmann, the president of the St. Louis Cardinals, and his wife, Mildred; Rev. John Meyer, executive of the Missouri District and his wife, Elsa; Mr. Ed Parent, a real estate agent in St. Louis, and his wife, Lois; Mr. Ed Stoppenhagen, the AAL general agent for the St. Louis area, and his wife, Ruby; Rev. Elmer Kraemer, the editor of *The Lutheran Layman* (the LLL newspaper), and his wife, Martha; and Marcia and I.

I really enjoyed that bridge club. Whenever the club was scheduled to meet, I would try to be home in order to be there. We would move around to the various people's homes, and I suppose there was as much conversation and socializing as there was serious card playing.

Someone once asked one of the members of that bridge group whether I was a good bridge player. "Ossie is a good Lutheran Hour speaker," was the reply.

Those bridge evenings were a great time of relaxation with friends, and I enjoyed them very much.

Over the years, though, the recreational highlights that stick in our minds are the vacation trips. Marcia and I had lots of those.

VACATIONING IN THE POCONOS

In the years when we lived in New York, I would spend a week giving lectures at Pocono Crest Lutheran Camp, just outside Pocono Pines, Pennsylvania. Usually, I would take the family with me, and we would have a good time together there.

One time, though, was not much fun: August 1955, the year Kate was born. A terrible hurricane that year caused a torrential rainstorm in the mountains. Forty people were killed, and 19 bridges were washed out. I had planned to go back to New York City on one Sunday to preach and then return to Pocono Pines. Marcia, though, afraid of being stranded when eight months and three weeks pregnant, went back to New York with me. The drive back was no fun—especially driving in the blinding rain over the top of a dam. It took us a long time to get home!

In later years, beginning in the early 1980s, we went regularly to another place in the Poconos: the large Mount Airy Lodge just outside the town of Mount Pocono, Pennsylvania, and just a few miles from Pocono Pines. The lodge's principal owner and manager is a wonderful layman named Emil Wagner. He was a charter member of The Lutheran Church of Our Savior in Mount Pocono. I first met Mr. Wagner through his pastor, Rev. Louis Meyer. Previously Lou had been an executive for the Atlantic District and had occupied a New York office in the same building and on the same floor as mine when I was public relations director for the LCMS. (I mentioned that back in chapter 6.) He also worked with us as a public relations representative for the Atlantic District at quite a few of the synodical conventions. We got to know each other quite well. Then Lou served a congregation in Bogota, New Jersey. In 1980, when he was already at retirement age, he accepted a call to Mount Pocono.

Anyway, on several occasions Lou or Emil invited Marcia and me to come to the Poconos, and Emil would put us up at his lodge for as long as we wanted to stay. Even though Lou Meyer is now living in Ridgewood, New Jersey, all I have to do is get in touch with him or Emil, and Marcia and I can go up to Mount Airy Lodge and stay there for a beautiful few days.

A third place in the Poconos we have visited several times was the summer home of our friends Rev. Dr. Ewald and Joan Mueller. Our friendship with the Muellers went all the way back to our New York days. I first met Ewald when I was helping Ade Meyer as a volunteer for the synodical public relations committee back in the '40s. When the committee first proposed to a Synodical convention that the church should have a full-time office and staff, Ewald, who was a pastor in Brooklyn at the time, strongly supported us. After the office opened in '48, Ewald and Joan, Lou and Ida Meyer, and Marcia and I sometimes would get together for just an evening of socializing. We were able to do that a number of times also in the Poconos until Ewald passed away.

We were together with the Muellers for the last time at Concordia-St. Paul, Minnesota, in 1990. Ewald received the Distinguished Alumni Award, and I received the Aeterna Moliri Award. Ewald was already in failing health at the time. We had a wonderful time there. The people at Concordia-St. Paul dotted every *i* and crossed every *t* to make that a wonderful occasion.

GONE FISHING

One of the benefits of moving to St. Louis in 1963 was developing a close friendship with Harry Barr, then president of the LLL. He owned an aluminum fabrication factory, and—as a side benefit for me—sat as a member of the Game and Fish Commission of the state of Arkansas. He began a tradition of fishing trips that continues yet today. But before I go into detail about those trips, I need to tell you about Harry himself.

Harry Barr is one of the great heroes in my memory. He was a prince of the Kingdom, a man with a real heart for the Lord Jesus Christ. His character was molded by his faith in Christ and the love by which faith exercises itself. That's the way faith makes muscle: with love. There are those who do not see it that way. They appear to believe that faith exercises itself by exercising the muscles of the mouth. But the way I see it, faith exercises the muscles of the heart.

That is a beautiful thing to see. It looks wonderful in a woman, but it also looks great in a man. It is very masculine. It is the kind of love that is willing to take a rap for Christ and to come back for more. That is the way Harry was, and I guess that is the way Christ expects us to be.

Harry did not have a legalistic bone in his body. That was the wonderful thing about him. Some laymen do have legalism in their makeup, because they have a sneaking hunch that maybe God is looking to them to make good for themselves. Some seem to believe that God is looking to them to redeem others, if in no other way than through criticism of others. But not Harry. He knew that only the blood of Christ could redeem him and anyone else.

I personally am thankful that Harry was president of the Lutheran Laymen's League in 1963. He served the LLL as chairman of "The Lutheran Hour" committee and in other ways too. Finally, in 1960, he was elected LLL president (and reelected again in 1962). As a recognized leader in the church he later he became vice-chairman of the Board of Directors of The Lutheran Church—Missouri Synod. He credited all this to his grandmother Barr. Scotsmen (which is what Harry was) usually aren't Lutherans, but Granny Barr was—and she insisted that her grandson too be raised a Lutheran.

Harry died in 1984. He had a heart attack while he was on a trip to Scotland. His pastor in Fort Smith, Arkansas, had his funeral sermon, but I also spoke at his funeral. At Harry's funeral, we cried—and we laughed too. I think that is the way he would have wanted it.

Harry had been in the air-conditioning business in Fort Smith, Arkansas, where he lived. Then he started an aluminum fabrication factory in order to take care of his three sons who were just growing up at that time. The remarkable thing was that all three of them fit beautifully into that business and have developed it so that they now sell all over the country. They are now a vinyl window and door manufacturing company and still make all kinds of other things. Tom Barr is the president, Dick Barr is the sales director, and Larry Barr is in charge of operations and data processing for the company. They all work together beautifully.

By the way, they all live on seven acres right in the middle of Fort Smith, with great woods and houses all over the property. I think the house where Harry and his wife lived burned down at least once, maybe twice, but they rebuilt and continued to live there. Harry's daughter, Marilyn, Dick's twin sister, a medical doctor, lives in the house with her mother, Irene, since Harry died.

Now, let me tell you about the fishing trips that came about because of Harry.

Our Arkansas Fishing Trips

Those fishing trips started when Harry was still a member of the Game and Fish Commission of the state of Arkansas. Harry's plan was to get a small bunch of leading Lutheran laymen together for some wholesome recreation as well as for mutual support. I suppose I was invited in part because I was "The Lutheran Hour" speaker and in part to provide some biblical input to the mutual support.

Those who go on these fishing trips consider it an honor to be invited. I believe there are others who would love to be invited, and if there were room, we would be glad to have them along. But we have to limit it to 10 or 12 people. It has to be an even number, because there are two to each boat.

The first trip was, I believe, to Beaver Lake in Arkansas. Our escorts were three game wardens who furnished the boats and the motors and everything else we needed for that fishing trip. That was great, having game wardens taking us around, because they knew where the fish were. A few years afterwards, though, that was no longer possible, because the members of the Game and Fish Commission decided to restrict the wardens' activities.

One time at another lake we had a wonderful time in the motel where we were staying, because it poured cats and dogs almost the whole time we were there. We did get out now and then to fish for crappies, and I think we must have caught about 80. There was no limit at that time on crappies. We could keep all we caught.

For about the past 20 years, we have been floating down the White River, a fast-flowing river coming out of the Bull Shoals Dam. We usually meet at Mountain Home, Arkansas. In recent years, some of the fishermen fly into St. Louis, and I drive us down to Mountain Home. Marcia always makes sandwiches for us to eat along the way. She makes different kinds and labels each one so that we know what kind they are. We always have sandwiches left over, even though these are fellows with man-sized appetites. She also sends along lemonade to drink with the sandwiches. Even though we could eat at home, since it is only a five-hour drive, we still take those sandwiches and eat them in the car.

That night we stay in a little old motel in Mountain Home. I take the group out to dinner that evening, and that is my last contribution to the event. The other guys take care of the rest.

The trip has become something of a ritual. We all wear caps that have "OCJH Fishing Trip" on them—except for one of our regulars, Larry Knutson, who always wears his cap from Dakota

Boys Ranch. And we always contend for the prize for who catches the largest fish. I have never won that. Of course, I would refuse it if I did. The person who wins has to furnish the prize for the next year.

The first morning there, we get up at five o'clock, and by eight o'clock we are on the river. We go in boats, two men to each boat, with a guide. We go to where the Norfolk River joins the White River, about eight miles from Mountain Home, and put in at the dock there. The next days we float down the river to Calico and other places beyond that.

We finish fishing each day at 5:00 in the afternoon. We have dinner together in a tent set up for us. We sleep in tents along the river for two nights, and the next noon we leave. We tell our wives that we really rough it, because we sleep in tents. Our wives laugh at that, because we do not have to do anything to prepare our meals or even our sleeping quarters.

We eat a lot of fish. The possession limit we can take home is 12. We have to eat like mad in order to keep on fishing! We catch rainbow trout weighing from one to three pounds, and we have caught some weighing five to six pounds; but we usually return those to the water so somebody else can catch them. The state of Arkansas gives you a little pin that you can put on your hat attesting to the nobility of this action.

I enjoy the evenings along the river, for those are the hours we visit. Mostly we talk about things of the Kingdom—not church affairs, but affairs of the Kingdom throughout the world. The rest of the group is always glad to talk about things like that. Laymen like to talk about the cause of Christ and what it takes to be a Christian in the modern world.

Sometimes one or the other will give a testimony to the power of Christ in his own personal life during the past year or so. One man's wife had just died, and he told us what it means to have Christ to comfort him during that time. A year or two later he told us what it meant to have another wife who is willing to take care of him and for him to take care of her as Christ intended in the institution of marriage.

It is a really great way to get together. These discussions sometimes move the men to tears. At other times we laugh boisterously. I would say the laughter far outweighs the tears.

Our fishing trips are a wonderful time of being together with real men. That's another thing I appreciate. You do not have to be a wimp to be a Christian. These are real men. They also appreciate, I think, that this is a real gathering of men who know something. They know the power of the resurrection in their own lives.

Discussions of Letters from Lutheran Hour Listeners

When I was still speaker on "The Lutheran Hour," sometimes I would bring along letters that had the names and addresses deleted. These would be letters that I had answered during that year, often letters posing difficult problems in which people were asking for help. I would read a letter, then I would ask them, "How would you answer that letter?"

We would often spend a half hour or more on one letter. They would suggest to me how they might have answered that letter. It was really encouraging to see Christian laymen come up with what I would consider to be very intelligent answers. In most cases, they answered almost every aspect of the problem, and in a few cases, saw something of the problem that I had overlooked in my own reply to that letter.

Sometimes the problem a person had was really the problem of someone else. At other times the problem of someone else was really the problem of the letter writer. Someone would write, "I know someone who needs help with this problem," and then outline it. You knew exactly who it was that had the problem. It was the person who was writing the letter but did not want to identify it with himself or herself. The men on those fishing trips would sense what the writer was really asking in the letter, then go ahead and help answer the problem.

That helped me a lot. I think it helped those men too. It helped them to realize that the Word of Christ is at the cutting edge on a broadcast. It may seem to be off in the distance, but actually it is very close to the lives of people. People sometimes do ask questions of a broadcaster that they would not bring to the attention of people in their own neighborhood, or maybe even of their own pastor.

I knew I could not solve all their problems by mail, and I never tried to do that. What I tried to do was to give them a general line they could follow with the problem that confronted them. I did not want to mislead people into thinking that I could somehow by magic words or something else solve every problem that they had. But I could give them the comforting assurance that there might be a good solution to their problem. Then I would say, "I think you need help," and I would refer them to a local pastor.

In most cases, the pastor responded nobly. In a few cases, the pastor never called on them at all. That is the way it was. I guess it shows that pastors are human too.

Anyhow, discussing those letters was one of the things that we did on those fishing trips.

Of the 10 or so on the trip, the regulars for many years were Harry Barr, Hy Firehammer, John Bleeke, Walter Rugland, Rupert Dunklau, and Dr. John Drager. A number of others were invited to come along each year. What outstanding men! John Bleeke became vice-president of The Chocolate House, a post from which he retired in Milwaukee; Hy Firehammer owned a General Tire agency in Benton Harbor, Michigan; Walter Rugland, now deceased, was president of AAL; Dr. John Drager is an oral surgeon in Alaska (I'll tell you more about him later); and I already told you about Harry Barr.

Of course, the makeup of the participants in those fishing trips has now changed somewhat. More recently it has included General Jack Vessey; Walter Roessler, an executive of General Motors in Michigan; Chaplain Connie Walker; Jerry Saegert, a lawyer and the son of Clarence Saegert, a very prominent LLL member in Texas; Dr. Ralph Reinke, the former president of Concordia Publishing House and of Concordia College, Seward, Nebraska; Larry Knutson, chairman of Dakota Boys Ranch; Chaplain James Shaw; and Pastor Paul Dunklau (the son of Rupert and Ruth Dunklau). Over the years others attending included President Jacob Preus of The Lutheran Church—Missouri Synod; John Schuelke, the executive director of the LCMS; and my sons, Peter, Paul, and John. The roster changes every year.

Dr. John Drager has been going on the White River fishing trip with us for 18 years. When he was first invited, he was still a young man. He regarded it an honor that he could join such notable people on these fishing trips. He is a lot of fun. He always likes to stop somewhere and talk to someone about buying property, but he never buys any.

On one of our fishing trips, as John Drager and his partner, Dick Barr, were going down the river, they saw some boat cushions and a tackle box come floating by. Then they saw an older man holding onto something and shouting that he could not swim. Another old man floated by treading water. Figuring this man was all right, they concentrated on saving the other fellow. They managed to get him into their boat. Later they saw the second man on shore with two teenagers. He had floated under their boat, and they had pulled him out of the water; but he was blue and did not seem to be breathing. Drager and Barr gave him CPR and managed to revive him. Someone then ran to a house up the hill and called EMS. They came and took over from there. We heard all about what had happened on the news on the radio the next day. The man was called "Uncle Harry." He was 89 years old.

The next day we called the hospital in Mountain Home, Arkansas, and received the good news that both fishermen were recovering nicely.

Those were the fishing trips Harry Barr organized. Even though he passed away, his sons have continued the tradition. Usually two of them will come along while the other one stays behind to take care of the business. They are great fishermen. They learned that from their father!

Alaska Fishing Trips

The other fishing trip I take annually is in Alaska, where we fish for halibut and salmon. That fishing trip is arranged by Dr. John Drager, one of the regulars on our Arkansas trips.

I first met John at a Lutheran Hour rally in Beloit, Wisconsin, where his mother, Patricia Drager, was rally secretary. Then I next met John and his wife, Carol, when he was a Navy man stationed on Staten Island. He attended a Lutheran Hour rally that was held in the chapel at Princeton University years ago. After that, he was stationed in Boston, and I was up there to preach for the baccalaureate of the Coast Guard Academy in New London. That is when I invited him to go on our annual White River fishing trip. We drove together to Hartford, Connecticut, took a plane out to St. Louis, and drove to Mountain Home to join the others.

John and Carol would come to hear me any time I was speaking anywhere near where he was stationed. He was a pipe smoker, as I was at the time, and every time he came, he always brought me a can of tobacco. Now he brings halibut and salmon. Both he and his wife, Carol, who has been a teacher all these years, have been wonderful friends through the years. Their children, Philip and Christine, both graduates of Valparaiso University, have been wonderful friends too.

John was stationed in Alaska for more than 10 years. As an oral surgeon and captain in the Navy, John took care of many Eskimo patients through the public health service while he was serving the military base. He recently retired from the Navy and has decided to stay in Alaska and open a private practice.

John arranges those fishing trips up there in Alaska. We take a cottage and fish for salmon for a few days on the Kenai River. On one of those days we go along the coast and spend four or five hours fishing for halibut in the ocean about a half mile off shore. Because halibut feed off the bottom of the sea, a person fishes for them by merely dropping the bait as the boat drifts along. Eventually a halibut will take the bait. Halibut generally average between 20 and 60 pounds. I do not know the size of the largest halibut ever caught, but 110 pounds is not unusual. In 1993 we caught about 200 pounds altogether. That year there were five of us, including Tom Barr, in a boat barely big enough to accommodate us and all those fish.

John is a strong LLL supporter and without a doubt the leading Lutheran layman in Alaska. He helps arrange my schedule when I go to Alaska. Usually I preach up there either the Sunday before or the Sunday after our fishing trip—sometimes both Sundays.

In 1993, I preached in Anchorage, then the following Sunday in Palmer, about 40 miles north, for the celebration of the wedding anniversary of Al and Eleanor Brooks. Eleanor is a wonderful writer. One of the things she does is to write postcards to people to encourage them when they need help or to congratulate them for some achievement. She is also a great missionary for the church, always inviting someone to come to a worship service.

Some years before, Eleanor was to be honored for the many marvelous things she had done. When she heard about it, she drove away and spent two days at a motel. She did not want to be honored!

This time they told me, "We're going to honor her, but we're not going to tell her we're honoring her. We're going to say that it's a reception for you."

I asked whether I could mention it in my sermon.

"You better not," they told me, "or she may get up and walk out."

I did include her in my sermon, though, in a little sentence about "the brooks rushing towards the sea." That completely escaped her, but when I said that, I heard several people in the congregation gasp. I think they expected her to rise from her seat and walk out.

After the service we went downstairs to the reception. She was talking to me, and all of a sudden it became apparent to her that this reception was for her and her husband.

In my little talk at the reception, I said, "I had it in the sermon that the Brooks were being honored here today, but I didn't make much of a point of it." A couple weeks later, Mrs. Brooks wrote to me and asked, "Where in the sermon did you say that?" No one in her family had caught it. (Since that time her husband, Al, has died, and she is going her productive way, but now alone.)

That same trick was pulled on another great lady, Edna Messerschmidt, who was church secretary at St. Philip Lutheran Church in Chicago, where Pastor Robert Rickman now serves, following in the footsteps of his saintly father, Vic Rickman, who was a member of my Public Relations Board and later chairman of the Board for Public Relations of The Lutheran Church—Missouri Synod. They had planned to honor Edna for 50 years of service in a number of capacities to that church. She probably did not know that this service was dedicated to her until I entered the pulpit and she was escorted to the seat of honor.

Anyway, those trips to Alaska usually provide us with enough salmon and halibut to put in our home freezer to last all year. I like that, for Marcia tends to fix fish on Friday, even though we are not bound by any regulation to do that. Which reminds me of a funny event that took place back in 1965.

After I had come back from the Vatican Council, I invited some of the priests I had met there from the St. Louis archdiocese to have dinner with us: Joe Baker, Father O'Meara, and Father Persich, the president of Kenrick Seminary.

Father Persich told me that on the previous Christmas, which happened to be on Friday, he and his two brothers, who were also priests, came home to have Christmas dinner with their mother. There were these three strapping fellows, all in their clericals. "Mom," they said, "we can have meat this Christmas."

"No, you can't," she said. "It's Friday."

"The pope has given a special dispensation that we can eat meat on this Christmas Day," one of them said.

She looked at those three strapping sons of hers, all in their clericals, and said, "I'm going to go and ask the priest."

Of course, all of us have been living with the memory of regulations about one thing or another that we think we have to observe. Otherwise we shall give up our faith. The fact of the matter is, all kinds of regulations of the church are of human origin and constantly need to be examined and if necessary appropriately changed. John and James left their nets for their father, Zebedee, to repair. They had more important things to do, and their father probably understood that the usual is not always necessary, while the necessary may be the unusual.

That's probably enough about fishing and fish.

THE *Schlachtfest* IN FRANKENMUTH

Another activity I have enjoyed very much over the years is the annual *Schlachtfest* (butchering festival) in Frankenmuth, Michigan. I think I have been going there for that in late January or early February for something like 20 years.

340

This annual sausage-making event is a long-standing tradition in the Bavarian community of Frankenmuth, which was founded in the 1840s by followers of Rev. William Loehe. While Loehe himself never came to America, he sent many Bavarians to this Michigan community, where they could practice their Lutheran faith in freedom. One of those whom he sent was Jakob Seidel, my mother's grandfather, whom I wrote about in chapter 2.

We leave for the *Schlachtfest* on Saturday morning. Marcia and I and anyone from St. Louis we have invited to join us fly into Detroit Metropolitan Airport. We are met there by Teddi and Marvin Moser, go to their house for coffee, and then Marv hands me the keys to his Lincoln Continental, and we drive to Frankenmuth, which is about 75 miles away.

We arrive in Frankenmuth sometime in the middle of the afternoon and check in at the Bavarian Inn Motel. I preach that evening and for two or three services on Sunday morning at St. Lorenz, the 5,000-member Lutheran church in Frankenmuth. After that, we usually have brunch at the Bavarian Inn, to which about 30 people may be invited.

That afternoon, the men go out to the Adolph Riess farm where two hogs are slaughtered in preparation for the sausage-making the next day. After the hogs have been butchered, the men who are there take turns using a special scraper to scrape the hair off the butchered pigs. I have my own scraper with my name on it, which was given me a few years ago. I actually use it when it is my turn.

That evening, Marcia and I sometimes go to visit the sick and shut-ins at their homes and in nursing homes. Wally Bronner, who with his wife, Irene, owns and operates Bronner's Christmas World in Frankenmuth, arranges these visits. Sometimes we spend as much as six hours visiting and comforting people who need consolation.

341

I always enjoy seeing these wonderful Christian people. They tell me that they listen to "The Lutheran Hour" every Sunday. Some are people who had been faithful churchgoers, but they can no longer get out to church because of illness or the infirmities of age. "The Lutheran Hour" has become their church, and that is an important function of the program.

St. Lorenz church also broadcasts its services, and most of these folks also listen to those broadcasts. They always tell me, "I heard you this morning."

Monday morning the *Schlachtfest* actually begins. The men who participate are a mixed group. Some of them are farmers who learned how to make sausage from their fathers or grandfathers. Others are men who had been raised on farms but have gone on to other professions. Then there are some management people from major corporations, school teachers, pastors—all kinds of people.

This is strictly a men's event. While we are doing the sausage-making, Marcia and the other women go shopping. They spend a good deal of time at Bronner's Christmas World, but they also go to some of the other shops and malls around Frankenmuth. At noon, the women have their own lunch together.

We men start making sausage at 9 A.M. at the Bavarian Inn. For years William Tiny Zehnder, who owns the restaurant, closed it down that day, and we made our sausage in the restaurant kitchen. In recent years, though, we have done our sausage-making in a room off the kitchen, and that works out just fine too. Tiny pays all the costs associated with the *Schlachtfest.*

We have a lot of fun at the *Schlachtfest,* but we also work hard. This is not a spectator sport. Everyone participates! In the morning, the men take turns manning the meat saw, removing the skin, separating the fat from the meat and the meat from the bones.

Great conversation accompanies all these goings-on. Sometimes there is a little blood too. The knives used for all of this are very sharp. In case somebody nicks a finger, Tiny keeps Band-Aids and towels nearby.

About 10:30 or so, we take a break. Tiny has coffee and other Bavarian liquids available in another room for anybody who wants them. Since it is still pretty early to be drinking other liquids, most of us drink coffee.

After the break, we go back and finish what we had been doing. About a half hour later, we start actually making the sausage. We add spices to the fat and meat combinations used to make the sausages, mixing them with our hands. The spicing is according to Tiny Zehnder's secret recipes written by his grand-mother in German. We grind the sausage using a powered sausage grinder. Everybody gets a chance to turn the crank to stuff the sausage casings. We make bratwurst, Polish sausage, blutwurst, liver sausage, and head cheese.

We stop around noon for lunch. The menu is always the same: boiled potatoes, sauerkraut, and pork cooked in the same pot, together with Bavarian rye bread. There is coffee and beer to drink. Tiny makes "poker beer" by putting a small, very hot poker into a half a glass of draft beer. This gives the beer a kind of smoky taste.

After lunch, we go back and finish our sausage-making. At about 4:00 we go back to the motel to clean up a little and to pick up our wives for the evening meal at the Bavarian Inn.

Before the meal that night there is a social hour. Tiny provides whatever is necessary for between 80 and 100 guests. After that, we sit down to eat. Applesauce and *sulzen,* a German delicacy that we also made that afternoon, is served. The buffet-style meal consists of the sausages we made, boiled potatoes, sauerkraut, and Bavarian rye bread.

The dessert is always apple pie. Tiny's wife, Dorothy, spends most of the day baking those pies. The only use of modern appli-ances in making the pies is that the apples are peeled and cored by a big apple peeling machine in the restaurant kitchen. Dorothy bakes her pies in the magnificent ovens in the restaurant kitchen.

After dinner, Judy Keller (Tiny and Dorothy's daughter) serves as master of ceremonies for the *Schlachtfest* program. She wears a headpiece that has a pig snout and pig ears. Whoever has been chosen to be "Schlacht King" for this particular year wears a similar headpiece. That person gets to invite anybody he wants to the next *Schlachtfest.* I was "Schlacht King" in 1994. That award and other equally important awards are given out during the program.

We also do a lot of singing, both in English and in German. I lead the group in singing "A Mighty Fortress." At the end of the program, Tiny gives some closing remarks. Then we sing "God Bless America."

After these festivities, any remaining sausage is sold. Usually I take some sausage home to St. Louis. On Tuesday morning after the *Schlachtfest,* we drive back to Detroit. The Mosers take us to the airport in time to catch our plane, and we are back in St. Louis that evening.

I really enjoy the *Schlachtfest.* Those Frankenmuth Bavarians are wonderful people. They're good Lutheran folks, and they know how to have a *great* time.

Well—as I said at the beginning of the chapter, referring to Ecclesiastes, there is a time to laugh and a time to dance. I thank our gracious Lord that He has provided Marcia and me with plenty of opportunity to do both as we enjoy the company of solid people in His kingdom. Because of what He has done, we appropriate Jackie Gleason's words: "How sweet it is!"

23

THE END OF 33½ YEARS

ACK WHEN I WAS AGE 62 OR 63, I HAD SUGGESTED THAT THE BOARD of Governors of the LLL should appoint an associate speaker for whatever contingencies might arise in the near or distant future. Although a person expects to keep on living at that age, the only thing a Christian can say for certain about the future is that it will be met with the Lord in control. As a result, in 1977, the LLL selected and appointed as associate Lutheran Hour speaker Rev. Wallace Schulz. I had nothing at all to do with the selection process. I left that strictly up to the LLL.

Pastor Schulz shared preaching duties with me on the program. He also spoke at some of "The Lutheran Hour" rallies. He initiated a program called the "Added Dimension" to try to make the rallies more occasions for evangelical outreach. During all our years of serving together, we have never had one cross word with one another.

Eleven years later though, in 1988, at age 74, I knew the time had come to retire from my position as Lutheran Hour speaker. The LLL knew it would happen someday, of course. That is why the Board of Governors of the LLL had appointed a search committee for an eventual new speaker. Once again, I left that completely up to others. I did not suggest any names or have anything to do with the process at all. I felt that it should be completely the decision of the LLL.

I announced my retirement on July 1, 1988. A number of factors precipitated the decision. One was that at the end of May, Marcia and I had returned from mainland China and the taping of "The Lutheran Hour" special "Christmas in China" (of which I will write more later). Also I was approaching my 75th birthday. And the time seemed right at the LLL. The search committee began doing its work with a new executive director (John Schoedel), who had taken office June 1. Dr. Dale A. Meyer, my successor, was chosen later that summer.

As part of my retirement announcement, I said that my last broadcast would be the Christmas special we had just taped: "Christmas in China." To me, that retirement day of December 25, 1988, was significant. The day I would retire from "The Lutheran Hour" after 33½ years would be my 75th baptismal birthday.

Before telling you about my retirement, let me fill you in on the recording of that year's Christmas special.

"CHRISTMAS IN CHINA"

A half year before the taping, I had been in mainland China as president of the United Bible Societies to dedicate, on December 5, 1987, the new Amity Press, a press built specifically for the printing of Bibles and Christian literature in Chinese. While there, I had talked with Bishop K. H. Ting and Han Wenzao, the vice-president of the China Christian Council, about possibly recording the Christmas special, for they would have to be the ones to get us the necessary approvals. They agreed to allow us to do that. As things worked out, I saw Bishop Ting again just two weeks before we left for China on May 17. He was visiting various U.S. churches, including the LCMS and our seminary in St. Louis.

"The Lutheran Hour" was, I believe, the first Christian group to be given official permission by the Chinese government to record a program inside China since the beginning of the Com-

346

munist regime. For that recording, Marcia and I went over to China, together with Rev. Michael Trinklein, our Lutheran Hour producer at the time, and his wife, Jan.

Steven Tsui, from our Lutheran Hour office in Taiwan, met us in Hong Kong. He was greatly responsible for getting all the recording equipment and cables necessary to establish a temporary studio at the seminary in Nanjing. The gear was all loaded on a big dolly that we took to the airport at Hong Kong, When we got there, China Airlines refused to take it. They said they did not have room for it on the plane.

Fortunately Steven Tsui, a native of mainland China, was with us. He spoke to the airline personnel in Chinese. He told them in measured, but nevertheless very direct language that if not every piece that was on this dolly arrived in Nanjing, the secret police in Nanjing would wonder why, because they had a list of everything we were bringing in. After that, the airline suddenly found room on the plane for everything on that dolly!

When we got to Nanjing, another near disaster happened. Mike Trinklein had a copy of the signed document that gave official permission for us to bring all this equipment into China, but somehow he had lost it. He looked everywhere, but he could not find it. Everybody else had gone through customs, while Mike kept looking for that piece of paper.

After a while this man who was the head of customs said to me, "Will you come out to the parking lot with me?" I did—and there at the edge of the parking lot were Han Wenzao, the vice-president of the China Christian Council, and all the others who were waiting for us. They had not been allowed through the gate into the area where we were, but they were waiting outside. The customs official waved to them, and one of them came running over with the original piece of paper giving the permission we needed.

The official walked back with me with that document in his hand. I thanked him for what he had done, and he smiled at me and was very friendly. But when we got inside the building, his whole demeanor changed. He again became the government official who does not know anybody, and he would not allow me to thank him again.

We went from there to the Theological Seminary in Nanjing, where we set up our recording studio. On the program, the seminary choir sang Christmas songs in both Chinese and English. I talked about Christmas in China with two professors at the seminary, James and Rachel Chen, and with Mrs. Mo Ru Xi, the associate dean. I concluded the program with a short Christmas message that ended with these words:

> With the power of God's Spirit, the light of Christ is poking into your heart at this moment, on the strong beam of God's grace, bringing you the joy of forgiveness and the sure hope of life eternal. For this Christ died, and for this Christ rose from the dead. For this Christ was born: to be your personal Savior.
>
> You have heard this Good News from me during many years past. Now you will hear it from others in the days and years to come. It was good to have the same Good News come to us today from Christians on the China mainland. They pay great tribute to the missionaries who brought them the Gospel of the Lord decades ago. Now they are witnesses, as all can be who trust in the Lord and His salvation—witnesses to friends and foes alike of God's indescribable gift to the world, even Jesus Christ. Let this be my last word to all of you on this broadcast: "A blessed Christmas to all of you in Jesus Christ, our Lord and Savior." Amen.

"Christmas in China" was carried on five stations in China. It was the first Christian program that had been carried on Chinese television for over 40 years. As a result of that broadcast, the International Lutheran Laymen's League was invited by the China Christian Council to help them conduct a cassette tape ministry. By the way, the Gaisers are among those who make it possible financially. The father, Robert, gave the start-up funds to the Lutheran Hour's tape ministry in India, and when China asked for our help, Robert responded again. His children Robert and Betty are carrying on the support.

"Self help" was the slogan of the day in the government of China in those days—and, therefore, also in the government-approved Christian community. By that slogan they meant that Western involvement was not welcome. However, we were allowed to do that because they knew us and trusted us. They knew that our interest is only in communicating the Gospel.

"BLOOM WHERE YOU ARE PLANTED"

A few weeks before my retirement the end of December 1988, there arrived at my office without any warning a blooming azalea plant. It came from a man I have never met, but from whom I received bitter letters over the years, sometimes as many as three a week. I always answered him with a Gospel note, telling of God and His kindness in sending His Son to be our Savior.

About five weeks before I received the plant, I received a letter from him—full of Christian hope!—with a $25 check for "The Lutheran Hour" enclosed. A week later a similar letter came with another $25 check enclosed for "The Lutheran Hour." Then came the plant with its beautiful blooms. The purpose of all of this, the man wrote, was to help celebrate my 75th birthday.

I wrote about that man in my last "Quarterly Letter to Pastors." I recounted what had happened, and then I wrote: "That reminds me to say to you now, as I said to the whole Lutheran Hour audience on a broadcast shortly before I retired as Lutheran Hour speaker, 'Bloom where you are planted.' "

It is a good motto for anybody, I think. It is something I have tried to do throughout my life. I never trained to be anything but a pastor. Probably it remains the greatest opportunity God has given me.

A SPECIAL CELEBRATION

On January 28, 1989, the International Lutheran Laymen's League planned a special celebration in honor of my becoming honorary Lutheran Hour speaker. About 500 people from all over the country attended that celebration. That afternoon a special service was held at my home congregation, Concordia Lutheran Church in Kirkwood, Missouri, in thanksgiving to God for the many favors He showered upon me during years of proclaiming the Gospel as Lutheran Hour speaker. All three of our sons participated in that service. Peter was liturgist, Paul preached the sermon, and John read the Scriptures. Our grandson, Tom, was trumpeter for the service.

That evening, I was honored at a banquet at one of St. Louis's largest hotels. Even I was impressed by those called upon to recognize my years of service. They were

Dr. Ralph Bohlmann, President of The Lutheran Church—Missouri Synod;

Mr. John Schoedel, Executive Director of the International LLL;

Mr. Roy Schmidt, President of the International LLL;

Mrs. Betty Duda, President of the International Lutheran Women's Missionary League;

Dr. William D. Kniffel, Director of International Operations for the International LLL;

Dr. John Erickson, General Secretary of the American Bible Society and Chairman of the Executive Committee of the United Bible Societies;

Chaplain (Major General) Norris Einertson, Chief of Chaplains, U.S. Army; and

Mr. Henry Scheig, Chairman of the Board of AAL.

Dr. Richard W. Bimler, executive director of the Board for Youth Services of the LCMS, was the master of ceremonies. Dr. Arnold Kuntz, past president of the Southern California District and a good friend of mine, was the banquet speaker. It was a long and wonderful evening!

One other presentation was made during the course of that banquet. Prior to that evening, unknown to me, people from the LLL had decided that they wanted to give something other than a tangible gift to me, "something to continue my legacy" (as they put it) into the next generation. Jim Miller, director of development for the LLL at the time, went to three of my fishing buddies and asked whether they would give a significant gift to begin a "Lutheran Hour Endowment Fund" in recognition of my service as Lutheran Hour speaker, which they agreed to do. By the time a presentation of this was made at the banquet that evening, others had agreed to participate, and the amount of the fund had grown to a quarter of a million dollars. This then developed into the "Hoffmann Society."

Following that evening, members of the LLL staff made personal visits to people asking whether they had remembered Lutheran Hour Ministries in their estate planning. Anyone who had done so was made a member of the Hoffmann Society. My involvement in all of this has been primarily to send thank-you letters and small gifts of appreciation to those who became Hoffmann Society members.

They will probably change the name of the Hoffmann Society after I die. My name there is not important. What is important is that the proclamation of the Gospel through "The Lutheran Hour" continues throughout the world. Primarily it is the gifts of laypeople of the church that, by God's grace, make everything possible.

"CELEBRATION OF CHRISTMAS" TOURS

One thing I added to my schedule in 1991 is the "Celebration of Christmas" concert tours, put together by Dave Anderson and his wife, Barbara, out in Phoenix, Arizona. I had met Dave in 1970, when I was the speaker at a Lutheran Youth Congress in San Francisco, sponsored by a youth organization he founded called

"Lutheran Youth Alive." After that, I spoke at many Youth Congresses sponsored by Lutheran Youth Encounters and Lutheran Youth Alive in the 1970s and early 1980s. I have always enjoyed speaking to those young audiences, and they have always been most attentive. I think it is because I do not speak down to them but can present the Gospel to them in a very human way.

As a result of those and many other contacts at gatherings of various kinds over the years where I was a speaker and Dave and Barb Anderson provided the music, Dave asked whether I would serve as narrator for this Christmas concert tour he was putting together. He explained that my presence would help to give credibility in places where people might not know him or his music. He said that I would be reading narration prepared by others and wondered whether I was willing to follow a script. I assured him that a script was no problem but rather a help in dealing with musicians. I was glad to agree to participate in his "Celebration of Christmas" tours.

That first year, he planned a tour through Illinois, Nebraska, and Minnesota. We had a concert every night for seven nights, traveling by van from place to place. Besides Dave and Barb Anderson, the program included Gospel singer Don Wharton and Cary Dietsche, an instrumentalist. The concerts also have included mass choirs of local people that were conducted at more recent concerts by our director and producer, Gary Lohmeyer.

I enjoyed those concerts, and I also enjoyed those days in the van with the concert team. Many times as we traveled down the road in Illinois or Nebraska or somewhere else in the Midwest, I would see a farmhouse and recall having had dinner there. Or we would pass a church where I had spoken or a community with a heritage I knew about, and I told my traveling companions about those people. My van mates told me they really enjoyed my travelogs as we traveled throughout the Midwest.

We faced some real problems that first concert tour in 1991. We often had to battle bad weather, but I remember one particularly bad afternoon. I had had to speak elsewhere in the morning and had to be in Kearney, Nebraska, that evening for our first concert. The drive from Lincoln to Kearney was in one of the worst ice storms I have ever seen. I was told that when they put the car up on a hoist the next day, they found a foot of ice had accumulated underneath.

That first tour had other problems too; but the crowning blow was our last concert, held in the Civic Center in St. Paul, Minnesota. The auditorium would hold probably about 6,000 people, and we had only 600 at the concert. When we finished, Dave asked me whether I would join them if they did "Celebration of Christmas" the following year. I assured him that I would, and that seemed to give him the encouragement he needed to try it again.

The second year we had large audiences everywhere we went. There were 1,000–2,000 people in the audience every night. That held true for the third year also. Although we had some problems with bad weather on our tour in 1994, especially in Minnesota, it was still a successful and enjoyable experience.

One day during our tour the second year, my traveling companions went together and bought me a black, Greek sailor's cap. I had told them that I had worn one for many years, but that earlier that year someone had inadvertently taken mine from the cloakroom at my church and had left a blue one in its place. I did not like that one as well, I told them, because it did not match my coat. I told them that receiving that gift on that particular day had special meaning for me, but I did not tell them why.

At the concert that night when I got up to do the narration, I began by saying, "Seventy-nine years ago in a little town in Nebraska, a little baby was born." It was only then that they realized that the reason their gift was special that day was because it was a birthday gift.

When Dave Anderson realized that, he immediately jumped up and led the entire audience in singing "Happy Birthday."

On our third tour, Cary Dietsche had put together a medley of Christmas carols and Christmas songs that he played on the electric keyboard. When he played "Have Yourself a Merry Little Christmas," there was the sound of finger snapping in the background. Someone, I do not remember who, got the idea that we should involve the audience in finger snapping. The way we worked it out was that our choir director, Gary Lohmeyer, would get the choir started snapping their fingers. Then he would come over to me and get me started snapping my fingers. I would then turn to the audience and direct them in finger snapping. It was a lot of fun.

The 1995 tour took us to Wisconsin, Illinois, Missouri, Nebraska, Colorado, and Arizona, and covered 15 days. Except for the trip to Colorado and Arizona, all travel was by van.

I have really enjoyed the "Celebration of Christmas" concert tours. Almost everywhere I go, people I have met before have come up to talk with me after the first half of the concert. Many times they will start by saying, "You probably don't remember me." Many times I do remember who they are and where I have met them before. If I do not, I will simply say, "No, I'm sorry, I don't. Tell me who you are." Most of the time when they tell me their names and a little about where we met before, I will remember them and be able to give some details of our previous time together—who else was at dinner that day, what we had talked about, something like that.

Many times during the day on those tours, I am able to arrange a visit with one or more people who are bedridden or confined to their homes because of illness. Someone from the community where we are makes the arrangements for me to do that and provides transportation for me. I always appreciate those opportunities to share my faith with people and to have them share their faith with me. That's a marvelous thing!

CONTINUING SERVICE TO THE LORD

When I retired as Lutheran Hour speaker, the LLL graciously named me honorary Lutheran Hour speaker and provided me with an office at LLL headquarters for as long as needed. They moved me back into the office I had occupied for all the years before the new studio was built in 1986. They provided me with assistance in the person of Gaylene LaBore, who had been my secretary when I first came to St. Louis and who still remains with me as my executive assistant.

When I retired as "The Lutheran Hour" speaker, I also retired as president of the United Bible Societies. But I am not retired from other activities. The Lord continues to use me in many ways. I still serve on the American Bible Society Board of Trustees and as chairman of the Society's Translations Committee. I remain on the editorial board of *Christianity Today.* I am a speaker at two or three Billy Graham Schools of Evangelism every year. I preach for many occasions, such as church anniversaries, church building dedications, Reformation services, and other occasions at churches all over the country. My calendar of speaking engagements is as full as ever.

I still assist with various projects in the League office when asked. The LLL staff even asks me to direct a staff choir for the annual staff Christmas service. I have been pleased to do that. We have some good musicians on that staff. We do not have much rehearsal time, but that choir sounds pretty good.

By God's grace, I shall continue to serve Him in these ways as long as I can. That's really, I think, what life is all about. You just do what the Lord gives you to do. You give the Lord the best you have. The Lord forgives your failures and gives you the power of the Holy Spirit to equip you for whatever He wants you to do. He just keeps on surprising you, opening one door after another.

24

SOME FAMILY NOTES

BACK IN CHAPTER 2 WHEN I WROTE ABOUT TAKING SON PAUL WITH ME back to my hometown of Snyder, Nebraska, I said, "It is important that we have a sense of where we have come from, for that's a part of who we are. Maybe I needed to remind myself again who I truly am behind the well-known voice and face: a small-town preacher's kid—and thankful for it." And just as we look to our forebears for insights, so I believe we need to look to our children and grandchildren for additional information about ourselves. Just as parts of my grandparents and parents live in me, so I can look to my children and grandchildren for parts of me there— and for self-understanding into the significance of those parts.

One of the blessings of retirement, even semiretirement, is that in recent years I have been able to spend a little more time with my children and grandchildren. Let me briefly fill you in on where they are and what they are doing today.

Our oldest son, Peter, is pastor of Good Shepherd Lutheran Church in Chicago. He and his wife, Elaine (nee Bicker), are the parents of five of our grandchildren. Three of those grandchildren are interracial adoptions. Carl, the oldest, was an early transracial adoption in Ohio. He served in the Air Force. Tom is in restaurant management, and Marcia, who recently was graduated from college, worked for Oprah Winfrey and is now a social worker. After Peter and Elaine had adopted those three children, they had two other biological children of their own: Paul, who recently graduated from a technical school and is an excellent automobile mechanic, and George, who is in junior high school. Elaine teaches at a Lutheran elementary school in Lansing, Illinois.

Our second son, Paul, is pastor of Holy Cross Lutheran Church in Los Gatos, California. He and his wife, Jane (nee Meyer, daughter of Pastor John and Elsa Meyer), are the parents of three strapping grandsons: David, Stephen, and Matthew. David attended the University of Washington on a football scholarship. He played linebacker for the Huskies and had the privilege of playing in three Rose Bowls. He was drafted by the Chicago Bears, then played with the Pittsburgh Steelers and the World Football League. Stephen followed in his brother's footsteps and played defensive lineman for the University of Washington Huskies football team. In 1995 Stephen was married to Heidi (nee Hills), who played forward on the Huskies women's basketball team. Younger brother Matthew attends Pacific Lutheran University, where he plays football and is majoring in communication. Jane is a registered nurse and is education coordinator for a San Jose home health agency.

Our third son, John, lives at home with us. He works for Lutheran Family and Children's Services, helps with all the chores around the house, goes to the office to pick up my mail when I am out of town, and many times serves as chauffeur to and from the airport. He is a great help to us.

Daughter Kate has been a legal secretary and is married to Brian Bates. He is a lawyer who works as an immigration attorney in Houston, Texas. They are the parents of two young daughters, Erin and Anne.

That is our family. They are truly a blessing to us.

The realization, though, that our children are becoming grandparents themselves forcefully reminds Marcia and me that many years have passed since our marriage on June 23, 1940. Time is taking its due from our bodies. Marcia has had problems in recent years with osteoporosis and is in constant pain. She tells me she is at least four inches shorter than she was before the osteoporosis began. In spite of all of that, she goes with me on many of the trips I take. As always, she is a wonderful traveling companion. We have traveled many ways together and have met many interesting people.

A STRANGE SURPRISE

The Lord reminded me of my aging body in a rather strange way. I was in St. John, Newfoundland, speaking for the Canadian Bible Society in late October and early November of 1989. While I was there, I had a pain under my tongue. I did not pay any attention, thinking it was just one of those things that would go away.

When I got back to St. Louis, I realized it was not going to go away. I went to my dentist and he said, "I'm not going to touch that," and sent me to my doctor.

My physician, Dr. Frede Mortensen, sent me to Barnes Hospital for a biopsy. When the results came back, they showed that I had a malignant tumor under my tongue. Dr. Mortensen referred me to a surgeon, Dr. Albert Ruehl. He did two exploratory surgeries to find out just how bad the situation was. On January 16, 1990, I had major mouth surgery at Barnes Hospital in St. Louis. I went in at seven o'clock in the morning, and the surgery lasted for 12 hours. They removed the cancer from my mouth, which included removing part of my tongue. Then they took skin off my thigh to cover the places on the floor of my mouth where the cancer had been removed. I was impressed when I found out later that Dr. Ruehl had never left the operating room.

I had to go back for surgery a second time, because some of that skin grafting did not take.

After the surgery, I had radiation treatments. When I went for my treatments, a friend of mine, Parker Wheatley, also was being treated there. For many years, he had had a religious TV program called "Eye on St. Louis." He was being treated for cancer of the nose. I did not know it at the time, but he told some other people that my cheerfulness at those radiation sessions provided great strength for him.

The radiation affected my teeth. For the first time in quite a while, I had to go to a dentist. I had not had a filling for 20 years, but now, because of what the radiation has done to my teeth, I have to go back to the dentist constantly.

Because they also took out a large part of my tongue, I could not lick a stamp anymore. I also had to learn to talk all over again. They wanted me to go to a speech therapist, but I told them, "Oh, I know better than any therapist how the tongue works. I taught linguistics, you know."

I worked a lot on the liquids, *l* and *r*. In linguistics, they play a great role. In fact, in many Oriental languages, there's no distinction between them, which is why it sounds like *l* when they are saying *r* and vice versa.

As part of my speech therapy, I spent a lot of time saying Psalm 90 every day out loud to myself. It was a comfort, both for its content and for the *l*s and the *r*s scattered all over the landscape in that psalm.

My surgery has never really bothered me that much. Once shortly after my surgery, my friend Lou Meyer phoned me to see how I was doing.

"Oh," I told him, "I have a little impediment in my speech, but so did Moses. I guess I'm in good company!"

The last time I went to see my doctor, he told me, "You're doing just fine. Come back in six months." At the oncology department at Barnes Hospital, which I visit once a year, the medical people tell me, "You're cured."

How grateful to our Lord and Creator Marcia and I are that we still have each other. We have, of course, lost others in our extended family.

MY BROTHER KENNY

Kenny died in 1970 of lung cancer at the age of 55. At the time he was pastor at Grace Lutheran Church in Cleveland, Ohio.

Kenny had married Violet Rubbert. Her mother had died in childbirth, and Violet had been raised by her grandparents, Mr. and Mrs. Ernest Rubbert. Ken and Violet had three children.

Kenny had vicared at Messiah Lutheran Church in south St. Louis, then had been called there as assistant pastor. He next became pastor at Concordia Lutheran Church in Kirkwood, Missouri, the congregation in suburban St. Louis which has been our home church since coming to St. Louis. My brother was pastor there when the church moved to its present location on Kirkwood Road. That was an important move, because it put the church on a main thoroughfare.

When Concordia first moved to the new location, they did not have a church building. The congregation worshiped in the new parish hall. Kenny left there before the church building was built to serve as chaplain at the hospital the LLL sponsored in Vicksburg, Mississippi. He went from there to two congregations in Maryland, then to Grace Church in Cleveland, Ohio, which turned out to be his last parish.

Prior to 1970, Kenny had been diagnosed as having lung cancer, but had responded to treatment and was doing pretty well. He sold his house and bought a condominium for his wife and children to live in. Then he got sick again and had to go into the hospital for the last time.

I went to visit him in the hospital about two weeks before he died. I reminisced with him about the old days when we were boys in Minnesota and went down the hills on the toboggan with our caps flying in the air, and other times like that.

I asked him about his faith. "Oh," he said, "when you need Him, the Lord is near." That is the way he always was.

When it was time for me to say good-bye to him, I had trouble finding words. "There are times when you don't need words," he said. I thanked him for that.

When I went out the door, I just waved to him, and he waved to me, and we parted. The great thing about faith in Christ is that you are absolutely sure another day is coming when you are going to wave again. In all His humanity, the Son of God rose from the dead, carrying our nature in victory over death. There is no reason in the world why, with confidence in Christ, people cannot go joyfully into the world that He has prepared for those who love Him.

When Kenny died, the members of his congregation were devastated. Marcia and I went to the funeral. When we came in for the service with my mother, who by this time was walking with a walker, one of the head ushers broke down and wept uncontrollably.

My mother did not cry. She was a real good soldier, and she took it. I have often thought that the mother of our Lord really went through a lot to see her Son go on ahead of her into death the way He did. Mary took that nobly.

Somebody told me a story once about a woman who died young and left a family, and she was very sorrowful. She got to heaven and they welcomed her there. Then they told her, "You have an hour or two before lunch. You can walk around in the garden and take a look at the flowers."

While she was doing that, an older woman came along. The younger woman said to her that she did not weep, but she still felt sorrowful, because she had left those children down there. The older woman said that she understood that very well.

"There's only one thing worse than that," she said, "and that's having your son die before you do."

The name of the older woman was Mary.

TAKING CARE OF MY MOTHER

After Kenny died, we brought my mother to live in St. Louis. She was living at the time in Cleveland. To explain that, I need to back up in time a bit.

When my father retired in 1957, he and my mother bought a house and moved to Saint Petersburg, Florida, where my father became an assisting pastor at Grace Lutheran Church. People at New Port Richey and also at Dunedin were eager to begin new congregations. As a result, my father became the founding pastor of Faith Lutheran Church at New Port Richey, which became one of the largest congregations in Florida, and also of Faith Lutheran Church, Dunedin. Generally, he and my mother drove to both places, conducting services in the morning at New Port Richey and at Dunedin in the afternoon.

After my father died in 1963, my mother continued to live in Florida for awhile, but she was bothered terribly by arthritis and had difficulty getting around. That had started already when the folks lived in Minneapolis, but it kept getting worse. We wanted to bring her to St. Louis from Florida. We even looked for an apartment for her, but there was nothing available near us. Kenny, though, said that there was this wonderful apartment in the Alcazar Hotel in Cleveland, which some people had bought and turned into a retirement home. We moved her there.

When I would go to visit her there, she never seemed to realize that I was no longer 12 years old. She still made meals for me the way she had when I was growing up. She did not eat Jell-O, but she would make a whole bowl of Jell-O for me and expect me to eat it all. Or she would make a pie for me and expect me to eat the whole thing.

She was quite a forceful woman, although she was only 5'2", and in later years shorter—probably down to about five feet. Her parents and all her brothers and sisters were small like that too.

The Hoffmanns were tall people, and they got taller with our family. John became 6'5", Paul is 6'5", and Paul's children are even taller. One of them is 6'6"—and they can handle their weight in wildcats!

Anyway, when Ken died, we again worked to get my mother to come to St. Louis. By this time, however, Marcia had had two heart attacks, and she could not lift my mother or take care of her all the time. Happily we learned that Lutheran Charities had just built Laclede Groves, a retirement/nursing facility, and we got her into the minimal care unit there. She was one of their first residents. She had her own room, could go to the dining room for her meals, and could come and go as she wanted. She even had a call bell in case she needed help.

In 1978, my mother went to visit her niece Ruth Gienapp in Concordia, Missouri, where Ruth's husband, Norman Gienapp, was a professor at St. Paul's College. Mother got sick while she was there, and they had to take her to Kansas City to the hospital. After that she could not go back to living in her room. She had to go into the hospital unit at Laclede Groves.

It was a very difficult time, both for her and for us. John, Kate, and Marcia went to Kansas City to bring her home. We had told Mother that she would have to go into the hospital, but she told Marcia that she was sure that Marcia could take care of things so she would not have to go into the hospital. Of course, Marcia could not do that. Marcia said that my mother cried and cried all the way home from Kansas City. It was very hard for Marcia.

My mother died on June 23, 1978, at the age of almost 93. We took her body to Saint Petersburg, Florida, to be buried beside my father. We used the same committal service that he had used all through the years for Lutherans who had gone to be with their Lord. The pastor who took care of all that for us was Pastor Milan Weerts at Our Savior Lutheran Church in Saint Petersburg, Florida.

SOME THOUGHTS ABOUT DEATH

I do not know that death is such a remarkable event. It will come to all of us. I do not keep thinking about death all the time. When it comes, it needs to be accepted as another door through which to go into the next room that Christ has prepared in the commonwealth that is His.

Death is a time of remembrance. That is human. When death comes, you remember all those times that you had together. And by the way, a lot of people at the time of death remember what they could have done—the kindnesses they could have shown, the forgiveness they could have extended, the understanding they really should have had. That is true of everybody. That is our humanity.

Sometimes in our humanity, we do not know what to say to grieving people. For example, what do you say to a mother and two little children standing at the graveside of her husband and their father who has died of a brain tumor? You do not come and say to them, "I understand how you feel." Nobody understands how they feel except God. One thing you can say to them without exaggerating one bit is, "Jesus Christ is Lord. I do not know how things will work out for you in your life, but I know they will. You do not have to worry about it. Jesus is Lord. He has been raised from the dead by the glory of His Father. He is around. He will guide and govern all your works, both personal and professional."

Some years ago, I put some of my thoughts about death and dying on an audiotape called "Take Heart in Your Grief." That was Elmer Knoernschild's idea, but I had to work it out. I worked a long time on that. It was very hard. It took a long time to get it in final form. That tape is still being requested from the International Lutheran Laymen's League by people who wish to share it with bereaved friends.

Actually, that "Take Heart in Your Grief" tape is probably not in final form even now. Nothing we do is really completely finished. Christ said "It is finished" (John 19:30), and He meant it *was* finished. Everything *we* do has to be revised, repaired, restored, renovated. Only Christ does not need to revise what He did. He suffered once, the just for the unjust to bring us to God. That truth needs to be told. What a privilege to do that throughout your life!

Epilog

I never tried to play the hero in positions I held or in any part of my life. We have only one hero: our Lord Jesus Christ. He's the one. After Him all of us come in second—or third—or fourth. That's the way it is. That's the way it ought to be.

Someone once asked me how I would like to be remembered after I die. I told him I had no dreams about that at all. That's all right, for it is not we who should be remembered. The one we proclaim should be remembered. I am really not too concerned about how I will be remembered—or whether I will be remembered at all. What difference does it make? "Whether we live, we are the Lord's. Whether we die, we are the Lord's. Whether we live, therefore, or whether we die, we are the Lord's" (Romans 14:8).

Having said that, what more is there to say but amen?